LESS
THAN
THE
LEAST

LESS
THAN
THE
LEAST

Memoirs of
Cornelius Hanko

Cornelius Hanko

Karen Van Baren, editor

Second Edition

REFORMED
FREE PUBLISHING
ASSOCIATION
Jenison, Michigan

Scriptures cited are taken from the King James (Authorized) Version

Reformed Free Publishing Association
1894 Georgetown Center Drive
Jenison, Michigan 49428
rfpa.org
mail@rfpa.org
616-457-5970

Cover design by Erika Kiel
Interior design and typesetting by Katherine Lloyd, the DESK

ISBN 978-1-944555-20-7
Ebook 978-1-944555-21-4
LCCN 2017941970

*Unto me, who am less than the least of all saints,
is this grace given, that I should preach among
the Gentiles the unsearchable riches of Christ.*
—Ephesians 3:8

Contents

Foreword to the Second Edition
of *Less Than the Least*

This book arose out of the efforts of many people. It began with a dear grandfather who loved to tell stories to his children and grandchildren about his life as a charter member of the Protestant Reformed Churches and his ministry in those same churches. Thankfully, over the years he wrote many of those stories, kept diaries, and saved a treasure trove of pictures, sermons, articles, family documents, and correspondence.

I first became aware of the broader value of his story when my history professor at Calvin College, Jim Bratt, suggested that I do my senior project on Grandpa's life. Professor Bratt is very interested in the history of Calvinism, and while he did not know Cornelius Hanko, he knew the Protestant Reformed Churches well. For that project I tape-recorded interviews with Grandpa and others who knew him. My sister Sharon Kleyn typed the taped interviews. Then I dug through Grandpa's personal files and wrote a paper. That was step two.

Grandpa was in his mid-nineties when my husband, Philip, suggested that I weave together all the material I had gathered on Grandpa's life into a series of articles for the *Beacon Lights* magazine. That was step three.

The *Beacon Lights* articles, each proofread by my father, Herman Hanko, were received with interest. Many people suggested that the articles be put into a book for wider distribution. The family decided to self-publish the book, with my uncle, Fred Hanko, doing the typesetting. Thus *Less Than the Least* was born. That was step four.

Mr. Dan Van Uffelen was the first to suggest that the Reformed

Free Publishing Association publish a second edition of the book, and for that I am grateful. I have since done much work to improve, polish, and expand the book with appendices; a better map of the Grand Rapids neighborhood in which Grandpa grew up (drafted by Trevor Van Overloop while he was a high school student); additional family history; and more pictures. All pictures not credited to others are from Hanko family members and the archives of the Protestant Reformed Churches and the Reformed Free Publishing Association. The comments at the beginning of each chapter and the footnotes are mine.

But all of this was not without the help of the staff of the publishing association and family members. What you hold in your hands is the result of many years of work by various people.

Grandpa would not have cared for any fame the book would have gotten him. His desire would have been that through this story of his life, you, the reader, would come to know God more fully, to love more ardently the truths of sovereign grace, and to pray more fervently for the church of Christ.

Karen Van Baren, editor

Preface to the First Edition of *Less Than the Least*

The content of this book originally appeared as a series of articles in the *Beacon Lights*, the magazine of the young people of the Protestant Reformed Churches. It is the result of the editing of several documents that Rev. Hanko prepared prior to his death in 2005.

Rev. Hanko prepared three or four such documents: two were memoirs of most of his life, while one or two were more detailed accounts of aspects of his work while in the ministry. Karen Van Baren, Rev. Hanko's granddaughter, wove all the documents into one narrative and edited them as she went along. This book is, therefore, an edited version of those documents.

Rev. Hanko's intent in writing them was really to prepare some more permanent record of his busy and active life, not just simply that the children, grandchildren, and great-grandchildren might come to know him a bit, but because his ministry spanned almost all of the sometimes turbulent history of the Protestant Reformed Churches in which he labored as a minister of the gospel. He was deeply involved in the controversies over common grace, which formed the occasion for the beginning of the Protestant Reformed Churches. He was also in the troubled controversies of the 1940s and 1950s when the denomination was split over the question of conditional theology.

Rev. Hanko wanted his succeeding generations to know the importance of the battles he fought in defense of the truths of God's sovereign and particular grace, so that the generations after him might appreciate their heritage and be faithful to it. Hence these memoirs are really an "insider's" look into the struggles of the denomination of which he was a part.

Because the requests for a printed copy came from all parts of the denomination, the family decided to make the memoirs available in book form. It is our hope and prayer that the book will be an inspiration to those who read it to be faithful to the heritage for which our fathers fought so valiantly.

Prof. Herman Hanko

Chapter 1

HERMAN AND JANTJE

Rev. Hanko begins his story with his birth in Grand Rapids, Michigan, in 1907. He then takes us back to the Netherlands as he explains the circumstances in which his parents, Herman Hanko and Jantje Burmania, were born and raised. The Netherlands that his parents knew was one in which the state church held religious sway and class divisions governed social life. His narrative continues with his parents' separate immigrations to the United States, their meeting, and subsequent marriage.

As I sit here probing into the past, my earliest recollection is of a small, dark bedroom with a bed in a corner. The shades were drawn, but the afternoon sun shone through the pinholes in the green fabric.

I have been told that I was born on Pentecost Sunday, May 19, 1907, soon after my dad returned from the morning service at Eastern Avenue Christian Reformed Church in Grand Rapids, Michigan. I have no reason to doubt it.

To provide a little context for the story, let me go back a couple of generations. Friedriech Wilhelm Hanko, my grandfather, was born in Prussia in 1822. He immigrated to Appingedam, Groningen, Netherlands. In 1851 he married Meike Beeker, who was from Hanover, Germany. Friedriech was a tinsmith. My father told me that Grandpa had made the silver candlestick that stood in the Roman Catholic Church in Stadt Groningen.

Grandpa raised his family in the *Hervormde Kerk* (the state church) in the Netherlands. From every impression we received, the family went to church but was not very spiritual. Herman Hanko, my father, was born into the family on August 1, 1861. He was the fifth of six children. Two of those children died before the age of three, leaving his two brothers Harm and Willem, and his sister was Jetske. Harm immigrated to America and lived in Roseland, Chicago, and had three children—Fred, Agnes, and Henrietta. Willem never came to America. He was married to a daughter of the Pijpers, whose descendants had immigrated to America and joined Oak Lawn Protestant Reformed Church while I was the minister there. My father sent them money from time to time until he heard that Willem spent the money on liquor, and that was the end of that. Jetske was married to Jan Pijp, the father of the late Gerrit Pipe of Fourth (Southeast) Protestant Reformed Church.

Grandpa was of the better class, since he owned his own business. He was insistent that my father should learn the trade of painting and decorating, but did not seem overly concerned about the spiritual welfare of his family. Having been away from home and in the military service, my father did not have much opportunity to grow spiritually. That may explain why he was accustomed to using vulgar language. This language was a great offence to his second wife—my mother—and he gradually learned to distance himself from such language.

At age twenty-seven my father married Jeltje (Thelma) Schriemer. They were blessed with the birth of two girls, Jantje and Maike (Jennie and Maggie), before they immigrated to America.

My mother, Jantje Burmania, was born November 22, 1872, near Harlingen, Friesland, to a poor farm hand, Cornelius Burmania, and his wife, Sena Bouma. Cornelius and Sena had two children besides Jantje: Lucy and Geeela. Geeela died at age 14, and later Sena died of tuberculosis. Cornelius then married Heinke Kolthoff and had eight more children, six of whom survived into adulthood.

As the family increased food became scarcer. My mother spoke of getting a piece of rye bread for supper with a small piece of pork. The girls would push the pork to the end of the slice, so that the last bite would taste the best. Then they were sent to bed, holding their stomachs so the hunger pangs would not keep them awake.

Mother's family belonged to the *Afscheiding* (the Separation) of 1834, which was led by Hendrik de Cock. Although the family was poor, her father sent the children to the Christian school. Mother told how they passed the public school on the way to the Christian school and were mocked as *fijner* (pure ones) or *doe akelige Cockseanen* (you hateful followers of De Cock).[1]

When Mother turned eleven, her father could no longer support her, so she was taken out of school and put to work. She found a job with a rich family in Leeuwarden. If I am not mistaken, her employer was the mayor of the town. He lived in a large, three-story house. The water for washing, cooking, baking, and baths had to be drawn from the canal. Mother ruined her back by hauling buckets of water from the canal all the way to the third floor of the house and suffered as a hunchback for the rest of her life. Years later her children would come into the house, take one look at their mother's face to see how intense the pain was on that particular day. If her face was severely drawn, they went about the affairs of the home without making undue disturbances. The sight of her pain-ridden face was deeply engraved in their minds for years afterward.

Her uncle, Doeke Bouma (brother of her father's first wife), showed deep concern for her spiritual welfare and often visited her. When Uncle Doeke came to see her, her employer allowed her to visit with him, but she had to keep ironing. On Sundays she prepared the whole family for church. After they had stepped

---

1 Those schools were not the same as public schools in the United States. They were supported by the government but operated by the state church.

into the coach, she hurriedly dressed and ran to church. The family sat in the rented pews. She often had to stand in the back of the auditorium throughout the service. [2]

At first my mother worked only for room and board, but as she grew older she received wages, which she frugally saved for the day she could go to America. Her trip was delayed for a time by her hospitalization for a ruptured ulcer at the age of seventeen. At about age twenty she had saved enough to travel to America as a third-class passenger in the bottom of the ship. When she arrived at the port of Hoboken, New Jersey, she was deloused along with the others who had traveled third class. Jantje found this very demeaning. She never cared to go back to the Netherlands, not even for a visit, for as she said, "I never experienced anything there but poverty."

She stayed first with her half-sister Lizzie Goeman, who lived in a house along Chicago Drive between Zeeland and Hudsonville, Michigan, near 62nd Street. Jantje quickly began looking for work. She needed to support herself, but she also wanted to save money so that her parents and her full sister, Lucy, could move to America.

Here we see the amazing hand of providence. My father had moved to America with his wife and daughters and settled in Grand Rapids to set up his painting and decorating business. The Hanko family had not been in the United States very long when Jeltje died in 1894, shortly after the birth of the third daughter. I later found a letter that Jeltje had written to family in the Netherlands, which letter had been returned to my father. In her letter she said that she likely would not live much longer, but that she had found the Lord and had peace in her soul. Father needed someone to take care of the house and children, so he hired Jantje—my mother—as a housekeeper.

---

2   At that time in the Netherlands it was customary for wealthy families to rent a pew in which to sit. Those who could not afford to rent a pew were forced to find a seat in the back or stand.

Jantje soon became attached to the three Hanko girls, Jennie, Maggie, and Henrietta, so that after a time and at least one rejection, Herman convinced her to marry him. Rev. Sevensma, minister in Eastern Avenue Christian Reformed Church, married them in 1895. Being a Frisian himself, he told my mother that in her case it was too bad that she had to give up her maiden name to take on a German name![3]

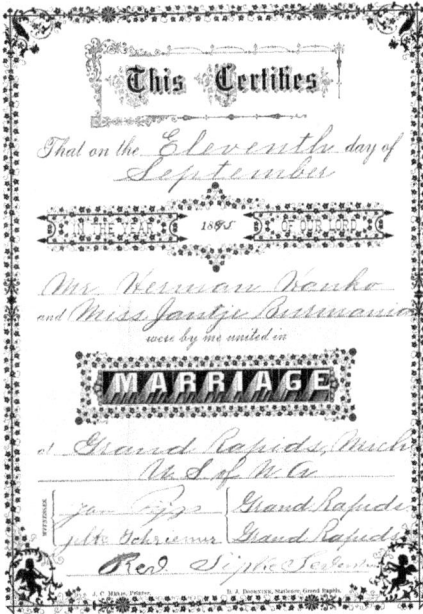

Herman Hanko and Jantje Burmania were married on September 11, 1895.

Jennie, Maggie, and Henrietta's grandmother lived only a few houses away. The elderly grandmother was at first very concerned whether a young woman in her twenties could take care

---

3   Burmania is a noble Dutch and Frisian name that can be traced back to the Reformation and beyond. Hanko family tradition includes a story of a Dutch noble with the name Burmania who refused to bow to the detested Catholic Philip II of Spain during the Dutch Revolt that was the beginning of the Eighty Years' War between Spain and the Netherlands. The pride of the Frisians is well known. By contrast, the name Hanko can be found in various European countries, including Germany, but is not native to the Netherlands.

of her grandchildren. Later she became extremely jealous even at the thought that another woman was imposing herself in the place of her dead daughter. When Jantje dressed the daughters in bright, neat clothing, she was immediately rebuffed and accused of caring nothing for the dead. In the grandmother's mind, the girls should wear black for at least a year out of respect for their departed mother.

The result was that especially the oldest daughter insisted on having her own way. When that failed she threatened to pack up and live with Grandma because Grandma was so much nicer to her than her stepmother. That went on for some time, until finally one day Jantje had had enough. She told the complaining daughter to get her belongings together and go to live with Grandma indefinitely. The daughter then had second thoughts, and from then on she did not try to hide behind Grandma to get her way.

Within the next nine years Fred, Sena, Lucy, Corie, and I

Young Cornelius Hanko

Cornelius Hanko c. 1910

were born to the union of Herman Hanko and Jantje Burmania, so ours was a very busy household.[4]

Meanwhile, the Cleveland Panic had devastated the American economy.[5] In the recession that hit the country following the panic, my parents lost their home and were forced to move elsewhere. They reached an agreement with a certain Mr. Johnson to purchase a two-story house nearby. The agreement was that Father would build a barn for the sum of one hundred dollars as a down payment for the house. Then by weekly payments the one-thou-

The house the Hanko family lost in the Cleveland Panic as it stood in the 1990s.

sand-dollar house would in due time become their own. Because of those bad economic times and the lapse in the home decorating business, Father had to work at cutting ice on Reeds Lake, near present-day Calvin College in Grand Rapids, Michigan, for a dollar per day. The ice was then stored in shacks to be sold for use in the preservation of food. Mother took in weekly washings to supplement the family's income.

It was not strange for us to have outsiders in the home with us. My dad often referred to our home as always having the welcome sign out. In fact, when my dad's sister Jetske died, her son, Herman Pipe, came to stay with us for a number of years before and after I was born. He was a gloomy fellow whose gloom deepened whenever he failed at business or love. Eventually he married and moved

---

4 Grandpa told the story from his viewpoint and did not include any information on those years. He was the youngest in the family.
5 The Cleveland Panic (1893–97) is named after Grover Cleveland, who was president at the time a recession hit the United States as a result of the country's going off the gold standard.

out of our home. Another regular visitor was Aunt Lucy, who had eleven operations and each time recuperated in our home.

In her younger days my mother was also the neighborhood midwife. She was called on from time to time to deliver a baby, for which she received little more recompense than a thank-you. She sometimes jokingly referred to a ten-cent set of salt and pepper shakers for which she had worked all night.

A mother for whom my mother was the midwife died soon after her baby was born. On her deathbed she asked my mother to take the baby, since she wanted it to have a good home. My mother consented, although she already had seven children to raise. After about six months, long enough for Mother to become strongly attached to the child, some relatives came and demanded the baby on the basis that they had more right to it than my mother. Since no adoption proceedings had begun, my mother could only turn over the child.

Mother was also known for her ability to make coffee in large quantities. In those days coffee was made in a wash boiler. To make the grounds settle to the bottom, a dozen eggs were added. At society banquets, or even at neighborhood weddings, my mother was asked to make the coffee. We sometimes received a free invitation to the wedding because of my mother's ability to make good coffee.

My father was quick-tempered and often impatient. I actually did not learn to know my father well until I was old enough to paint with him in the summer. Then I was sorry that I had not learned before to know his inner kindly nature, his understanding, and also his generosity. His generosity went far beyond my mother's, who always feared that the wolf of poverty was at the door.

We could always confide our cares and woes to Mother. She could be very stern and make a sharp distinction between right and wrong. As teenagers when we wanted to go out in the evening, we would first have to tell her where we were going and when we would be home. She held us to that, saying, "I trust you, and I am praying for you."

Herman and Jantje Hanko

So the family lived happily together. Mother especially exerted a spiritual influence on the family. She knew how to comfort in times of distress, but she also knew how to admonish in no uncertain terms. She was very matter-of-fact and very down-to-earth. Her stern disapproval of all that was wrong, her quiet admonitions, and above all her exemplary walk of life could not pass unnoticed. One sees the marvelous work of God in gathering his church in the line of continued generations. As a parent works out his or her salvation with fear and trembling, a mark is left upon each child, as either a blessing or a condemnation, but a mark that is never entirely erased.

A mother who was given only the most basic education can nevertheless be used by God to gather, defend, and preserve his church from generation to generation even as the promise came to Abraham. A mother has not lived in vain when in the great day of days she can say, "Behold I and the children which God hath given me" (Heb. 2:13).

9

Chapter 2

GRAND RAPIDS, MICHIGAN

In this chapter Rev. Hanko takes us inside the Dutch enclaves of Grand Rapids, Michigan. When the Dutch settled in the United States they banded together by the province from which they had come. Thus there was the Groninger buurt, or neighborhood, settled by many of the people from the province of Groningen.

The story of his childhood in Michigan must be understood in the context of turn-of-the-century America, where the common American did not enjoy the luxuries of electricity and automobiles. Life for those immigrant families was often hard; still, it was a step up from the grinding poverty they had suffered in the Netherlands. All businesses were family owned and operated. Often a family took up residence behind its business. The need for community was satisfied by life in the closely-knit Dutch enclaves, most of whose members worshiped in the Christian Reformed Church.

All of southeastern Grand Rapids was divided into three parts.[1] To the south of my home were the Frisians,[2] who occupied the Oakdale Park area around Hall Street. To the north

---

1 The author makes a tongue-in-cheek reference to the opening line of Julius Caesar's *Gallic Wars*: "All of Gaul is divided into three parts."
2 The Frisians were from Friesland, a province in the northern part of the Netherlands.

of us in the Brickyard[3] were the Zeeuws.[4] They occupied the area around Fulton Street.

We lived in the Groninger buurt in the area chiefly bounded by Eastern Avenue on the west, Fuller Avenue on the east, Franklin Street on the south, and Wealthy Street on the north. Our house was at 903 Ella Avenue, which was later changed to 1065 Bemis Street.

The street was very narrow, with the sidewalk along the road. On the south side of the street were mostly barns, since the streets were so close together. On the corner of Diamond Avenue and Bemis Street was Baxter

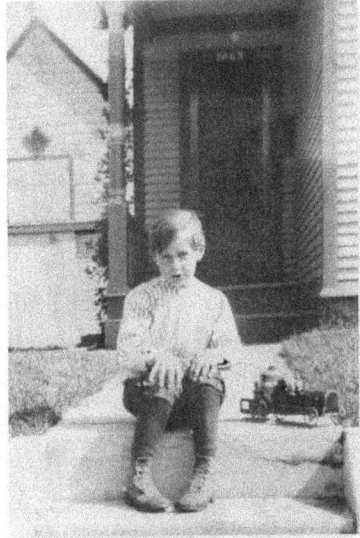

Cornelius in front of the house on Bemis Street

Christian School; beyond that was the black section, and on the corner of Bemis Street and Eastern Avenue stood our church, Eastern Avenue Christian Reformed Church.

Fuller Avenue was the eastern boundary of the city. Beyond the city boundaries lay pastureland and trees. Every day we saw cows passing our house to be pastured beyond the city limits. At Dunham Street were woods, which extended to a golf course, which is now East Grand Rapids. Calvin College was built among those woods. At Franklin Street was a sandy area full of sand burrs that extended to the sand banks where Adams Street Protestant Reformed Christian School was later built. Beyond that

---

3   The Brickyard was an area on the eastern edge of the city where bricks were made from the clay there to facilitate the growing city of Grand Rapids.
4   The Zeeuws were from Zeeland, a province in the south.

area were a brick factory and Silver Creek, where we children hunted for polliwogs.

Eastern Avenue was our main shopping center. The west side of the street was lined with stores from Franklin Street to a little beyond Logan Street.

On the corner of Franklin Street and Eastern Avenue stood the grocery store of Oom Bakker, related somehow to my mother. Going north was Pastoor's meat market, then Kuiper's smithy. Next to that was Zaagman's funeral home.

On the corner of Dunham Street was Kolkman's furniture store, then a few houses with a confectionary next door, which also sold bottled beer. Then stood Kok's bakery, Hoorn's bookstore, Zondag's bakery, Vander Laan's meat market, and on the corner of Sherman Street, Vander Veen's grocery. On the north corner of Sherman Street stood a drug store, then Kwant's Dutch supply store. On the corner of Baxter Street was a paint store with a barbershop next door, and then the ladies' hat shop of *Vrouw Knol*.[5]

North of that, across from Vander Veen Court, stood a bank, then Eerdmans' bookstore and Hoeksema's shoe store (of which we will hear later). On the corner of Logan Street was Hamstra's tin shop and hardware. The only store beyond that was a very small place where Noordewier had a shoe shop.

On the east side of Eastern Avenue between Baxter Street and Sherman Street were Trompen's clothing store, a barber shop run by Carter, a black man, and Zins' drug store on the corner of Sherman Street. Carter and Zins were the only two non-Hollanders in the neighborhood.

Across from Zins on the southeast corner stood Steel's lumberyard, in front of which was a watering trough for horses. Exactly one block south of that was the dormitory for students

---

5   Vrouw is Dutch for Madame.

who attended Calvin Theological Seminary, where my sister Lucy later worked.

On the northeast corner of Eastern Avenue and Bemis Street stood the Christian Reformed church that was the center of attention in the 1924 controversy. On the south side of the street was the parsonage where the pastor, Rev. Groen, lived.

Although Eastern Avenue was considered the shopping center, there were also many small neighborhood stores in the area. On Logan Street, beginning close to Eastern Avenue and going east, there was a hay and feed store; about a half block down was a grocery store (at one time run by Richard Newhouse and Bert Korhorn); next to it was located Vander Wagon's shoe store. A short distance farther and in front of his house stood Wiersma's grocery store, which had a bell hanging over the door that called him from the house whenever a customer arrived. Beyond Diamond Avenue, on the other side of the street, was Van Winsheim's front-room grocery, and then not far from Fuller Avenue was another small grocery store. Those stores had square boxes of cookies, mustard in a crock, and sugar, vinegar, molasses, and kerosene in large barrels.

But one was not compelled to go from Bemis Street to Logan Street for neighborhood shopping, for on the south side of Baxter Street, across from Baxter Christian School, was Hulst's grocery store. On the northeast corner of Diamond Avenue and Baxter Street was De Vos' grocery store. The owner was the grandfather of Richard De Vos from Amway Corporation. He often served as elder in Eastern Avenue Christian Reformed Church and First Protestant Reformed Church. A half-block north was Westra's grocery store. Those three stores sold penny candy. Across the street one could visit the dry goods store of Nieboer and the meat market of Monsma.

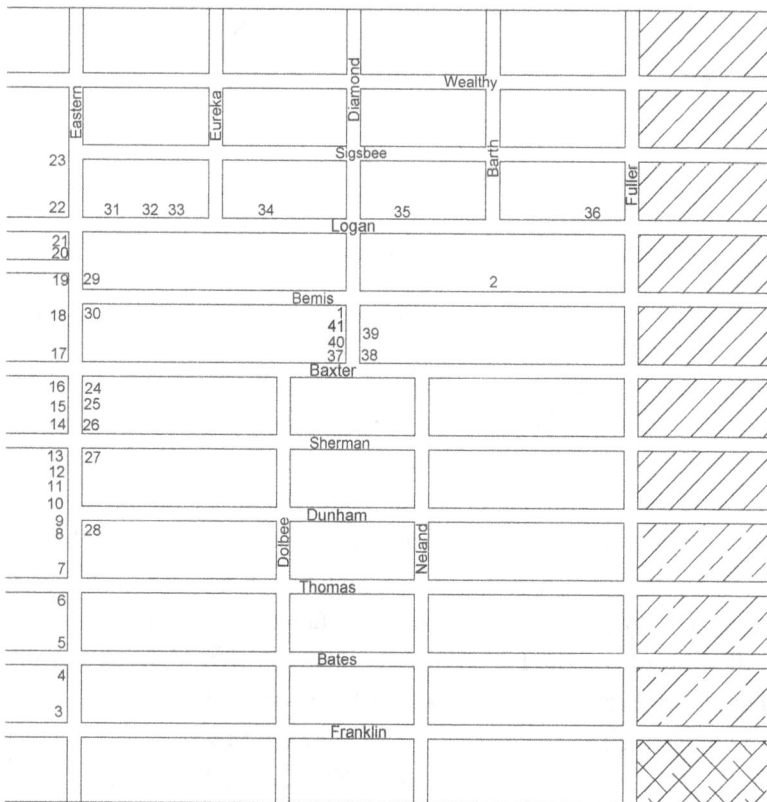

Map showing the author's neighborhood (the Groninger buurt) in Grand Rapids, Michigan, at the turn of the twentieth century. The map was drawn by Trevor Van Overloop according to the memories of the author.

Even so, mothers in the home usually did not have to go that far to obtain supplies for the needs of their families. Milk was delivered at the door every day except Sunday. Those close to the dairy received their milk from a can poured into one of their pans. On Tuesday the fish peddler came down the street blowing a horn. The Polish banana peddler with his two-wheeled cart and loudly shouting "Bananaaa" also drove by. On one of those days Kooistra came with a little pad and a stubby pencil, which he put into his mouth after writing each order. Later in the day he delivered the groceries in a little cart. Almost any time one could

1. Baxter Christian School
2. Cornelius Hanko's childhood home
3. Oom Bakker's grocery store
4. Pastoor's meat market
5. Kuiper's smithy
6. Zaagman's funeral home
7. Kolkman's furniture
8. confectionary store
9. Kok's bakery
10. Hoorn's bookstore
11. Zondag's bakery
12. Vander Laan's meat market
13. Vander Veen's grocery store
14. drug store
15. Kwant's Dutch supply store
16. paint store
17. barbershop
18. *Vrouw* Knol's ladies' hat shop
19. bank
20. Eerdmans' book store
21. Hoeksema's shoe store
22. Hamstra's tin shop and hardware
23. Noordewier's shoe shop
24. Trompen's clothing store
25. Carter's barber shop
26. Zins' drug store
27. Steel's lumberyard
28. Dormitory for students of Calvin seminary
29. Eastern Avenue Christian Reformed Church
30. Rev. Groen's parsonage
31. hay and feed store
32. Grocery store run by Newhouse and Korhorn
33. Vander Wagon's shoe store
34. Wiersma's grocery store
35. Van Winsheim's grocery store
36. grocery store
37. Hulst's grocery store
38. De Vos' grocery store
39. Westra's grocery store
40. Nieboer's dry goods
41. Monsma's meat market

also expect a visit from Oebele Westra, who slaughtered cows and delivered large slabs of pot roast in a basket covered with a bloody towel. He was not what one would call neat in his appearance. One received the impression that he had not changed his clothing after slaughtering the cows. His grunt always attracted our interest.

Then toward the end of the week the bakery wagon stopped, and the vegetable peddler came by with his "Appois, tatoes, all kinds of vegebles!" The oilman, the iceman, the beer wagon, and many others made deliveries. All morning long the housewife stood ready with her coin purse. The ice cream wagon with its shrill whistle came every so often to lure the kids of the neighborhood. On our street the ice cream man had very few, if any, customers. There were also the sprinkle wagon to settle the dust on the dirt streets, the man who swept up the horse manure, and the men from the honey wagon who from time to time came to clean out the outhouses.

There were very few automobiles at that time. Not many families owned one. The common means of transportation was the horse and wagon. We had a chestnut-colored horse, a wagon for my father's paint equipment, and a buggy for special occasions. For example, on Labor Day Dad took out the buggy, in which we rode to the mission festival on the north end of the city. At the festival there was a large, decorated wagon that served as a platform for the band and the speakers. There were also confection stands for the children.

When winter settled in the wagons were converted into sleighs. The wheels were removed and runners were attached to make it possible to travel on the snow-covered streets. The man for whom I worked had a box sled to peddle milk in the winter. A lantern was placed in the center and the milk cases were covered with blankets. The deliveryman sat fully exposed to the wind and cold.

All the fire engines in the city were horse-drawn. The firemen's sleeping quarters were upstairs in the fire house. They slid down a pole when the fire bell rang. The horses were in stables behind the engines. The harnesses hung in front of the engines, ready to be dropped on and tied to the horses. Soon those stately horses were dashing on their way. Two pulled the ladder wagon and two pulled the steam engine. If the firemen thought the fire was large, a fireman began already on the way to build a fire in the boiler to get up steam, which added pressure to the fire hoses. A fire always drew a large crowd of spectators.

It was a thrill for the boys to go to a busy street, like Eastern Avenue, and ride people's sleighs by standing on the runners. Often the driver did not appreciate having riders, so one eye always had to be alert for a sudden sweep of the whip. But who would want to miss the fun of a free ride?

Into this turn-of-the-century Grand Rapids I was born.

Chapter 3

HOME LIFE

In this chapter Rev. Hanko takes us inside his boyhood home and his family's routine. No doubt, life in his home was similar to that of many homes in that Dutch Calvinist community—orderly and scheduled.

The typical Dutch home had a task and a meal for each day of the week. Monday was wash day. At four o'clock in the morning the wash kettle was placed on the cook stove to boil the clothes. The wash tubs were arranged on the hand wringer. Water was brought in from the cistern, and the lines were hung for the clothes to dry outside. When my father came in from his morning chores, my mother asked him about the weather. Rain meant that clothes had to be hung inside, most likely in the upstairs bedrooms. One common answer of my father was, "It could rain; it could turn out well." We children were awakened by the strong smell of soap. How I hated those Mondays, especially because the kitchen table and all the chairs were pushed into the corner to make room for the washing paraphernalia. Wash day also meant that I had to turn the wheel of the washing machine until it was time for school.

Usually by the time we arrived home from school in the afternoon the washing apparatus was being put away for another week. The evening meal that day consisted of brown beans, which had been cooking on the back of the stove all day. The beans were served with bacon, followed by rusk and milk.[1]

---

1 A rusk is a piece of twice-baked bread.

Tuesday was ironing day, which meant that the ironing board was out most of the day. In those days sheets, pillowcases, dresses, cotton shirts, and other clothes were ironed. Each cotton shirt took twenty minutes to iron. We had advanced from flatirons heated on the stove to a gasoline iron, which from time to time became empty and had to be filled while it was hot. The result was that sometime the whole thing would catch fire. When she was little, my sister Henrietta was so afraid of that newfangled tool that she would stand by the screen door ready to run out every time the iron had to be refilled. Since this was the day the fish man came, we had fish with potatoes and vegetables for supper.

Wednesday was sewing day. The girls' dresses were homemade. The long stockings were knitted. Sometimes even the men's shirts were homemade. For special dresses and shirts a sewing woman would come for a day to help my mother. The warm meal for Wednesday consisted of potatoes, roast beef, and beans or peas.

Thursday was shopping day whenever my mother was compelled to go downtown to shop. That was an all-day affair, since there was usually quite a list of things that had to be purchased for the family. I recall one occasion when my father suggested that Mother should not go hungry all day but should stop in the five-and-dime store to buy a sandwich. That was indeed a very special treat. My mother could not stop talking about how good that sandwich tasted. And the coffee! It did cost ten cents, but to her mind it was well worth it.

On a Thursday when there was no shopping to do, the married girls came over. Maggie and Henrietta came all the way from the south end by streetcar. Henrietta, who had a heart of gold but tended to scold, could be heard coming up the street saying to her son, "If you don't behave, we're going right back home."

On Friday the whole house had to be turned on end for cleaning. All the furniture was moved, everything in the room was dusted, and the floor and carpet were swept or cleaned by the carpet sweeper. The bedding was changed, and the bedrooms were given a good cleaning. All but the kitchen had a thorough going over.

On Saturdays the kitchen got its weekly cleaning. All the chairs were moved to the living room, and the table was pushed into the corner. The floor was scrubbed, the stove polished, and the rest of the room dusted. After that there was baking to be done. Mother baked seven huge loaves of white bread, one or two raisin loaves, and also a cake. There is nothing quite as good as the smell of baking bread in the oven. Even the flies, attracted by the smell, were thick on the screen doors and eager to come inside.

We all had chores to do. My duties were to grind a pound of coffee for the week while learning my catechism, polish all the shoes of the family, chop wood, fill the wood boxes for the weekend, fill the coal pails, and take care of the lawn. My sisters had to polish the silverware, sand the wooden forks, and fill in with other duties. On Saturday afternoons during the school year Mother checked the girls for lice they might have picked up. If there was evidence of lice, she combed the girls' hair with kerosene and a fine-toothed comb, which made the girls pull up their legs and scream.

There was one exception to the Saturday chores for Corie and me. If the store downtown had a special Saturday bargain on Fels-Naphtha soap (six bars for twenty-five cents), we would walk downtown to buy the soap.[2] The trip involved the entire morning, since children always find a lot to see and to entertain them on their journeys.

We had a happy home. We often spent evenings around the kitchen table, everyone engaged in his or her own endeavor. Fred and the older girls often had fun teasing and chasing each other.

---

2   Fels-Naphtha was a laundry soap used to pretreat stains.

It was a good thing that Dad could replace a pane of glass, for more than once someone accidentally crashed through a window.

Every Dutch housewife spring-cleaned her home. As soon as the weather proved to be a bit favorable, the urge for the annual house cleaning became overpowering. Room by room, every nook and cranny of the house underwent a special cleaning. The beds were taken apart, the springs and mattresses brought outside for an airing, and the carpet or rugs hung on the line to be severely beaten with the carpet beater until not a speck of dust could be seen. In the living room every piece of furniture was removed, curtains washed, carpets hung out to be beaten dust free, floors mopped, and ceilings, walls, and furniture thoroughly washed. Despite the weekly cleaning, no housewife was considered to have done her duty until the entire house had undergone a spring cleaning or renovations of some sort.

Late summer and autumn were busy times in the kitchen. Beans were strung and canned. Other vegetables, peaches, and various fruits were also canned. There were also jellies to be made. I particularly recall the grape bag, hanging and dripping for a day or two. Later in the fall twenty bushels of potatoes were stored in the cellar, and carrots and beets were placed in sandboxes.

As soon as his work slowed down my dad took a day off to cut up huge chunks of pork fat, which we rendered for a winter's supply of lard. The stench clung to the rooms. The good part was that we ate the crunchy cracklings hot from the fire.

Then there was the all-day job of setting up the hard coal stove in the living room. The stove, stripped of all its decorations, was hauled out of the corner of the bedroom into the kitchen, and then the work began. All the mica squares on the doors were cleaned, and all the black parts and metal trimmings were cleaned and polished. Finally the stove was moved into the living room, set up in the corner with all its decorations, and filled with hard coal, ready for lighting. The hard coal burned with a pleasant glow, which lit up the entire room at night.

The first Christmas that I remember I received, along with the usual knitted black stockings and mittens, underwear, shirts, and a blackboard on a stand. A year later I received a Berry cart, which was given by the Berry Varnish Company to customers such as my dad who had purchased a certain amount of varnish. My cart was often a source of entertainment among the kids of the neighborhood because it was the only one of its kind.

Since my mother's parents lived in Byron Center, Michigan, we paid them an occasional visit by train. We took the streetcar to the west side of Grand Rapids and there boarded the train. In the afternoon at four o'clock there was a train that took us home.

My step-grandmother, Mrs. Schriemer, died when I was about seven years old. A hack (wagon) with two beautiful black horses came to pick up my parents and me and bring us to the home of the departed. After a short service at the home we were transferred by hack to the church. All the women who were closely related to the departed wore heavy black veils over their faces. The men wore black suits or black bands around their arms. When the minister announced the psalm to be sung, the ladies took out a black-bordered handkerchief and carefully reached under their veils to wipe away their tears. After the service we had a long ride to the cemetery where the committal was held. The black hearse pulled by stately black horses led the way to the cemetery. It was customary in those days for the minister to take a handful of dirt, spread it over the casket, and say, "Dust thou art and to dust thou shalt return." Afterward we were taken back to the home of the departed for lunch and then back to our home. It was a wonderful experience for me, and I proudly looked out of the window of the hack.

Grandfather Burmania (after whom I am named) died in Byron Center, his adopted hometown. He had suffered from hammer toes toward the end of his life. His stockings had to be put on in a special way so as not to pain his toes. His widow, Heinke Burmania, wanted the coffin opened to see if his stockings had been put on properly, but her request was not granted.

His funeral followed the same pattern as Grandma Schriemer's. His grave can still be found in the cemetery in Byron Center.

In the summer of my sixth or seventh year, my parents and I went to see Uncle Harm and his daughter, who lived on 103rd Place in Roseland, Illinois. We traveled by interurban to Holland, Michigan, then by boat across Lake Michigan to Chicago, arriving there in the morning.[3] I remember visiting some of the parks in the Chicago area. The streetcar rides were especially exciting. On the way home Lake Michigan was rough and wavy, and we all became seasick. Even in the interurban I was still very uncomfortable. When we arrived home I was eager to lie down.

Sometime before our trip to Chicago, my father had gone there alone to attend the funeral of his sister-in-law. What stood out in the memories of the family members was that while he was away Sena came down with black diphtheria, which was almost always fatal. Since my father was not at home, my mother did not dare to incur the expense of calling a doctor. For three days and three nights, with unceasing prayer and almost no sleep, she swabbed Sena's black throat with iodine, hovering over her almost constantly. Amazingly, Sena recovered.

In the meantime my brother Fred, who was eleven years older than I, had graduated at fifteen years of age from the eighth grade. Passing every year was by no means assured in those days. He evidently had a struggle to get through the grades, mainly because of his bad eyesight. It was likely caused by the many ailments he had as a small boy. He had trouble with the glands in his neck, which would swell sometimes and require lancing. He was on a steady diet of cod liver oil, so that the storekeeper asked him who in the world could take so much cod liver oil, which Fred bought by the gallon.

---

3   The interurban was a local train that connected nearby cities. The old interurban track between Grand Rapids and Byron Center is now part of the Kent Trails.

After Fred graduated from eighth grade, he naturally went into the painting business. He then began to drive the horse-drawn wagon to work early in the morning and back from work after five o'clock. That poor horse had to stand on the street for at least eight hours, with the only interesting time being noon when the feed bag was suspended from his neck. The horse traveled over the gravel and cobblestones at a merry pace. He was as meek as a lamb and readily allowed himself to be harnessed to the wagon every morning to make another trip somewhere in the city.

Sometimes Fred and Dad painted homes beyond North Park. That meant getting up before six o'clock in the morning so that the entire family could gather around the table for morning devotions before they left. Then they made the long trip to the north end and worked in the bedbug-infested houses in that part of town. My mother was always afraid that Dad and Fred would carry some of the pests along with them in their clothes, which they hung in the back hall. The men were very careful not to take any more clothing into the houses than was absolutely necessary. As they took the dirty beds of customers apart, the bedbugs and cockroaches would run helter-skelter. The only bugs they ever took home with them, as far as I know, were cockroaches, which never went farther into the house than the back hall.

By the time I was born my three older half-sisters had already left home to do housework among the richer class of people. Jennie married Nick Bolt when I was just over a year old. They had one child, John, who spent much of his time at our house, because that was where the action was. Maggie worked for a number of years at a house on Fuller Avenue near Lake Drive. She also slept there and only came home Thursday afternoons. Later she married Pete Kladder. Henrietta worked and lived on Sigsbee Street across from the Sigsbee Christian School until she married Rich Helder.

When Sena graduated a year or so after Fred, she also went out to do housework on Cambridge Boulevard. Later she worked in Klaasen's dry goods store on Wealthy Street near Charles Street. I made a little money peddling fashion sheets for Klaasen after school.[4] Sena later married Charles Van Dyken.

When Lucy finished school she worked in the Calvin College dormitory on Eastern Avenue at Dunham Street. She came home every night. She had more than one boyfriend, but the friendships did not last until Bernard Woudenberg came around.

Corie (or Cornelia, after my grandfather) worked in Katie Scheepstra's dry goods store on Diamond Avenue near Wealthy Street. She also had various boyfriends, some for a longer time, some for a shorter time, but she finally settled on Otto Vander Woude, who was attending Calvin College at the time. They were married and had four children. First they lived on Bemis Street, where she was quite a help to my aged mother. Later they moved to Prince Street.

When I was seven I fell out of the neighbor's tree. On the way down my arm was torn open by a broken branch. The neighbor lady saw that and quickly submerged my arm in a tub of rainwater. She wrapped the bleeding arm in a clean towel and sent me home. My mother called the doctor, who advised giving me a half-cup of whiskey at once. When he arrived he took a look at the arm and suggested another half cup of whiskey. After laying me on the kitchen table, he put in twelve stitches. Evidently the liquor was to make the sewing virtually painless. I walked around with a bandaged arm for the rest of the summer.

I was soon old enough to work in the summer. My first job was with a lawn tender who lived on Lake Drive. My brother fixed up his old bike and made it fit to ride so that I had transportation. Every morning I went to rake four area lawns.

Later I worked for the same lawn tender six days a week in the summer, at twenty-six cents a day. He went from one lawn to another cutting the grass with a lawn mower. I followed him with

---

4   Fashion sheets advertised women's clothing.

Cornelius Hanko c. 1917

a lawn trimmer and shears. I had to trim the edges and sweep up the grass. The lawn tender was a man of few words; he rarely spoke and then only when necessary. He expected me to see what he was doing and then to follow suit. If he picked up a lawn mower, that meant cutting lawns. If he picked up rakes and other tools, that meant weeding flowerbeds. When it was time to quit we put away the tools. No words were wasted.

After a few years our neighbor, who was also a lawn tender, hired me to work for him in the neighborhood of Morris and Madison, where a slightly higher class of people lived. He paid me twenty-five cents an hour. Because I received more pay than the other boys, I was made their superintendent and was not allowed to do menial work.

So the rhythm of life continued. We worked, we ate, we slept, we went to church, and when we grew old, we died. Although the times have changed drastically, the rhythm of life remains much the same. As Solomon said, "There is no new thing under the sun" (Eccl. 1:9).

Chapter 4

CHURCH LIFE

In this chapter Rev. Hanko describes a typical Sunday in his home and at church. The reader will recognize many similarities in our lives today, including some of the characters he describes. Yet there are many differences to capture our interest.

Sunday was a special day. As much as possible the family made all preparations for Sunday on Saturday. We checked Sunday clothing, peeled potatoes, prepared vegetables and meat, and did whatever else had to be done. At ten-thirty in the evening my father arose from his chair, wound the clocks, and no matter who was there, announced that it was bedtime.

Sunday morning we each had an egg. Generally, we also ate fresh-baked bread and a slice of raisin bread. At eight o'clock the church bell rang for everyone to adjust his or her clock. There was a time when the three girls who were still home wore tight shoes that came almost to their knees. Because the girls were already strapped into their corsets, they could not bend down to string them. So it was my task to tie their shoes. We each received money for the collections, along with two peppermints, and Corie and I started out for church to save seats for our parents.

Our church was a white, wooden structure. It had fourteen steps to the front entrance; there were two side entrances and two back entrances. One evening the church caught fire. Whatever the cause, much of the fire was between the siding and the inner wall where the firemen could not get at it. It smoldered for

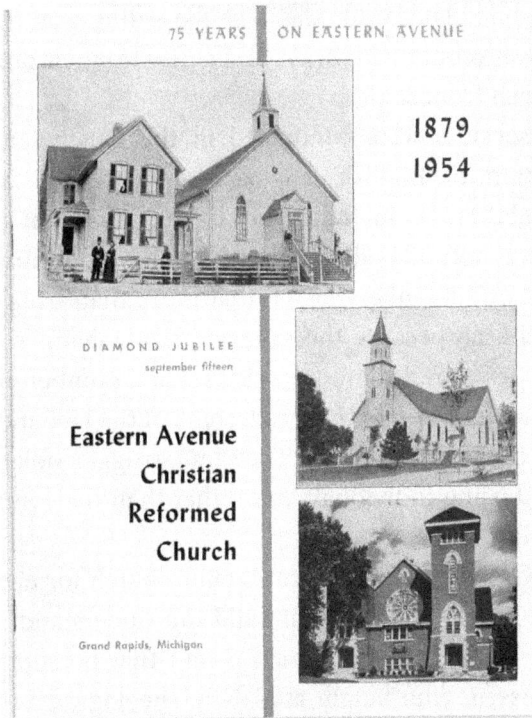

75 YEARS ON EASTERN AVENUE

1879
1954

DIAMOND JUBILEE
september fifteen

Eastern Avenue
Christian
Reformed
Church

Grand Rapids, Michigan

The cover of this anniversary booklet shows Eastern Avenue Christian Reformed Church as the author knew it growing up and as it looks in more modern times.

Johannes Groen's parsonage as it stood in the early 1990s

quite a while. The result was that the siding was removed, the exterior was rebuilt with brick, and a new front entrance replaced the fourteen front steps.

The services were conducted in the Dutch language. The introduction of English language services came with a bitter struggle. Many, including my father, were convinced that if English was introduced into the churches, modernism was sure to follow. The members feared that more than usual in Eastern Avenue church because the minister, Rev. Johannes Groen, was known to lean toward modern views. For a number of years after English services were introduced, some of the Hollanders refused to attend the English service. The same struggle took place before we started using individual cups rather than the common cup at communion.

Rev. Groen served Eastern Avenue church for eighteen years from 1900 to 1919. Although I did not understand at the time, he was a "Janssen man," which meant that he supported Prof. Ralph Janssen, who taught at Calvin Theological Seminary and favored a higher critical view of scripture. Often I heard criticism of Groen's liberal preaching, but I never really understood why. Outsiders referred to his church as "Johnnie Green's Opera House."[1]

Rev. Groen always addressed the congregation as "esteemed audience." When he reached his last point he always said, "And finally esteemed audience," which sometimes meant that he was almost finished preaching. However, that also could have meant that he would continue preaching for fifteen more minutes. During the singing of the last song, he put a velvet cap on his head, evidently because he had been sweating.

The first elder always led a visiting minister to the pulpit and shook hands with the minister to show the congregation that he was officially appointed to preach. The first elder was usually Mr.

---

1 Johnnie Green is the English translation of Johannes Groen.

Bishop, the kerosene peddler, who sat in the first row along the north side of the center aisle in the sanctuary. During the service he had the habit of turning the end of his beard up to his mouth and licking it. On the opposite end of the pew sat our catechism teacher, Mr. Sevensma. He always held his hand on the head of his son to keep him quiet.

Behind the elders sat Mr. Karsies, the baker on Logan Street.[2] Whenever the organ gave out during an electrical storm, which happened quite often, he would step forward and lead the singing. In the meantime, Mr. Hoek would hasten from under the south balcony to the back of the organ to start pumping the bellows that produced the air for the organ. If he succeeded in getting there first, which was not always the case, he would remain the official organ pumper throughout the service. In fact, he would bring a chair up on the pulpit to be ready for the next act.

Later Mr. Karsies had throat cancer, which required an opening in his throat to breathe. He still wanted to lead the singing. When the occasion demanded his leadership, he stood up, solemnly place his finger on the opening in his throat, and give the pitch.

When the Griffioen family (my future in-laws) began coming to Eastern Avenue church, they entered in the side door used by the elders. Usually there was no empty row for the whole family to sit together, so Pa Griffioen would spread the children around. He always saw to it that Arie sat by him because Arie could not sit still.

Under the north gallery sat Mr. De Good, the janitor of the Christian school on Sigsbee Street. He always smoked his pipe until he got up to the church door. Then he slid the pipe into the

---

2   When an attempt was made to run the tracks of the streetcar along Eastern Avenue to Wealthy Street, Mr. Karsies rallied the Dutchmen by ringing the church bell. *Vrouw* Guit and others came out with shovels and pitchforks and dug up the rails as fast as they were laid. It was deemed improper to run a noisy horse-drawn streetcar in front of the church on Sundays.

inside pocket of his suit coat and sat down. One time he failed to knock out all the ashes. Shortly after he was seated he began to hit his coat as hard as he could. Then he hurried out. Just what damage was done, we never heard.

In the middle section behind the elders on the opposite side from Mr. Karsies sat Prof. Ralph Janssen and his family. He was deposed from Calvin seminary in 1922 for denying the infallibility of the Bible and the miracles.[3] Behind him sat Rev. J. Vander Mey and his family. When Rev. Hoeksema was the minister of Eastern Avenue, Rev. Vander Mey opposed Rev. Hoeksema and brought a protest against him. At the Classis of 1924 at which Rev. Hoeksema was deposed, Vander Mey made a statement that almost caused the hair of the delegates to rise from their heads, yet the statement was more truth than fiction. He said that Rev. Hoeksema had a different God than he had.

The deacons sat in the south section of the auditorium. In earlier years they had a black velvet collection bag that they extended on a pole and passed along from aisle to aisle. The people could quietly drop their money into the bag. When the pole was extended to its full length, the bag was carefully lifted over the heads to the next row. When the collection was finished, the bags were hung alongside the organ room.

We always sat in the front row of the south balcony directly across from the pulpit. This was an ideal spot on communion Sundays. Five tables were set up around the pulpit, the center one for serving. The bread and wine were not distributed to the congregants in the pews, but they came forward in turns to the tables to be served. Usually Rev. Groen asked the congregation to sing

---

3   Rev. Herman Hoeksema had been appointed by the theological school committee along with six other ministers to study Professor Janssen's teachings. The majority of the committee drew up a report condemning those teachings. The report was adopted by the synod of 1922. The majority report was chiefly the work of Rev. Hoeksema. For more information on the Janssen case, see Herman Hanko, *A Study of the Relation between the Views of Prof. R. Janssen and Common Grace* (Th.M. thesis, Calvin seminary, 1988).

the verses of Psalm 25, since there were usually eleven or twelve turns of partaking at the tables. The elders would first take their places about the table. Then the deacons and others were invited to fill the chairs around the other four tables. Even in the second round, people were reluctant to come forward to partake of the sacrament because that was considered bold and presumptuous. But by the time the seventh or eighth round was reached there was a rush to come forward, so that some had to return to their seats. No one wanted to be first, nor did anyone care to be last.

On baptism Sundays the father and mother of the infant came in with their baby and took their places in the front row of seats, which had been provided with a small footstool for the mother. Usually the baby cried because it sensed the tenseness of the mother. Then a grandmother or a neighbor lady got up and took the baby out. She usually stood in the hallway at the back entrance until the baptism form had been read. Then she dutifully brought the baby to the parents. It was very common for the mother, or even both parents, to leave as soon as the baptism service was ended.

Before church started, Mother prepared a big pan of rice for Sunday dinner. The rice was made with milk, baked in the oven, and came out with a beautiful brown crust over it. In later years, during more prosperous times, we had potatoes, pork roast, and green beans.

There was time for a short nap before the two o'clock service, the second of three services. Everyone in the Hanko family went to the second service until the time the English service was introduced in the evening. Then the older sisters and brother Fred went to the evening service instead of the afternoon service.

On Sundays we never considered writing letters, playing games, or playing outside. I well recall that someone reported that our large wooden telephone that hung on the wall in the kitchen was out of order. On Sunday afternoon a repairman came into the kitchen and began to work on the phone. My father came from the living room, took one look, and in a loud voice demanded the man to leave the house. He was so amazed at Father's Yankee-Dutch scolding that he quickly packed up and did not return.

Our catechism teacher was Mr. Sevensma, a hunchback and a cripple. He was very stern and terrified his catechumens. We always had to address him with more than one word. We had to say "Ja, Mr. Sevensma" or "Neen, Mr. Sevensma." He made scathing remarks to those who failed to learn the lessons. He picked his nose while telling the story and also had his own unique applications of the lessons. For instance, Eutychus, who slept during Paul's preaching and fell from the third loft and was taken up dead (Acts 20:9), was an example of what happened if one slept in church.

In the summer we had a very special event, the annual Sunday school picnic. We children met in the church and walked to Wealthy Street, where we boarded waiting streetcars, some of them open cars, which took us through downtown Grand Rapids to John Ball Park. We received twenty-five cents in tickets that could be spent at the park. Ice cream cones and Cracker Jack cost a nickel. There was also a large wash tub filled with lemonade. The mothers and some of the fathers came for dinner. After the dinner a minister gave a speech, and then the children played games. Streetcars took us home again.

On Christmas afternoon at five o'clock in the afternoon we had a Sunday school Christmas program. All the speeches and songs were in Dutch, although the Sunday school lesson was taught in English. After the program we each received an orange and a box of candy.

Sometimes people speak of the "good old days," as if the church then was spiritually much better than at present. That may have been true from certain aspects, since sin does develop from year to year in the church, as well as in the world, and brings constant need for reformation. But there was much in those days of which one could hardly approve.

There were the neighborhood "toughies." They did not hesitate to steal, as long as they did not get caught. They sought every opportunity to obtain beer and to have their pleasures. On Sunday they sat in the back row of the church balcony, where they slept, talked, or played cards. The consistory appointed a muscular individual to keep order among them and when necessary to strong-arm them out of the church. He had the authority to make arrests, although I do not know of any instance in which he did that. There was still a carryover of that practice when we worshiped in First Protestant Reformed Church.

Strangely, the consistory did nothing about those outlaws. The elders took the attitude that because the unruly ones were not confessing members, but only baptized members, they were not subjects of discipline.

We ended our Sundays in the twilight singing Dutch psalms, with Father as *voorzinger* (lead singer). My dad had been in a choir in the Netherlands, so he enjoyed singing. He often read to my mother from the religious paper *De Standaard*[4] or from some religious book. In the winter the hard coal stove with isinglass (mica) windows glowed in the corner of our home. What a wonderful way to end the Sabbath!

---

4 *De Standaard* (*The standard*) was a Christian newspaper written and published in the Netherlands and edited by Dr. Abraham Kuyper.

Chapter 5

SCHOOL DAYS

Rev. Hanko began school when Christian education was in its infancy in the United States. Nevertheless, the education he received was superior and equipped him for his life's work as a pastor.

On a Saturday afternoon in the latter part of January 1912, my sister Sena washed and dressed me for a shopping spree. The shopping that day involved going to Wiersma's store on Logan Street to buy the necessary equipment for starting school. Boxes of cookies, cases of candy, a balance scale with various weights, a barrel of kerosene, a barrel of molasses, and every other object that might attract a neighborhood customer stood around. We bought a slate, slate pencils, and a pencil box. Proudly I walked home with my new possessions, eager for Monday and the start of a new adventure.

The next Monday morning I ventured off to Sigsbee Street between Diamond and Eureka, where the old, brown, wooden, four-room schoolhouse stood to serve the lower grades. It had double seats for two children to occupy, a blackboard, a crude wooden floor, and a straight-laced teacher, who wore her hair in a bun and a dress that touched the floor.

At Diamond Avenue and Baxter Street stood a white brick building that housed the upper grades.

In those early years the teachers had no more than an eighth-grade education. It was some time later that a high school education was required to teach, and still later that a college degree was demanded.

I went off every Monday morning with a nickel for the weekly tuition payment, which was carefully recorded on a sheet of paper. Since I was the fifth child of the family going to school, my tuition was cheaper than the other students' tuition.

Since I started school in February instead of the usual September, I was placed in the first grade, which made me the youngest student in the class and required me to plug along a bit harder to keep up.

The school board expected that the small children had not learned English at home, so the first semester's teaching was in Dutch. I hardly needed that because I had an older brother and sisters who spoke English. The teacher wrote the lessons on the blackboard, and the children copied them onto the slates. Whenever a lesson was complete, a pan of water was passed around the room for everyone to wash his or her slate. You can imagine what a confusion that created when some twenty or thirty children were blowing and puffing and swinging their slates in the aisle to hasten the drying process. At times the teacher pleaded for quiet lest she should lose her mind.

We passed quite soon from slates to pencil and paper. The teacher taught reading by showing us a large picture with identifying words printed underneath. The class stood in front of the room and pronounced the words. Spelling words were written on the blackboard, and we were required to write them a number of times. A test would determine how well we knew how to spell the words.

At recess a pail of water and a dipper were set on the porch to quench our thirst. The janitor stood by with a knife to sharpen pencils that needed attention. His left thumb was black from holding the lead of the pencil against the knife.

I can well recall that when I arrived in the fourth grade the first word of the spelling lesson was *geranium*. That floored me.

I decided that if that was the first word I would never make the grade; but somehow I did.

There was no special school or training for the children with learning difficulties. They could sit in a class for three or four years, only to be moved up a grade because they outgrew the seats in the room. Some of those children were very quiet, but some created disturbances in the class, so the teacher was at times almost driven frantic. By the time some of the students reached fourteen or fifteen years they were too strong for the teacher to handle, so their parents were advised to keep them home or to find something else to occupy their time.

One day a classmate and I were playing by the back fence of the school grounds. Sigsbee Street was up a hill from Logan Street. The chicken coop in the backyard of Logan Street was below the school grounds. First we watched the chickens. Then the notion arose in our minds to throw stones at the chickens. That was a pleasant pastime. We were not always successful in hitting a chicken or a rooster, but when we did the bird would become quite perturbed. We were so occupied in our sport that we did not notice the big fellow from the house, climbing up the wall until he was almost to the top. I raced off, and instead of mingling with the other kids I hid behind the school door, where I was soon discovered and brought to the teacher. I do not recall what punishment I received, but it was likely a number of slaps on the hand with the ever-present ruler.

While I was still in the primary grades, those grades moved from the Sigsbee Street building to the Baxter Street building. A new section of red brick had been added to the Baxter building, so that all the grades could then be in one school building. We all helped to move, some carrying waste baskets with supplies, others carrying other paraphernalia, until we had arrived at our new school. The father of Tom and Sid Newhof bought the old building on Sigsbee and made it into a barn in the back of their lot. Tom built a house for himself in front of the old school building.

The old Sigsbee schoolhouse was used as a storage shed.

Baxter Street Christian School in more modern times

Baxter Street Christian School graduation picture;
Cornelius is in the second row, second from the right.

In 1920 I graduated from the eighth grade of Baxter school. In those days a writing diploma was given to those who by the time of their graduation had finished in an acceptable manner all the lessons in the Palmer Method book.[1] I was near the top of my class.

But that did not mean much the next semester, when I went to Grand Rapids Christian High School located at the corner of Madison Avenue and Franklin Street. Previously, Calvin seminary had occupied the building on that corner. After a new, larger building was erected at Franklin Street and Giddings Avenue to be used by the seminary and the college for instruction in the fine arts, Calvin no longer used the Madison Avenue building, and it became the home for the Christian high school.

There were three hundred students enrolled in the high school during my first semester, far more than had been anticipated. The result was a tremendous shortage of teachers and of seats in the classroom. When the classes met, young teenagers lined up along the walls. Besides, there was no teacher prepared for teaching algebra and Latin, even though those courses were offered.

Substitute teachers were brought in from time to time, but very few students were able to get a hold of the basics of algebra and Latin. Nearly the whole class, except for those whose parents had been able to help them through, took the courses over again. By the second semester everything was far better organized, except the assembly room, which was used for a study room and had so many students gathered there that the disturbances were not conducive to quiet study.

In many ways these were happy years. The high school was more than a mile from our home, but I usually enjoyed the walk, since it was not uncommon to meet other students on the way. I made many new acquaintances, so the days and weeks slipped swiftly by.

---

1   The Palmer Method was a method of penmanship instruction taught in American schools in that era.

Chapter 6

WORLD WAR I

World War I (1914—18) was sparked by the assassination of Austrian Archduke Franz Ferdinand at Sarajevo. It seemed that all the nations of the world were divided into two camps. The Allied powers were led by Britain and France, and the Central powers were led by Germany. After a few months of hard fighting across Western Europe, the battle line remained stationary for almost three years until the United States entered the war on the side of Britain and France. The United States entered in answer to Germany's policy of unrestricted submarine warfare. Rev. Hanko recounts his experiences in wartime Grand Rapids.

In 1914 there were rumblings of war in Europe. Soon England, France, and Germany were engaged in an all-out war.

There was a long spell in which the two opposing armies in the trenches had reached a stalemate. Neither side made significant progress. Possibly it was like the time will be before Christ returns, when the whole world is engaged in the final battle of Armageddon, but neither side dares to unleash its lethal weapons.

People in our community hoped that the United States would stay out of the war. That was especially true in our home, since my father was definitely pro-German, as could be expected when one considers his background. But then came the sinking of the

39

Lusitania,[1] and the United States was as involved as all the other nations.

Strong propaganda encouraged patriotism, much more so than in World War II. The Germans were described as beasts, far less than human. Even the churches became involved by stressing that God was on the side of the Allies. Dr. Beets told how the Germans sent poison gas into the trenches of the Allies and God turned the wind about so that the gas came right back at them.[2] One election day Beets gave a radio speech on Genesis 3:9: "And the LORD God called unto Adam, and said unto him, Adam, where art thou?" He raised the question in the sermon, "Adam, where art thou on election day?" Children especially were aroused to patriotism with all kinds of ditties, sayings, and songs.

On one occasion Rev. Herman Hoeksema was asked to speak and encourage the buying of Liberty bonds. The common consensus was that he would refuse, or if he did speak he would oppose the idea. Some took tomatoes and eggs to throw at him while he spoke. He made a strong defense of submission and obedience to those who are in authority, thus silencing his critics.

That overzealous patriotism brought another form of trouble to Rev. Hoeksema, minister in Fourteenth Street Christian Reformed Church in Holland, Michigan, when he refused to have the American flag in the church. His argument was that the church of Jesus Christ was not at war with the Germans, particularly not with the believers in Germany. Some people threatened to tar and feather him. Later he was assured that he would have been tarred and feathered if he had not warned them that he carried a gun to protect himself. That gun was still lying loaded in

---

1   The *Lusitania* was a British liner that was carrying many American passengers. It was sunk by a German submarine in May 1915. Over a thousand lives were lost. That incident was one of the causes for America's entering the war on the side of the Allies.
2   Dr. Henry Beets was a Christian Reformed minister and secretary of missions.

the drawer next to his bed when he went to Pine Rest Christian Hospital almost fifty years later.

A minister in Sully, Iowa, was sought for something unpatriotic that he had said from the pulpit. He had to flee into the cornfield, and his church was set afire.

No minister in Iowa was allowed to preach in any language other than English unless the sermon was repeated word for word in English. An interpreter sat nearby to hear whether that was done accurately.

In that kind of atmosphere the young men hastened to enlist for the service or else waited eagerly for the draft. Anyone not in the service was considered a slacker or a no-good. My brother Fred would have done anything to get into the army, but he was rejected because of poor eyesight. The girls wanted a "soldier boy," and they looked with scorn on any boy who was not in the service.

My mother lived in fear that sometime my father would explode against all that fanaticism and find himself in jail. She must have done a lot of praying for him, for he had a very hot temper.

Almost every home had a flag in the window with a blue star for each son in the service. If the young man of the house was killed in action, the blue star was replaced with a gold star. In those days the immediate family was not the first to be notified. However, every daily paper carried a list of the casualties that had been reported. Two of my sisters were engaged to boys in the service. As soon as the sisters came home from work they took up the paper to check the list of casualties. Whenever a letter came the girls were ecstatic, but they soon realized that it had taken a week or more for letters to reach them. Much could have happened since the boys wrote those letters.

For a number of weeks in the winter of 1917, schools and churches were closed because of a coal shortage. The authorities maintained that so much coal was being shipped across the sea that there was insufficient coal for public gathering places.

Because of the closing of churches and schools, a few of the neighbors came into our kitchen for worship on Sunday mornings. My dad would conduct the service and read a sermon. Thereupon we would all enjoy a cup of coffee and a piece of cake.

Everyone was put on rations. Sugar was so scarce that we kids went around to the neighborhood stores in the hope of picking up a pound or two. We could purchase flour only if a like amount of a substitute was also purchased. We bought flour by the hundred-pound sack, because my father used flour for paste in hanging wallpaper. So a hundred-pound sack of flour brought along with it a hundred pounds of cornmeal, oatmeal, or the like. We had cornmeal for breakfast and cornmeal for lunch. We ate cornmeal mush, cornmeal muffins, and cornmeal bread. We were so tired of eating cornmeal that we thought we would never want to see it again.

Then, to make matters worse, the influenza epidemic hit in the winter of 1918–19.[3] Once more schools and churches were closed for six weeks. Almost no one went to work. Nearly every home had one or more sick with the flu. Doctors could not keep up with the calls that came in. They worked day and night. But the worst was that they knew of no cure. They tried the usual medicines, and they tried the most caustic medicines, all to no avail. Hundreds died. Funeral services were held outside. Very few went to the cemetery.

A little girl in our neighborhood died also. Her coffin was placed by the front window for the neighbors to see. The minister preached the funeral sermon in the street.

A gloom hung over all. Everyone wondered, "Will it strike us next?" There were some homes in which the whole family was stricken, and one home in which there were five deaths. My future mother-in-law, Mrs. Alida Griffioen, gave birth to a child in a room shut off by sheets while others in the family had the flu.

---

3 The flu epidemic referred to here was actually a pandemic of the Spanish influenza, which killed more people than the fighting of World War I.

Ministers were in a quandary regarding what to do. Rev. Groen was so afraid of catching the flu that he refused to visit anyone. Rev. Peter Jonker Jr. of Dennis Avenue Christian Reformed Church was out almost day and night visiting the sick. He placed a ladder next to an upstairs window in order to visit someone upstairs. He wore himself out to the point that he could hardly preach. The consistory allowed him to preach old sermons for a while.

Our family was spared. We sat at home, trying to seek a bit of entertainment among ourselves. But sitting home day after day can grow very wearisome. I remember walking along Wealthy Street just to get out, but the streets were void of pedestrians. The street was "like a painted ship on a painted ocean."[4] It hardly seemed real. The break came on Sunday, when we had our home service in the morning. To prevent further spreading of the sickness, no more than seven people were allowed to meet together; but we did invite in some neighbors. Those were times when prayer was no longer a mere formality, but a cry of the anxious soul pleading for the sick and bereaved.

As the nation struggled to deal with that public health disaster, it also had to contend with sick and crippled men returning from the war. One political cartoon showed two large millstones with people being poured in at the top and mangled corpses dropping out of the sides. Over it stood the caption: "Will war never cease, will peace never come?"

But actually the war was grinding to a close. On November 6 we received a false report of the armistice. The country went wild, absolutely berserk. Young and old sought to give expression to the release of their tensions. Schools closed, shops closed. An unofficial holiday was called. Since there was no radio or television to turn to, everyone awaited eagerly for the next special

---

4   The author here quotes a line from Samuel Taylor Coleridge's poem *The Rime of the Ancient Mariner.*

edition of the paper, for us the *Grand Rapids Press*. It seemed as if the whole city poured downtown to get the latest news as it came out.

We boys went to the *Press* office, bought ten or twenty papers, and sold them on the streets. Although the price was three cents, almost no one bothered to ask for change. People were ready to give a nickel or a dime just to obtain the very latest news. An unorganized parade ran along Monroe Avenue. Some trucks carried effigies of Kaiser Bill being hanged.[5] Others gave expression to their joy in other ways. But there were no thanks given to the Almighty except in the churches.

Five days later, on November 11, 1918, when the true report of the armistice came through, people had little energy left to celebrate again.

When the boys came home, there was a grand parade in downtown Grand Rapids. They came in full uniform, metal hats and all. The churches had special welcomes. In Eastern Avenue Christian Reformed Church, there was a program with a band, various drills with guns and bayonets, and bugle calls, followed by eating ice cream and cake.

Many young men did not return. For those who did return, life was not easy. Those boy soldiers had undergone anxious hours and terrifying experiences. Some had fallen for the French lassies.

My sister Sena noticed that her boyfriend was cold and aloof. On Memorial Day they sat together on the lawn. He had no desire to go anywhere. In their letters they had addressed each other as "Hubby" and "Wifey," but there was no more of that. After a few weeks he told her that he was not interested in her anymore. I saw her dropping his letters one by one into the stove to be burned. Later he married a French girl. My sister Henrietta

---

5   Kaiser Bill refers to Kaiser Wilhelm, Germany's ruler at the time of World War I.

was also planning to get married to her boyfriend from Byron Center. One Sunday afternoon she was visiting at the home of his parents. Henrietta and her fiancé were not getting along. The father called his son outside and said, "It is better to separate in peace than to live together in trouble." My sisters had waited at least three years for their wedding days. They had used their spare time to fill their hope chests. Then all their dreams were shattered.

Sena soon met and married Charles Van Dyken. But for Henrietta the situation looked very precarious. She was twenty-eight years old by that time. Her hopes of getting married were almost zero. She knew a fellow on our street who was nothing more than a bum. She started going with him, much to the chagrin of my parents. My mother was very insistent, saying, "If you marry him, you need not step into this house again." She did give him up, but she said to our mother, "If I'm an old maid it will be your fault," to which my mother responded, "I would rather have that on my conscience than see you marry that bum."

Not very long afterward, Henrietta's girlhood sweetheart, Rich Helder, appeared on the scene. He also had been in the war. In fact, he had stood in line while one man after another was called to meet the enemy. Those men never returned. He would have been the next one, but no more men were needed. One night he sat in a barn that was struck by a bomb. He and his buddies wondered how they had escaped alive.

It was not long after their reunion that Henrietta and Rich were married. I am sure that my sister's strong attachment to Mother was due to the fact that Mother had kept her from a foolish marriage.

Those war years were hard for the family, but a much more difficult battle was coming. That one would be fought in the church.

Chapter 7

REV. HOEKSEMA COMES TO EASTERN AVENUE CHRISTIAN REFORMED CHURCH

The next four chapters in this story relate the background to and the history of the origin of the Protestant Reformed Churches. It is obvious from the length of these chapters that those events were earthshaking for the teenage Neal Hanko. He treats those matters in depth and with passion; very little editorial comment is needed.

Eastern Avenue Christian Reformed Church still stands as a well-preserved edifice, a reminder of better days, in a very unkempt neighborhood with shabby, deteriorated houses and run-down, boarded-up stores. It is difficult to imagine that sixty or seventy years ago that was a very neat and clean environment occupied almost entirely by Dutch people, who still spoke and worshiped in their native tongue.

Those Dutch folks who had come from the Netherlands during the nineteenth century were mainly of the Secession (*Afscheiding*) of 1834 or of the Separation (*Doleantie*) of 1886. Members of each party knew their doctrinal position and were determined to maintain it over against the other. In their visits together they often discussed such issues as infralapsarianism and supralapsarianism, mediate and immediate regeneration, the conditional covenant, presupposed regeneration, and temporal and eternal justification. (Would that we could discover similar conversations on doctrine in our day.)

Many of the ministers of the Secession preached a general, well-meant offer of salvation to all who hear the word. They argued that although God must work faith and conversion, man must believe and repent. Therefore, it can be said that God offers his salvation to all who hear, even with a sincere pleading, *upon the condition that man repents and believes.* As a result those Secession ministers no longer spoke of eternal predestination, first denying divine reprobation and then election.

Those of the *Doleantie* followed Abraham Kuyper in their teaching, including his presumptive regeneration and common grace theories. His followers strove for a synthesis, a harmony between the church and the world, sometimes referred to as "spanning the gap between Jerusalem and Athens." That is plainly a denial of the antithesis.

Our minister, Rev. Groen, had been the minister of Eastern Avenue Christian Reformed Church for eighteen years. He was a follower of Kuyper and among the most liberal of the ministers in the Christian Reformed Church. Besides being a Ralph Janssen man, he was known to defend women's suffrage and the labor union, both of which at that time were still strongly opposed by most members of the denomination. After his retire-

Rev. Johannes Groen
(Christian Reformed
ministers' database)

ment Eastern Avenue congregation was vacant for a year and a half. Many recognized the false teachings of Rev. Groen and were ready to accept a minister like Rev. Herman Hoeksema, who was known for his strong conviction of the truth.

Herman Hoeksema trained for the ministry at Calvin seminary. During that time he met Rev. Henry Danhof, a staunch defender of the Reformed truth, and heard him preach. In 1919 Rev. Danhof gave a paper entitled *De Idee Van het Genade Verbond* (*The idea of the covenant of grace*) at a ministers' conference. He extensively described the covenant as a relationship of friendship between God and his people in Christ. In later years Rev. Hoeksema developed this fundamental truth far more fully. It is cherished by the members of the Protestant Reformed Churches as their heritage.

Young Rev. Herman Hoeksema
(*Christian Reformed ministers' database*)

After graduating from Calvin Theological Seminary Rev. Hoeksema became the minister of Fourteenth Street Christian Reformed Church in Holland, Michigan. As members of the Eastern Avenue congregation, we had made our first acquaintance with him when he preached for us during our vacancy in 1919. He declined many calls while he was in Holland. A year after making our acquaintance, he accepted the call to Eastern Avenue Christian Reformed Church and remained with us for many years. Little did he or we realize the trials and blessings that would follow in and after the birth of the Protestant Reformed Churches.

At that time I was a teenage lad. Now after many years I can look back with a deep sense of gratitude to God that I knew Rev. Hoeksema as my pastor, as my theological instructor, and above all as my spiritual father. He caused me to see the errors into which the church at that time had fallen, and he instructed me in the blessed truth of God's sovereign grace, especially as that is revealed in God's covenant.

The consistory of Eastern Avenue Christian Reformed Church;
Rev. Hoeksema is front and center.

Changes took place in the congregation when Rev. Hoeksema took up the shepherd staff among us. For years catechism teaching and sick visiting had been left to the elders. When Rev. Hoeksema took charge, he was determined to teach all of the catechism classes, lead some of the societies, and visit most of the sick. In fact, he was very unhappy with the instruction that had been given to the youth of the church, which was often nothing more than a telling of a Bible story with a moral applied.

For the first time in my life I had a minister for my catechism teacher. Rev. Hoeksema stepped into the room that first evening, looked about with his sharp, piercing eyes, and immediately brought his catechumens to quiet attention. He insisted not only on order in the classroom, but also that they knew the lessons and gave him their full attention.

Rev. Hoeksema preached his inaugural sermon in Dutch on Colossians 2:1: "For I would that ye knew what great conflict I have for you." In the evening he preached in English on Isaiah 40:5–8: "The voice said Cry, and he said, What shall I cry?" He

49

concluded that sermon by saying, "Thus I conceive of my task in your midst. To this task I pledged myself when I first entered the ministry of the word. And therefore in God's name we assume this task of delivering this twofold message. We will proclaim that all flesh is as grass. We will witness against the attempts of human strength. And we will maintain that the word of our God and it alone stands for evermore."

It soon became evident to the majority in the congregation that they heard preaching that was quite different from what had previously been proclaimed. Rev. Hoeksema was not only a great orator, a forceful speaker who spoke with conviction, but he was also a meticulous exegete, whose exposition of the scriptures was clear and concise. Even the common people who had had little education could understand and be edified by his strongly doctrinal preaching.

There was an awakening in the church. There was an eagerness to hear the preaching of the word. Finally the congregation was hearing the sound preaching of the word and was being spiritually fed. That was food and drink for which our souls had yearned while we walked for many years in a dry and thirsty land. God had indeed sent us a man for that time.

There was also a new emphasis. The new minister laid a strong emphasis on the sovereignty of God. God, not man, stood on the foreground in his sermons. There was a new emphasis on the doctrine of predestination, a truth that was rarely heard in the past. And there was no less a strong emphasis on the antithesis—the marked, spiritual difference between the church and the world. Along with that there was an emphatic denial of the teaching of common grace. Practically the whole congregation had assumed that common grace was an accepted doctrine in the church. The fact that common grace was being denied in the preaching raised many an eyebrow, as if to ask, "What strange thing are we hearing?"

The Men's Society was the first to take action. The men

approached their new minister and asked him to explain to them the whole matter of common grace. He invited them over to his home for an evening, furnished coffee and cigars, explained his position, and patiently answered their questions. Not all were convinced, but from that time on my father was a staunch supporter of Hoeksema. My mother, who had been raised in the doctrines of the Secession, could never quite accept those new views. She actually remained a follower of Hendrik de Cock until the day she died. But she did enjoy Rev. Hoeksema's preaching.

In the context of those ongoing doctrinal discussions in Eastern Avenue, four professors from Calvin College presented a protest against Prof. Ralph Janssen, accusing him of error in his instruction. He had studied in Germany under modern theologians and had imbibed much of their modern teachings. He denied the miracles and the infallibility of scripture. Since the four professors served a protest against their colleague with very few grounds and had not spoken with him about his erroneous teaching, synod dropped the matter.

Not content with that, the professors appealed to the churches. They and four ministers, including Rev. Danhof and Rev. Hoeksema, wrote a pamphlet entitled *Waar het in de Zaak Janssen om Gaat* (*What the Janssen case is all about*).

The curatorium of the theological school appointed a committee of seven men, three who favored Professor Janssen and his teachings and four who opposed him. The committee met, but Janssen refused to cooperate with them. In the meantime, Rev. Hoeksema made an intensive study of the students' notes, and since he was editor of the rubric "Our Doctrine" in the *Banner*, he wrote there condemning Janssen's errors. The committee finally went to synod with majority and minority reports. At the synod of 1922 Professor Janssen's teachings were condemned and he was deposed from office.

On the surface it seemed as if the cause of truth and righteousness had prevailed. But that was not the end of the matter.

Chapter 8

THE CLASSES
AND SYNOD OF 1924

The church had won a great victory with the deposition of Professor Janssen. Rev. Hoeksema had played a leading role in that victory, but in doing so he had gained some powerful enemies. Rev. Hanko describes how those enemies set out to ruin the young and brilliant minister.

N ow that he had been suspended from his office as professor of theology at Calvin seminary, Professor Janssen and his supporters turned and attacked their chief opponent, Rev. Hoeksema, on his denial of common grace. Although Rev. Hoeksema had publicly written about the subject in 1918, at that time not a single voice of objection had been raised. Now his enemies told him that he should first remove the beam (his denial of common grace) from his own eye before he sought to take out the sliver (Professor Janssen's higher critical views of scripture) in his brother's eye. The result was that his opponents wrote brochures, which were in turn answered by Rev. Hoeksema and by Rev. Danhof, who was known to agree with Hoeksema in his denial of common grace.

To clarify the issue that brought about an extremely necessary and important reformation in the churches, I quote Rev. Hoeksema regarding that history.

In order to understand the reformation that gave rise to the Protestant Reformed Churches, it is necessary that we are somewhat acquainted with the history and condition of the Christian Reformed Churches [sic] from which they were separated, and especially with those events that led up to that secession.

Let us, then, go back as far as about 1918, the year when, not without struggle, the error of premillennialism was officially condemned by the synod of the Christian Reformed Churches.

Even before this time, it must be recorded, the Christian Reformed Churches had never been wholly purged from the leaven of Pelagianism and Arminianism. The churches were, indeed, officially Reformed, united on the basis of the Three Forms of Unity as their standards, but the actual condition was by no means in full accord with this official stand. The error of two irreconcilable wills of God, according to which, on the one hand, God willed that all men should be saved, while, on the other hand, He had predestinated His own from before the foundation of the world and reprobated the others, had found a ready acceptance in the churches. So deeply had the error, that the gospel of salvation is a well-meaning offer of grace on the part of God to all men, struck root, and so generally was it accepted as Reformed truth, that it was openly and officially taught in the Theological School of the Christian Reformed Churches, and that denial of this evident error was considered a dangerously extreme or one-sided view, if not a downright heresy. Indeed, we do not misrepresent the matter when we state that a strong Arminian tendency had always existed and strongly asserted itself under the pretense of being Reformed and with the claim of being sustained by the Reformed Confessions…

About the time of which we are writing other evils developed. There was a gradually growing spirit of confessional indifferentism, largely caused by ignorance of the Reformed truth and not infrequently manifesting itself in open disdain of and antagonism against the Reformed principles; and as might be expected, there developed a pronounced tendency toward a falsely conceived 'broadmindedness' together with the manifestation of a spirit of worldly-mindedness, that would hide behind the name of 'Calvinism' as a shield. Especially during the years of the World War, of which several of the leaders of the Christian Reformed Churches were enthusiastic supporters, with its spread of much false and pernicious propaganda, its confusion of the truth with purely humanistic philosophy, its hastening of the inevitable process of Americanization for the churches, long, perhaps, too long restrained, these evil tendencies received a new impetus and asserted themselves with a new confidence and emphasis. There began to appear what may be called a latitudinarian party in the churches, a group of men that assumed a certain leadership, who opposed the antithesis, stood for a 'broader' view of the Christian's life and calling in the world, and strove to abridge the gap between the world and the Church. These men were wont to speak of the urgent need of a 'restatement' of the truth; they lauded the movement of the *jongeren* in the Netherlands, who clamored for something new though they knew not what; and they frequently appealed to the alleged development of a 'new mentality,' that required new methods of approach, new forms and new truths. This 'broadminded' party, it must be recorded, did not appear to have any sympathy with the views of Doctor Abraham Kuyper Sr., until they discovered that this theory of *Common Grace* offered them a philosophy that would support the latitudinarian views in the name of Calvinism. The antithetical conception of Kuyper they fairly disdained. Common grace became the warp and the woof of their life-view. 'Calvinism' and 'Common Grace' became synonyms. Only they that believed and emphasized the theory of common grace were the true Calvinists. And all that opposed them and refused to believe and proclaim this theory of common grace, they proudly and disdainfully branded as Anabaptists! By a dexterous hocus-pocus, Calvinism, always known the world over for its doctrine of predestination and particular grace, had been changed overnight into a philosophy of common grace![1]

Across from the parsonage on Eastern Avenue were two stores. The one was Hamstra's hardware store, where ardent defenders of their pastor met and discussed the ecclesiastical problems of the day. Next door was a shoe shop owned by Wobko Hoeksema, where he entertained his brother, Rev. Gerrit Hoeksema, and other opponents of Rev. Herman Hoeksema.

In early 1924 there arose out of those meetings in the shoe store a protest against Eastern Avenue's pastor. The protest was signed by three members of the congregation, including Wobko Hoeksema. When the protest came to the consistory, the protestants were asked whether they had talked personally with their pastor about their disagreements. When they responded that they had not, they were told to do so. Rev. Hoeksema offered to meet with each protestant separately, but only one accepted the invitation. It soon became evident that the man did not even understand the content of his own protest. When the consistory rejected that protest, its backers proceeded to bring it to the May 21, 1924, meeting of Classis Grand Rapids East.

The men accused their pastor of committing a public sin by his denial of the theory of common grace. That charge of heresy was a serious accusation presented without proof. Therefore, the consistory demanded that they either prove their charges on the

---

1 Herman Hoeksema, *The Protestant Reformed Churches in America: Their Origin, Early History and Doctrine* (Grand Rapids, MI: First Protestant Reformed Church, 1936), 14–16.

basis of scripture and the Reformed confessions or retract them. Since they refused to do either, they were placed under censure. They also protested their censures to the classis.

Although it is not good order to treat a matter that is unfinished in the consistory, classis entered into the content of the protest of the three members of Eastern Avenue church.

The classis met in Eastern Avenue church for two days. The women of the congregation, most of them supporters of Hoeksema, fed the delegates. At lunch the second day a woman said, "We should not feed you men who are trying to depose our minister." The delegates regarded that as a threat and moved the meeting for the third day to the Sherman Street Christian Reformed Church.

There were other protests against Rev. H. Hoeksema, one from Rev. M. M. Schans and one from Rev. J. K. Van Baalen. In the discussion Rev. Schans remarked that Rev. Hoeksema had a different view of providence than the rest of the delegates. Rev. J. Vander Mey, a member of Eastern Avenue, also spoke against his pastor and accused him of having a different God from the rest of them.[2] Although the classis was shocked at the statement, there was more truth to it than they realized.

As an aside, I mention that Rev. Vander Mey no longer served in his office as minister but was the financial secretary of Calvin seminary and a collector of money, particularly in the Midwest. One day he stopped at the home of the great-great-grandmother of Prof. Barry Gritters and, looking at the books in her bookcase, remarked, "Mother, I don't see one book of Dr. Abraham Kuyper here." Mrs. Gritters was a staunch defender of the Secession of 1834, so her reaction was, "That name is not mentioned in this house. Get out of here." When Rev. Hoeksema first came

---

2 The author refers to the fact that the god of common grace is "a different God" from the God of sovereign and particular grace. Vander Mey maintained that God loves and is gracious to all men without distinction and objected to his pastor's view that God is gracious only to the elect.

to Eastern Avenue, Rev. Vander Mey sent him a card saying, "Of all your sermons the last one I heard crowns them all." Shortly thereafter he also joined the opposition against his pastor.

The meeting of synod was scheduled for the latter part of June and early July. The protests were hastily sent to that gathering. A lengthy debate was held at synod on the subject of common grace. It became evident, as one delegate later admitted, that most of the delegates failed to understand the issue at hand but simply assumed that common grace had always been an accepted doctrine of the churches.

Synod of 1924 *(Archives of Heritage Hall, Calvin College)*

Rev. Henry Danhof was a synodical delegate, and he took the opportunity to defend his convictions. On one occasion he remarked that he considered himself to be a spiritual son of Prof. Foppe Ten Hoor.[3] Ten Hoor responded, "I never knew that I had given birth to any spiritual sons." Rev. Hoeksema was refused

---

3 Foppe Ten Hoor was a professor at Calvin seminary under whom Hoeksema and Danhof had studied. Ten Hoor was known for his opposition to using worldly philosophy to develop the Reformed faith.

the right to speak because he was not a delegate. Since the issues deeply involved him, he felt that he should have the right to defend his stand. Finally he was allowed one evening to state his convictions. He spoke for about two hours, and from that time on was forbidden to speak.

The synod of 1924 formulated and adopted the well-known three points of common grace. Briefly summarized, the points state that God has a favorable attitude toward all men, revealed in the preaching, which proclaims that God loves all who hear the gospel and earnestly desires their salvation; that God by the working of the Spirit restrains sin in the hearts of wicked men; and that the wicked are able to perform civic good.

The synod did not fail to add that Rev. Danhof and Rev. Hoeksema were basically Reformed in their teachings with a tendency toward one-sidedness. Nor did the synod demand the censure to be lifted from the three protestants of the Eastern Avenue congregation who had accused their minister of public sin. The synod also expressed that a more thorough study of the matter of common grace should be made. Finally, synod issued a warning to the churches that a wrong and one-sided presentation of the theory of common grace could lead to worldliness.

If when traveling on the freeway one deliberately turns off on a wrong exit because it looks appealing, the result will be that unless he backtracks, he will find himself going farther and farther from the right road. Little did the delegates of synod realize how far the pernicious doctrine of common grace would lead the church astray, not only into worldly-mindedness, but also into rank Pelagianism and Arminianism, as well as into liberalism and modernism. They would one day lose their Reformed heritage completely.

That assembly made a significant and ecclesiastically destructive decision by adopting the three points of common grace. All that had been gained by condemning the views of Professor Janssen, which were based on the common grace theory, was lost by that unhappy decision.

Before taking up the events that followed the decision of the 1924 synod, I will make a few brief remarks about the three points. The first point states "with regard to the favorable disposition of God toward mankind in general...that besides the saving grace of God, shown only to the elect unto eternal life, there is a certain kind of favor or grace of God which He shows to His creatures in general.[4]

This statement is misleading to say the least. No one denies that God is good to his creation or handiwork, as we read in Psalm 145:9, but this psalm adds "but all the wicked will he destroy" (v. 20). As innocuous as this theory might seem to be, it is a significant world-and-life view that determines our conception of God and the antithesis and of our attitude toward the world around us, and much more.

It was also maintained that common grace has nothing in common with special grace. Yet the first point speaks of "a general offer of the Gospel." From this eventually followed a denial of all five points of Calvinism and the teaching of a general love of God for all mankind with eagerness on his part to save everyone.

The second point speaks of "the restraint of sin in the life of individuals and in society."[5] This does not refer to an outward restraint whereby God in his providence upholds and governs all things, but refers to an inner restraint that checks sin in the heart of the reprobate so that he is no longer totally depraved.

The second point opened the way for the third point, which says that "the unregenerate, though unable to do any saving good...are able to do civil good."[6] This is a very flattering view of the world in general, but also appeals to our sinful flesh. We like to think that this world and we ourselves are not so bad after

---

4 *1924 Acts of Synod of the Christian Reformed Church Held from 8 June to 15 July, 1924, in Kalamazoo, MI*, trans. Henry De Mots (Grand Rapids, MI: Archives of the Christian Reformed Church), 145–46.

5 Ibid., 146.

6 Ibid.

all. But read Romans 3:9–18. Many evils, such as questioning the infallibility of the scriptures, have followed out of the heresy of the third point.

At the conclusion of each point synod wrote that our Reformed fathers from of old have advocated these opinions. That is not true. The fathers did indeed speak of a common grace, but as Wilhelmus à Brakel, seventeenth century Dutch Reformed theologian, pointed out, common grace was generally understood to mean nothing more than that God gives good gifts such as rain and sunshine to the elect and reprobate alike.

Regarding the general, well-meant offer of salvation on the part of God to all mankind, à Brakel stated that this would be a contradiction in God, for God cannot will to save only the elect and also will to save all men. Moreover he pointed out that this must necessarily be a denial of total depravity and a denial of particular atonement.[7]

The summer of 1924 found me, as in previous summers, painting houses with my dad and brother. Although we were somewhat shocked that synod had made common grace an official doctrine of the church by adopting the three points, we were comforted that Rev. Hoeksema and Rev. Danhof were declared to be fundamentally Reformed, even though tending toward one-sidedness. We thought the matter would be put to rest by those decisions.

---

7 Regarding the calling and the well-meant offer of the gospel, see Wilhelmus à Brakel, *The Christian's Reasonable Service in which Divine Truths concerning the Covenant of Grace are Expounded, Defended against Opposing Parties, and Their Practice Advocated as well as the Administration of the Covenant in the Old and New Testaments*, trans. Bartel Elshout (Ligonier, PA: Soli Deo Gloria, 1993), 2:205–8. The Dutch is found in *De Redelijke Godsdienst* (Leiden: D. Donner, 1893), 2:1893

Chapter 9

REV. HOEKSEMA
IS DEPOSED

---

*The author relates the months-long process that ended
in the deposition of Rev. Hoeksema. It is an eyewitness
account, and a moving one, although not without its
humor.*

The decisions of the 1924 synod did not settle the problems in
Eastern Avenue Christian Reformed Church. Synod had spoken. The consistory demanded Rev. Vander Mey to confess his
sin of distributing copies of his protest throughout the churches.
The consistory also demanded the three protestants to retract
their accusation of public sin. Since all parties involved not only
refused, but also showed a hostile attitude, the consistory brought
the matter to Classis Grand Rapids East, which convened on
August 20, 1924. The consistory requested classis to rescind its
former decision that the consistory be advised to lift the censure
of the three protestants.

Classis did not advise the consistory of Eastern Avenue to
lift the censure of Rev. Vander Mey, but classis did advise the
consistory to lift, as soon as possible, the censure of the three
protestants, on the ground that synod had sustained their accusation against their pastor. Classis did exactly what synod had
refused to do. By the decision of classis Rev. Hoeksema was actually accused of public sin because of his denial of common grace.
That was the first step toward the deposition of Rev. Hoeksema

and his consistory and the expulsion of the congregation of Eastern Avenue from the Christian Reformed denomination!

The Eastern Avenue consistory felt compelled to call a congregational meeting for all confessing members, male and female, on September 2. At that meeting the decision of classis would be explained and opportunity would be given to all confessing members to sign a protest against the action of classis.

Eleven members formulated a protest against that congregational meeting, which accused the consistory of mutiny and rebellion, as well as allowing women to vote at a congregational meeting (although in reality there was no vote taken). The consistory treated the protest at its meeting of September 12.

Fifty confessing members brought a second protest to the consistory meeting of September 12. The protest was against the congregational meeting; it requested the consistory to demand Rev. Hoeksema to abide by the word of God and the confessions in his preaching and writing and to announce from the pulpit that he would submit to the three points; and it requested the consistory to submit to the classical and synodical decisions regarding the censure of the three protestants.

Classis Grand Rapids East repeatedly met, recessed, and met again. It should be understood that Rev. Hoeksema and his consistory resided in Classis Grand Rapids East. (Rev. Danhof and Rev. George Ophoff, who joined them in their stand, resided in Classis Grand Rapids West.) The classical meetings could be compared to a correspondence course between the Eastern Avenue consistory and the classis. Classis met, heard the answer of the consistory, placed it in the hands of a committee from the theological school, and recessed, only to meet again when the committee was ready to report.

One cannot help but ask why those ecclesiastical assemblies dealt with Rev. Hoeksema and his consistory in such a strange, improper, and illegal manner. It is obvious that they wanted to avoid with all their power a direct confrontation with Rev.

Hoeksema. The reason is evident. Rev. Hoeksema stood intellectually head and shoulders above all the leaders of that day. They all knew that if he were given the opportunity of a public discussion or debate, his strong oratorical ability and intellectual acumen would convince many listeners. It would even expose those leaders in their foolishness and errors. They avoided that with might and main, and therefore they consistently refused to allow him to speak in his own defense. Although that was not demanded of the other ministers and consistories, Classis Grand Rapids East demanded Rev. Hoeksema and his consistory to sign the three points of common grace that synod had adopted.

Those were crucial times. Many visitors attended every session of classis. Women took crocheting, sewing, or knitting along and stayed all day. At five o'clock they went home to make supper so their husbands could attend the evening sessions.

Some supporters of Rev. Hoeksema and Rev. Danhof began the Reformed Free Publishing Association to publish the writings of these men. Hoeksema no longer had a voice in the *Banner*, as he was forced to resign as the author of the rubric, "Our Doctrine," in the early 1920s in connection with the Janssen case. The publishing association began a new magazine called the *Standard Bearer*, which became the unofficial voice of the Protestant Reformed denomination.

Every Sunday, especially in the evening, the auditorium of Eastern Avenue was filled beyond capacity. Visitors came from various churches to hear our pastor. Not only were seats placed in the aisles and in front of the platform, but some people sat on the platform and on the steps leading up to the platform. Those who could not be seated stood in the hallways, so that repeatedly the fire chief came to clear the hallways.

One professor at Calvin seminary came to hear Hoeksema preach. In his sermon Hoeksema took a dig at Socrates and other philosophers. The next day that professor came to class and said, "Our beloved Socrates was dragged through the mud again last

THE STANDARD BEARER

EDITORIAL STAFF
Rev. H. Danhof
Rev. H. Hoeksema
Rev. G. Ophof
G. Van Beek

REFORMED MONTHLY

PUBLISHED BY THE REFORMED FREE
PUBLISHING ASSOCIATION
GRAND RAPIDS, MICH.

Communications relative to subscriptions should be addressed to G. Vos, 707 Thomas St., S.E., Grand Rapids, Mich. Communications relative to contents of Magazine should be addressed to Rev. H. Hoeksema, 524 Eastern Ave., S.E., Grand Rapids, Mich.

Vol. I, No. 1   OCTOBER, 1924   Subscription Price $1.50

MEDITATION

JEHOVAH'S GOODNESS

The Lord is good to all......but all
the wicked will He destroy.
Ps. 145: 9a, 20b.

Emphatically, according to the Hebrew original, the poet, who is the inspired author of this psalm, puts it: "Good is Jehovah".

The Lord is goodness essentially.

Apart from any relation to His creatures, conceived all by Himself, in Himself, for Himself, as the absolutely Self-existent, Self-sufficient, Independent One, the Lord is good. His essence is goodness, His eternally adorable Divine Being is only good. Could we enter into the amazing profundity and explore the fathomless depths of His infinite Being, the deepest depths of the incomprehensible divine essence would reveal nothing but goodness.

He is the Light and there is no darkness in Him. He is Truth, Righteousness, Holiness, Purity, Love, Grace, Mercy and Eternal Life, and there is no Lie, Unrighteousness, Defilement, Corruption and Death in Him.

He is Summum Bonum, the Highest Good, not in a mere superlative sense, not in a sense that would compare Him with other goods or goodnesses, that might perhaps be conceived as existing next to Him though in a far inferior degree; but in the sense that He is the Sole Good, that there is no good apart from Him or without Him. He is the ultimate and absolute criterion of all good. He is not good in the sense that He answers to a certain standard of goodness that might be applied to Him, but Himself is the only Standard of all that is called good.

He is good because He is God.

Very perfection in all His adorable virtues......

Good is Jehovah!

The Lord is good!

And because the very Being of His adorable Godhead is goodness, the Divine Nature in all the glorious attributes thereof is purest perfection and immaculate goodness. Neither is there any reason of want in God why He should need an object unto which to reveal and upon which to lavish His goodness. For as the Triune God He lives from everlasting to everlasting the perfect life of Infinite goodness in and thru Himself. Never there arises from the unfathomable depths of His perfect Essence the slightest thought that is not good, perfect, true. Never the faintest thrill of imperfection there is in the Will of Jehovah. Never the most imperceptible discord there is in His divine feeling. Never there is the tiniest ripple of evil on the stream of life flowing from His divine heart.

No shadow of darkness ever bedims the light of life, perfect and infinite, of the Divine Family. Father, Son and Holy Ghost, each eternally subsisting in the unchangeable Essence of limitless goodness, thinking in the Perfect Mind, willing with the Perfect Will are living in absolute Self-sufficiency an uninterrupted divine life of purest goodness, dwelling in a Light that is never in any wise bedimmed.

Yea, good is Jehovah!

Everlastingly, solely, unchangeably good!

Because the Lord is good, the absolute good in Himself He is also good to all His creatures.

Good is Jehovah to all!

He is the Overflowing Fount of all good.

All the good His creatures ever receive is solely from Him and is only good because He is good, assumes an attitude of goodness to them. He is full of richest benevolence which He lavishes in profuse abundance upon all the wide creation. His goodness profuses the silvery lustre thruout the starry heavens and arranges their marvellous harmony night upon night. His goodness decks the sun-with that glorious attire of wondrous gold, day after day. His goodness adorns the lily of the field with purest beauty such as Solomon never possessed and clothes the royal cedars of Lebanon with strength and majesty. His goodness causes the royal eagle to renew its strength as it sweeps the firmament with powerful wing; and fills the mouth of the young raven crying to Him for food. His goodness remembers the roaring lion and the chirping sparrow on the housetop. His goodness clothes the meadows in velvety green and covers the fields with golden grain. His goodness made man a little lower than the angels, adds keenness to his mind and strength to his arm and fills his heart with gladness.

The first issue of the *Standard Bearer*, October 1, 1924

night." In the eyes of the professor, Socrates, by God's common grace without a speck of special grace, had come right up to the portals of heaven.

Even the children on their way to Franklin Park for a Sunday school picnic walked along Eastern Avenue and Franklin Street shouting, "One, two, three, four! Who are we for? Hoeksema!"

The controversy created a stir far beyond the local congregation. Common grace was discussed in the homes at mealtimes, even when visitors were present, on the street corners, and in the grocery stores. Whenever one saw a group of people together in earnest discussion, one could be sure they were discussing the topic of the day. Those in favor of common grace would ask, "If an unbeliever pulls another man out of the ditch, is he doing good?" We would say, "No." They would say, "Is he doing any good if he leaves him in the ditch?" We would answer, "No, he isn't doing any good then either."

Even in Calvin College and in the seminary, which I was attending at the time, there was a lot of tension. The professors did not fail to make cutting remarks about Rev. Hoeksema and Rev. Ophoff. Among the students there was constant debate. Professor Volbeda's son was always ready to agree with me,[1] while Professor Berkhof's son took up the defense of the classis.[2] When the ministers were deposed, we who continued with them were virtually ignored.

When the time of Hoeksema's suspension neared, Prof. Clarence Bouma,[3] a cousin of my mother's, came over when my mother was alone and told her that I should not be allowed to stay with Hoeksema. Bouma said that I was needed in the Christian Reformed Church, and Hoeksema would never amount to anything anyway. When I came home she was crying because she felt bad about that unsettling conversation. I told her that I had decided to go with Hoeksema. Earlier that had been in some doubt, but after I met privately with Rev. Hoeksema, my mind was made up.

---

1   Samuel Volbeda was professor of church history and practical theology at Calvin seminary. He later became its president.

2   Louis Berkhof was a professor in Calvin seminary and also served as its president. He is known for his work in systematic theology and is considered the primary author of the three points of common grace.

3   Clarence Bouma was the son of Doeke Bouma. Doeke had visited Jantje when she was a young girl working as a maid in the Netherlands. Clarence became a professor at Calvin seminary in 1924. His daughter is Thea Van Halsema, author of various books, including *This Was John Calvin*.

I made confession of faith on a Thursday evening in December, the day before Rev. Hoeksema was suspended from office and his consistory was deposed. The next morning I was at school for an early class. Immediately I was informed by one of the students, who evidently was in the know, "Today your minister will be suspended from his office." That was followed by the question, "What are you going to do?" I answered that when Rev. Hoeksema was put out I was put out also. He and a few others told me, "Then we shake hands now for the last time."

As was expected, on December 12, 1924, Rev. Herman Hoeksema was suspended from the office of the ministry of the word and sacraments and his consistory was deposed. On January 28, 1925, he was deposed.

Earlier in January Classis Grand Rapids West had deposed Rev. Danhof and Rev. Ophoff and their consistories, First Kalamazoo and Hope. The *Grand Rapids Press* carried information regarding Classis Grand Rapids East and Classis Grand Rapids West on the front page of the evening papers whenever possible. Under the headline, "Rev. Ophoff Prefers Death," his final words to classis were recorded: "Mr. President, if you were to place me before a gun to be shot or before me the three points to adhere to, I would choose the former. I can't sign the three points. If I did I would be tearing the Bible into shreds. I would be stamping the Word under foot. I would be slapping God in the face."[4]

Even those depositions were contrary to the Church Order. It has always been maintained that according to the scriptures and sound Reformed principles, Christ rules his church. Christ opens and closes the gates of the kingdom of heaven. He calls the minister of the word, the elders, and the deacons to their respective offices. Christ does so through the consistory, which is the ruling body in the church that represents Christ. A classis or a synod is

---

4 *Grand Rapids Press*, January 23, 1925.

not a higher authority. They are not governing but advisory bodies. No classis or synod has the right to exercise discipline over members of the congregations or the right to discipline office-bearers. Classes and synods can only *advise*, and if that advice is not adopted, they can declare a particular congregation outside of the denomination. That is the extent of their rights.

Classis Grand Rapids East and Classis Grand Rapids West went far beyond that.

The next Sunday the congregation of Eastern Avenue met with mixed feelings. There were tears, but there was also joy. Tears? Yes, ninety-two members with their families were no longer with us. Some had refrained from coming to church for some time already, but now the recalcitrant ones left entirely, went their sinful ways, and met separately in Sherman Street church. But there was more, for we were illegally, even cruelly cast out of the denomination in which many of us had been baptized and reared. There was no doubt in our minds that when they cast out our pastor and consistory, we also were cast out.

Our pastor, consistory, and we have often been accused of withdrawing from the Christian Reformed Church. That is not true. Our minister and our consistory were deposed because of their convictions. As a result we also were placed outside of the denomination because of our convictions.

More than that, in some instances husband and wife stood diametrically opposed to each other, families were permanently broken up, and friendships were ended. A split in the church is a very painful experience. My three half-sisters and my full sister Sena with their families all remained in the Christian Reformed Church and became bitterly opposed to us. On birthdays we still came together, but as soon as any reference was made to church or doctrine the older ones became angry and threatened to go home.

Many of us could not refrain from singing, "Friend and lover are departed / Dark and lonely is my way; / Lord, be Thou my friend and helper, / Still to Thee, O Lord, I pray."[5]

Yet there was joy, and the joy far outweighed the grief. It was indeed a relief that peace was restored in the congregation. The offense of the presence of the protestants was removed. We could worship once more in complete harmony and unity. The struggle that had been foremost in our prayers and had caused many sleepless nights was over. We realized that the Lord had done great things for us.

Our God had brought about a reformation! Well may I add, a very necessary reformation. On that first Sunday our pastor chose as the text for his sermon John 6:67: "Then said Jesus unto the twelve, Will ye also go away?" We were forcefully reminded that we should not come along because of sympathy or sentiment or for any ulterior reason. We should not remain with the congregation because of the cruel injustice that had been performed. Before the face of God we should take our stand out of conviction, deep conviction of the truth, and love for the sovereignty of our God.

At the close of the service the rafters fairly rang with joyful praise to God in the strain of the psalmist, "Thou art, O God, our boast, the glory of our power; / Thy sovereign grace is e'er our fortress and our tower. / We lift our heads aloft, for God, our shield is o'er us, / Through Him, through Him alone, whose presence goes before us, / We'll wear the victor's crown, no more by foes assaulted, / We'll triumph through our King, by Israel's God exalted."[6]

---

5 No. 240:5, in *The Psalter with Doctrinal Standards, Liturgy, Church Order, and added Chorale Section,* reprinted and revised edition of the 1912 United Presbyterian *Psalter* (Grand Rapids, MI: Eerdmans, 1927; rev. ed. 1995).
6 No. 422:6, in ibid.

Chapter 10

BEGINNING ANEW

Rev. Hanko now tells of the "Gideon's band," out of which arose the Protesting Christian Reformed Churches. The small group eventually became a new denomination called the Protestant Reformed Churches.

The Lord had brought about a reformation. Yet at the time it seemed so small, so insignificant. We were like a small Gideon's band over against the large host that still opposed us.

True, there had been other ministers who during the conflict had encouraged Rev. Hoeksema to stand firm and hold his ground. One minister preached for us on the Sunday evening before Rev. Hoeksema's suspension. At the close of his sermon he urged us to continue to stand with our minister in defense of the truth, regardless of the consequences. But he himself did not. Another minister preached for us on a Sunday evening after Rev. Hoeksema was suspended from office, but later he confessed to his church that he had erred in doing so.

Rev. Ophoff had been asked to meet with a few Christian Reformed ministers in the Grandville Avenue Christian Reformed Church. He attended the meeting while his elder waited outside, nervously pacing the street. The meeting evidently lasted quite a while. When Rev. Ophoff made his appearance, the elder's first question was, "Did you give in?" Ophoff responded, "Of course not." Later Rev. Ophoff revealed

Rev. George Ophoff (1921)

that a rather large congregation was offered him if he would remain in the Christian Reformed Church. Eventually one of the ministers mentioned above accepted a call to that large congregation.

There were still others who gave every indication of breaking with the Christian Reformed Church if Rev. Hoeksema was cast out. But one by one they dropped away. Was it because the movement was much smaller than they had anticipated?

People on both sides of the issue of common grace wrote many pamphlets. Some of them were written before Rev. Danhof and Rev. Hoeksema were deposed, and some were written afterward.[1] Rev. Hoeksema and Rev. Danhof wrote a brochure entitled *For the Sake of Justice and Truth* to explain the recent controversy and their plans for the future.[2] Various other booklets were written in defense of the three points and the errors of common grace and the well-meant offer. Professor Bavinck in the Netherlands wrote *Common Grace*.[3] Rev. H. J. Kuiper published a series of three sermons that he had preached in defense of the three points.[4] Prof. Louis Berkhof published a brochure entitled *The Three Points, Reformed in All Parts*. Rev. Hoeksema answered Berkhof in *The Triple Breach in the Foundation of*

---

1 The pamphlets mentioned in this paragraph were originally written in Dutch. The author included the Dutch titles as well, but here I give only the English translations of the titles.

2 See Henry Danhof and Herman Hoeksema, *For the Sake of Justice and Truth: A Message of Clarification and Direction*, trans. Marvin Kamps, in Henry Danhof and Herman Hoeksema, *The Rock Whence We Are Hewn: God, Grace, and Covenant*, ed. David J. Engelsma (Jenison, MI: Reformed Free Publishing Association, 2015), 239–90.

3 Prof. Herman Bavinck was professor in the Free University of Amsterdam.

4 Rev. Kuiper was a minister in the Christian Reformed Church and editor of the *Banner*.

the Reformed Truth.[5] Rev. J. K. van Baalen wrote *The Denial of Common Grace: Reformed or Anabaptist?* Van Baalen accused Hoeksema and Danhof of being Anabaptist.[6] To that the ministers responded with *Not Anabaptist but Reformed.*[7] Van Baalen also wrote *Novelty and Error: The Denial of Common Grace.* Prof. William Heyns wrote a series in the *Banner* on the preaching of the gospel, which was also published in a pamphlet.[8] Hoeksema answered Heyns in a series of articles in the *Standard Bearer.*[9] Heyns also wrote a series of articles on the covenant, which Hoeksema answered in 1927 in a series of articles in the *Standard Bearer,* which were translated and published in book form in 1971 as *Believers and Their Seed.*[10]

Regarding the brochure of Heyns on the gospel, it is interesting to note that, completely contrary to the Reformed view that God has one will in Christ, Heyns stressed the idea of *two wills in God*: *God wills to save only the elect and wills to save all mankind.* It is amazing to see how that error developed throughout the

---

5 See Herman Hoeksema, *A Triple Breach in the Foundation of the Reformed Truth: A Critical Treatise on the Three Points Adopted by the Synod of the Christian Reformed Church in 1924,* in Danhof and Hoeksema, *The Rock Whence We Are Hewn,* 349–471.

6 Rev. van Baalen was minister in Munster Christian Reformed Church in Indiana. He was one of Hoeksema's fiercest opponents and probably wrote the most against him.

7 See Henry Danhof and Herman Hoeksema, *Not Anabaptist but Reformed: Provisional Response to Rev. J. K. van Baalan concerning the Denial of Common Grace,* trans. Daniel Holstege, in Danhof and Hoeksema, *The Rock Whence We Are Hewn,* 85–155.

8 William Heyns taught in Calvin College and seminary. He popularized the conditional view of the covenant.

9 In 1933 the mission committee of the Protestant Reformed Churches published the articles as *Het Evangelie* [The gospel]. The English translation, Herman Hoeksema, *The Gospel or the Most Recent Attack against the Truth of Sovereign Grace* is unpublished, but is available at http://www.prca.org/resources/publications/books/item/3159-the-gospel-het-evangelie-herman-hoeksema.

10 Herman Hoeksema, *Believers and Their Seed: Children in the Covenant,* rev. ed., trans. Homer Hoeksema (Grandville, MI: Reformed Free Publishing Association, 1997).

years in the Christian Reformed Church. At a later date Rev. R. B. Kuiper spoke on "The Balance That Is Calvinism,"[11] in which he completely undermined the five points of Calvinism by trying to point out that true Calvinism teaches total depravity, but also the good that sinners do; unconditional election, but also that God wills to save all mankind; limited atonement, but also that Christ died for all mankind; irresistible grace, but also that grace is resistible.

Still later the synod of the Christian Reformed Church took the stand that God *loves and wills to save all mankind.*[12] There are even voices heard in the church world today, that since Christ died for all men and by God's common grace loves all men, *there is a possibility that some, possibly many, are saved outside of the preaching of the gospel, that is, without faith in Jesus Christ.* This is so very obviously contrary to all the teachings of scripture, in which it is stressed that salvation is by faith in Jesus Christ alone (Gen. 15:6; John 3:16, 36; Acts 16:31; Eph. 2:8–9).

Regarding the threat of worldliness, of which even the 1924 synod had warned the churches, soon the Christian Reformed Church spoke of the labor unions as neutral societies and allowed their members to join. Later the theater was condoned and the liturgical dance was introduced into the worship services. Evolutionism is now taught in Calvin College and Calvin seminary and in the churches. More recently, women have been ordained as ministers, elders, and deacons in the churches. It would seem as if Professor Janssen lived too soon. Liberal theology has taken over in the Christian Reformed Church, even as Rev. Hoeksema had predicted.

---

11 Rev. Kuiper was a minister in the Christian Reformed Church who later taught in and was president of Westminster seminary. The speech referred to was given at a Calvin College graduation in 1952.

12 The Christian Reformed Church took this stand in the mid-1960s when it dealt with the "Dekker Case." Harold Dekker defended the proposition that the atonement of Christ was for all men regarding sufficiency and intention, but not efficacy.

We may well ask, since Rev. Hoeksema was no longer in the denomination, why was there continued antagonism against him and attacks made on him?

First, the theory of common grace as developed by Abraham Kuyper was used to defend the inclination in the church toward worldliness and culture. Besides, there was a strong element in the church that preached a general, well-meant offer of salvation on the part of God. Both segments tenaciously clung to their errors. Rev. Hoeksema continued openly to deny and oppose both.

Second, Rev. Hoeksema was a staunch defender of the truth and appealed strongly to scripture and the confessions, which teach no semblance of a theory of common grace, much less a general, well-meant offer of salvation on the part of God. His opponents realized that their appeal to scripture and the confessions was very weak, while his arguments could not be denied. Soon they gave up trying to answer his arguments and practiced the silent treatment to try to prevent him from influencing the church constituency.

Even in the Netherlands his writings were reviewed, particularly the brochure entitled *A Power of God unto Salvation*, yet no one entered into his arguments or tried to refute them. Well aware of the decision of the Christian Reformed Church in 1924, they ignored the whole issue with a pompous wave of the hand.

Third, we know that Rev. Hoeksema had employed some very strong language in his defense of the truth. He had told the members of Classis Grand Rapids East that the Reformed truth had to be sought among them with a lantern. Twice he had become so aggrieved by their obvious efforts to cast him out that he had walked out of the assemblies. He had also walked out of the 1924 synod when it refused to allow him to defend his own case after he had spoken once. Rightly or wrongly, the members had taken offense.

Fourth, Rev. Hoeksema's journalism was powerful and would

surely influence those who seriously read his defense. In his writings he plainly revealed his disgust with the flimsy arguments used by his opponents against him. They felt hurt, if not ashamed. They continued to refer to him as stubborn and self-willed. Often he was called a dictator, and it was commonly known that they referred to his church edifice, later built at the corner of Fuller and Franklin, as "Pope Herman's Cathedral."

We can only conclude that Rev. Hoeksema was the man appointed and prepared by God for his time. God had prepared a Luther who did not compromise like Melanchthon, a Calvin who was not a proud boaster like Servetus, and a Gomarus who was not a suave individual like Arminius. Surely reformers are human, and their strengths are often their weakness as well. But their honest, undaunted spirit is guided by the Spirit of Jesus Christ in preserving the truth of the scriptures.

Yet the history immediately after 1924 was not all strife and grief. There was also a bright side. Soon after the expulsion of Rev. Ophoff, Rev. Hoeksema, Rev. Danhof, and their consistories from the Christian Reformed Church, a meeting was held by the three consistories in which it was decided to send a protest to the denomination's 1926 synod and in the meantime to adopt the name Protesting Christian Reformed Churches.

Rev. Henry Danhof
(*Christian Reformed
ministers' database*)

The congregation loved Rev. Hoeksema dearly. They saw an aspect of his character that did not always become evident in public debates. In the Sunday services and in the catechisms and societies, the people learned to know him as he was. In the public worship services his prayers were a sincere pouring out of his soul to God. He never failed to emphasize the greatness, glory, and blessedness of God. Over against that, without fail, he made a humble confession of his and the congregation's sins. In his sermons he expounded the text thoroughly, was strongly doctrinal, and yet presented the truth in such a clear and concise manner that all were edified. His preaching was God-centered, antithetical, with the proper emphasis on predestination and on God's providence.

Hoeksema made it a practice to preach on the Heidelberg Catechism in the Dutch services in the morning. Later, when supply was available, English morning services were added, which he also took when the need demanded. In the afternoon services he preached a Dutch sermon for those who had difficulty understanding English. Those services were well attended. For some time he expounded the prophecy of Isaiah in the afternoon services, to the delight of his audiences. Often he used such down-to-earth examples that smiles would appear on the faces of the audience, and sometimes a slight titter passed through the congregation. On one occasion when he had not preached at the afternoon service for some time, he came on the pulpit and expressed his joy at being able to preach for the congregation again. A spontaneous voice arose from the audience, "We also are glad."

The evening service was in English and was also well attended. He preached on the history of the Old Testament from Genesis to Judges, not only explaining the historical events, but also interpreting them in the light of the whole of scripture. He enjoyed series preaching. He carefully and thoroughly expounded such books as Romans, Galatians, Ephesians, James, 1 and 2 Peter, and Revelation. In fact, he made a lifelong study of the book of Revelation, the fruit of which now appears in the incomparable volume *Behold, He Cometh.*[13]

The ministers were kept very busy. Rev. Ophoff remained a faithful and diligent laborer. He also worked hard as coeditor of the *Standard Bearer.* Besides the work in their congregations,

---

13 Herman Hoeksema, *Behold, He Cometh!: An Exposition of the Book of Revelation,* 2nd edition (Grandville, MI: Reformed Free Publishing Association, 2000).

writing articles, and giving lectures, there were requests from various areas for more information and possible organization. Soon congregations were organized in Byron Center, Roosevelt Park (later Southwest Protestant Reformed Church), and Hudsonville, Michigan. In answer to a request from the Midwest, Rev. Hoeksema and Rev. Danhof went to northwest Iowa and organized a congregation in Hull. Later Doon, Rock Valley, and Sioux Center were added. A church was also organized in Waupun, Wisconsin.

To this fledgling denomination God called me for my life's work.

Chapter 11

TROUBLE IN
THE SEMINARY

*Rev. Hanko continues his story with the beginning of the
Theological School of the Protestant Reformed Churches.
The first year was a difficult one as problems arose quickly
in the faculty and student body.*

For some time already I had felt a call to the ministry, more
particularly to be a missionary in some foreign field. With
that in mind I had enrolled in a seminary preparatory course at
Calvin College. Since the controversy with Rev. Hoeksema had
come to a head, and I was a defender of his position, I spoke
to him about my problem. He told me that the intention of the
combined consistories of the Protesting Christian Reformed
Churches was to start a seminary as soon as the second semester at Calvin had ended. He also informed me that missionaries
would be needed, and he urged me to look forward to attending
classes in our own seminary as soon as the school opened.

A call went out for men who were interested in seminary
training. God sent ten men to appear before the consistory of
the Eastern Avenue Protesting Christian Reformed Church to
seek entrance into the seminary, and all ten were accepted. A
unique group it was. Five were married men, two of them with
families; five were single. They ranged in age from teenagers to
middle-aged men. Some had a year or more of college training;
others had only an elementary school education. The married

77

men were Andrew De Vries, Arie Griffioen (my future father-in-law), Andrew Kuivenhoven, William Verhil, and Gerrit Vos. The younger single men, besides me, were Gerard Borduin, John Griffioen, Richard Veldman, and Leonard Vermeer.

The three ministers, Rev. Danhof, Rev. Hoeksema, and Rev. Ophoff, readily agreed to instruct those men to serve in the churches. The ministers made a schedule according to which Rev. Hoeksema was to teach Monday afternoons the subjects of Greek reading, New Testament exegesis, hermeneutics, and New Testament history. A separate class was held for beginning Greek. Rev. Ophoff consented to teach Wednesday afternoons the subjects of Hebrew grammar, Old Testament exegesis, Old Testament history, and English composition. Rev. Danhof came from Kalamazoo by interurban train Friday mornings to teach an introduction to dogmatics, dogmatics, homiletics, and church history.

There was great enthusiasm among both professors and students as the school opened the first week of June 1925. It was a new venture, and everyone was eager to see the reformation grow. Besides, there would be a great need for preaching and ministers when new churches were organized. All went to work with determination and zeal, prayerfully seeking the guidance and blessing of the Lord upon their work.

The meeting place was not ideal. The classes met in the basement of Eastern Avenue church in a large assembly room with seating capacity for about two hundred people. There were no desks or tables for writing. There was one advantage—a platform with a pulpit. We had no library, not even one reference work. For books we had to go elsewhere or purchase our own books. But no one seemed to mind.

We did not use those facilities for very long. In December we lost the church property and had to find another meeting place. There was an old elementary schoolhouse in the area of Kalamazoo Avenue and Oakdale Street, which was about to be torn down, but the second floor was made available for our use. Andrew Kuivenhoven took advantage of that and moved his small family into part of the second floor. There was one room with desks and a chalkboard that became our classroom. It was little better than our former facilities, but it would serve our purposes.

But a cloud hung over the seminary. There was a rift among the professors, which soon became evident to the students. Somehow a tension had developed between Rev. Danhof and Rev. Hoeksema. Was it jealousy on the part of Rev. Danhof, since he was the senior minister, and Rev. Hoeksema was receiving requests to lecture at various places? Was it a clash of personalities as they worked so closely together? We did not know.

We did know that Rev. Danhof had two nephews, Ralph and Benjamin Danhof, who had joined the Protesting Christian Reformed Churches. Benjamin Danhof had been a minister in Allendale, had withdrawn from the Christian Reformed Church, and had taken a few families with him. Later he received a call from our Hull congregation, which he readily accepted. Ralph Danhof had come to us as a candidate for the ministry in the Christian Reformed Church. Rev. Henry Danhof wanted the consistory of Eastern Avenue to start a new congregation consisting of members of Eastern Avenue who lived in the area of Dennis Avenue, so that Ralph Danhof could serve there. The consistory refused to do that because there were other requests for organization, and those churches would need to be supplied. Soon Ralph was requested to work in Waupun, Wisconsin. He agreed to do that.

Two young men of the Eastern Avenue congregation had seen Ralph Danhof coming out of a theater, which they reported to the consistory. Rev. Henry Danhof heard of it and demanded that the matter be treated by the combined consistories because Ralph was a candidate for the ministry. The consistory of Eastern Avenue insisted that it was a discipline case that belonged to its jurisdiction. That small incident helped to disturb the already troubled waters.

The first Friday morning that Rev. Henry Danhof began his classes, he informed the students that he did not intend to come all the way from Kalamazoo to Grand Rapids to teach four subjects. Also, he felt that the students must be prepared for the ministry as fast as possible. He would teach from nine to five, with an hour break for lunch, thus covering eight subjects, four more than he was asked to teach.

The result was that we students diligently took down extensive notes all day Friday. In order to preserve them, we had to type the notes the very next day. Since that was Saturday and some of the men worked, they had no time to prepare for the classes of Rev. Hoeksema on Monday. When students complained to Rev. Hoeksema, he quite properly answered with a shrug of the shoulders, "That is not my problem. I expect you to be prepared for my classes."

Rev. Hoeksema was a very capable teacher. It was a pleasure to attend his classes and receive his instruction. For Rev. Ophoff teaching was an entirely new venture. He had some new subjects, such as Hebrew grammar and Old Testament exegesis. But he also applied himself with diligence, working far harder than any of us realized. Rev. Danhof, as well as being a theologian, had a very broad knowledge of many subjects, among which was astronomy. That also became evident in his teaching.

Bible texts were assigned to all the students with the intention that as soon as sermons were prepared, they could be delivered in practice preaching sessions. Those sessions were held on Friday. Before the end of the school year students were being sent out to speak a word of edification in the churches. Both professors and students realized that those fledglings were incapable of making a thorough exegesis of a text, but the need in the churches was evident. However, the professors did not spare us. Our sermons and delivery were sharply criticized. I recall one incident

in which Rev. Danhof told one student that he had put everything he knew in one sermon; he had left nothing for another
sermon. On another occasion Rev. Hoeksema told a student to
put his sermon in a drawer, lock the drawer, and throw away the
key. But the professors also appreciated our serious efforts and
offered valuable advice to improve our messages and the delivery
of them.

The churches graciously understood and were appreciative
and glad to be supplied on the Sabbath. They encouraged us men
as much as possible.

My first venture into preaching occurred when I was nineteen
years of age, on a Sunday morning
in Byron Center. I took a friend with
me, and we arrived a bit early. We
stood by the coal stove in the town
hall, where the church was meeting, since no one else had arrived
yet. The janitor came in, took one
look, and asked in a surprised tone,
"What are you boys doing here?"
I answered, "I am going to preach."
With still greater surprise the man
asked, "You, preach?" When I
arrived in the consistory room, one

Rev. Hanko preached his first
sermon in the building on Harlow
and Prescott in Byron Center.

of the elders looked askance at the "preacher." The other, reading
his mind, said, "It's all right. Rev. Hoeksema said so."

Another student had to preach at Hope church at Riverbend,
where Rev. Ophoff was the minister. The student was standing
in the consistory room when he noticed the organist coming
through with an English psalter in her hand. He asked the consistory, "Are the services in English this morning? Rev. Ophoff told
me they were to be in Dutch." One of the elders looked at him in
amazement and said, "What does Rev. Ophoff have to say about

our services? You evidently belong in the schoolhouse across the road."[1]

On Monday Rev. Hoeksema always eagerly awaited the report of the students on their experiences the previous day. The same young man who had gone to the wrong church remarked one day, "The service lasted only an hour. I did not know what more to say, so I said, 'Amen.'" Rev. Hoeksema responded with a smile, "That's right. When you are finished, quit. Do not try to drag your sermon out."

There was a young man who attended the seminary for a short time but showed very little interest in the work. One day Rev. Hoeksema asked him point blank, "Why are you here?" He answered, "I was laid in the cradle to become a minister." Rev. Hoeksema shook his head and said, "Your mother cannot receive a call to the ministry for you." He responded, "Do you mean that?" Rev. Hoeksema answered, "With all my heart." Greatly relieved, the young man picked up his books, and we did not see him again.

Another small incident gave the students an occasion for a hearty laugh at their professor's expense. Rev. Ophoff had to drive to seminary from the southwest part of Grand Rapids near John Ball Park. One morning something held him up, and the students were watching through the window for him to arrive. He soon appeared in his car, but two police officers on motorcycles drove right up behind him. He stepped out of his car and urged them to give him a ticket, explaining, "Hurry, I'm late and I must get to my students." The officers were so completely baffled by his reaction that they passed off the incident with a mere warning to stay within the speed limit.

There was still remaining tension in the seminary. In the

---

1 The schoolhouse was where Hope Protesting Christian Reformed Church was meeting after losing its church building to Hope Christian Reformed Church after Rev. Ophoff was deposed.

early months of 1926, Rev. Danhof took aside three or four students and invited each one individually to accompany him to the Midwest that summer to organize churches. When any of them raised the objection that he had just begun to preach or was actually incapable of preaching a Dutch sermon, all objections were brushed aside with the answer, "You can help." Evidently Danhof wanted to go out on his own.

A combined consistory meeting was planned for the third week in May. Rev. Benjamin Danhof came a week earlier and met with three students in the home of his parents. Evidently the subject of the theological school was brought up, and the students must have complained that Rev. Hoeksema and Rev. Ophoff showed partiality to some students. A protest was drawn up and signed. Rev. Henry Danhof was informed by phone of the protest. He replied, "Do what you will, but keep me out of it."

The next day other students were informed of what had happened and were asked to sign the protest. The protest was entirely new to the other students, and it did not have a single ground. One of the students informed Rev. Hoeksema of the protest, so that before beginning his class on Monday he told the students about the document, stating that the protesting students had not contacted him or Rev. Ophoff before presenting their charges. He gave those who had signed the document an opportunity to withdraw their signatures in a written statement. One student withdrew his name. The other two refused.

The next day the combined consistories met in Kalamazoo. A committee was appointed to deal with the protest. Each student in turn was called before the committee and asked about affairs in the school and whether he thought one or the other professor had shown any particular prejudice. The final result was that the protest was cast out, and the school term came to a sudden halt.

That was a trying year. There were times when I was inclined to give up and return to Calvin. In retrospect I marvel that I did not give up, but I can see that the Lord was testing me regarding whether or not I would be willing to face the trials of the ministry. Ever since that year I have been thankful that the Lord gave me grace to continue.

In August another meeting of the combined consistories was held in which Rev. Danhof was reconciled with the other professors and promised to continue teaching in the school. Also, at the meeting the name Protestant Reformed Churches was adopted.

Soon afterward Rev. Danhof informed the faculty that he would no longer teach in the school or write in the *Standard Bearer*. In other words, he had withdrawn himself completely from our fellowship. His church would be an independent congregation.

To add insult to injury, Rev. Danhof rented the Woodmen Hall on Wealthy Street near Eastern Avenue church, where he publicly revealed all his grievances. Not only a goodly number of our people were present, but also four professors from Calvin College. Shortly afterward Rev. Hoeksema went to Kalamazoo, where he publicly answered the charges that Rev. Danhof had made against him. One can imagine the delight of outsiders in seeing our churches crumble at the outset. Rumors ran wild that they would not last long. Some gave the churches five years, some ten years. Others thought the entire movement would die out at the death of Rev. Hoeksema. In spite of those evil predictions, God has preserved and blessed us even until this very day!

Rev. Henry Danhof was the minister of the independent Protesting First Christian Reformed Church in Kalamazoo from 1924 to 1945, when he retired. In 1946 the congregation, including Rev. Danhof, returned to the Christian Reformed Church. Danhof went back on the condition that he would not have to sign the three points. He would not ask for any ministerial status, except he asked for the privilege of preaching the Dutch service in the church. That was allowed, but he had no other duties or functions in the church. It did not take long and he was criticizing the preacher. He soon was suspended for a second time.

Now the two remaining ministers, Rev. Ophoff and Rev. Hoeksema, were burdened with more work. As if their load had not already all but exceeded capacity, they now were called to take over all the classes in the theological school. They also took over most of the writing for the *Standard Bearer*. George Ophoff, son of Rev. Ophoff, once remarked, "One thing that stands out in my memory of my dad is the light that shone from under the door of his study almost all night."

Rev. Benjamin Danhof went back to Hull and placed a notice in the town paper stating that his congregation was not and had never been affiliated with the protesting churches. He also announced from the pulpit that the congregation had become independent. Some members objected, but those who approached the consistory on the matter were placed under censure.

The consistory called a congregational meeting to decide whether or not to return to the Christian Reformed Church. One of the members who was under censure attended that meeting and was told to leave. He refused. Rev. Danhof started toward him to force him to leave, but he took hold of a leg of a chair, lifted the chair, and dared Rev. Danhof to throw him out. The minister drew back and the man was allowed to remain.

The congregation, which formerly consisted of about thirty-nine families, was reduced to twelve families who remained loyal to the Protestant Reformed Churches. The others returned to the Christian Reformed Church and offered the new church edifice and the parsonage, with the debt of twelve thousand dollars, to the faithful remnant. Although especially during the Depression that was a great burden to the faithful remnant, they bore it willingly. Today the Hull congregation has a new church building and has become a large and thriving congregation.

Ralph Danhof also returned to the Christian Reformed Church. Obviously the Lord no longer had any purpose for those men in our churches. Under the blessing of the Lord the work could well go on without them, as it did.

Chapter 12

SEMINARY TRAINING

The trials continued through the spring and summer of 1927. The trials came in the form of sickness and death in Rev. Hanko's family. However, his training for the ministry continued, in spite of that difficult first year.

In April 1926 my sister Lucy, who had married Bernard Woudenberg, had their first baby in our home. It became evident almost at once that the child had certain infirmities that would result in an early death. About a month later the baby died. About that time my mother's stepmother in Byron Center also died.

On May 30 of the same year, my brother Fred died after an operation for a ruptured ulcer. For some time he had complained of pain in his stomach. One Saturday he was at his job when severe pains gripped him. They were so agonizing that he could not drive the car. My dad called me to come and drive him home. The doctor was called. Fred was taken to the hospital, but the doctor failed to diagnose the cause of the pain. On Sunday another doctor was called in to perform the operation, but the infection had already spread through his abdomen. On Sunday morning he died. He had planned to marry in three weeks.

My parents grieved sorely over the loss of their son. My father felt as if his right hand had been taken from him. Because of my father's sorrow, I felt compelled to keep him active by working along with him as much as possible. Daily he had to be brought to the job in the morning and taken home at night.

Father took very little interest in his business anymore. He was getting on in years and had intended to pass the business over to Fred. He soon gave up, especially as his eyesight was failing on account of the diabetes he had had for some time.

There were now only two professors at the seminary, but peace and harmony were restored. Five of the ten students who attended classes the first year dropped out, but three new ones entered the seminary in the fall of 1926: Andrew Cammenga, John De Jong, and Bernard Kok. Everything ran much

Frederick Hanko,
Rev. Hanko's only brother

smoother, and even the practice preaching was a much less terrifying experience. During the first year, practice preaching was very uncomfortable. Not only did we have to bear the sharp criticism of the professors, but while we were delivering the sermon, most of the students lay back in their seats with their legs on the desks. About all one could see of them was their feet. All that changed drastically during the second year. Emphasis was placed on the fact that we were dealing with the word of God and holy things. There was much more reverence in the entire experience.

Shortly after the second year started, I came down with rheumatic fever. I had pain sometimes in the ankle, sometimes in the knee or elbow. For one week I lay in bed and took pills that caused me to perspire to the extent that every day the bedding was wet and yellow with sweat. By the end of the week I was so weak that I could hardly walk. The first time I preached again I had to stand on one leg during the sermon. At that point I was also teaching catechism for First church on Saturday mornings in a store building on Wealthy Street.

By March 1927 there was a crying need for preaching in Iowa—Hull, Sioux Center, and Doon. Gerrit Vos, Richard Veldman, and I were requested to go to Iowa to take care of the three churches. There was a small house in Doon across from Henry Kuiper that became known as the parsonage. From there we took charge of the three churches, even teaching catechism and leading the consistory meetings. Old Model T Fords were made available to us for traveling to Hull and Sioux Center.

Seminarian Hanko trying his hand at plowing during his stay in Iowa.

Seminarian Hanko resting atop farm machinery in Hull.

Gerrit Vos returned home early because of trouble with his back. But Richard Veldman and I stayed until June 1927. School had already finished when we returned, so each of us took our exams separately in the consistory room of First church. When I finished my last exam, Rev. Hoeksema asked me if I would be willing to go back to the Midwest for the summer. Although I had been quite homesick at first in an entirely Dutch environment, I thought a bit and then consented to return. Andrew Cammenga accompanied me then.

During the summer months of 1927, Gerrit Vos was appointed to serve temporarily in the Sioux Center congregation, while William Verhil received and accepted a temporary call to Hull.[1]

By the time we returned to Michigan the third school year had begun. But we still had to preach, not only in the Grand Rapids area, but also in South Holland and Oak Lawn, Illinois, and in Waupun, Wisconsin. Every other Sunday we were out of town to preach. In the early spring of 1928 calls for supply came from Pella and Oskaloosa, Iowa. So once more I was drawn away from school and had to try to keep up with the studies and to supply those two churches. I had the morning service in Pella, ate lunch with the congregation in the consistory room, and then took the bus to preach in Oskaloosa at night.

In Oskaloosa a man was dying. He was not a member of the congregation, but he attended the services regularly. I was warned in advance that the woman living with him was not his wife. I was told that he had left his wife in the Netherlands and gone to America with the other woman. In case he should want to make some confession, I would know the background. He died, and shortly after, the woman confessed her sin and joined the church.

---

1 Gerrit Vos and William Verhil were sent out into the churches even though they had not completed their training. When the seminary produced its first graduates, they came back to finish their training.

Once more I failed to end the school year with the rest of the class. But at least it was a good experience as an internship for the ministry.

I spent six weeks of the summer of 1928 in Waupun, Wisconsin. Although the group there was quite mystical, it had joined the Protestant Reformed Churches because of their stand on total depravity. The consistory did not meet before the services, but the seminarian stood in the back of the church, where Elder Wildeman whispered into his ear the various announcements. The singing was at a very slow tempo and almost mournful. Between each line the organist played a brief interlude and a longer one between the verses. If the sermons of the day met with the approval of Mr. Wildeman, he stood up at the end of the afternoon service and proposed that the congregation sing the doxology to the student. If the seminarian failed the test, there was no doxology sung.

In the evening the elite, the more spiritual element of the congregation, met together. One by one they spoke of their former sinful walks, of their dramatic conversions, or of some spiritual experiences. The student was required to be present, but he was to listen in silence.

What stands out in my memory is the family visitation that I was asked to carry out there. The people of the congregation, with their mystical tendencies, dreaded family visitation. One lady who was in her eighties told me that it was the first time she stayed for family visitation, and the only reason she stayed then was because she wanted to find out what the young kid would say. In another family of ten children the only ones we found home were the parents. When asked where the others were, we were told that it was impossible to keep them home when the *dominie* came.[2] The youngest of them was four years old. So the elder and I arranged to call on the family at suppertime. The mother agreed

---

2 *Dominie* is the Dutch word for Reverend.

to have everything in readiness at six o'clock sharp so we could come into the house, sit down at the meal, and thus prevent anyone from getting away. The plan succeeded to a point. All went smoothly until I began to talk to the oldest girl, who turned her back to me and after a while got up and left. The next oldest child stayed but was unresponsive. So it was down the line of children. But at least we tried.

Then there were two girls from another family, one of whom was married. Her husband refused to go to church, and her baby was not baptized. I asked her whether her husband prevented her from having the baby baptized. The answer I received from him is better not repeated. The younger girl looked and dressed like a harlot. Soon it became evident that she was virtually as she appeared. The excuse was, "I am not converted." That seemed to be a coverup for much of the evil in the congregation. When I admonished the two girls for their sinful walks, the mother interfered by reminding me that after all, they were not yet converted. Never in all the years of ministry did I experience anything like those six weeks in Waupun, and never did I lose more sleep after my family visits.

You may wonder whether during that busy time I had any opportunities to date. In the fall of 1927 I met my future wife, Jennie Griffioen. Sometime during the first semester, fellow student Arie Griffioen invited Leonard Vermeer and me to visit him in his home. Arie's two oldest daughters impressed me as complete opposites. The older one was quiet and reserved, and the other loud and giggly. Shortly afterward I was invited to attend a wedding, and I took the older daughter, Jennie, with me.

I was still crippled from the effects of rheumatic fever when we went together to Central High School to attend a program given by the Young Men's League of the Christian Reformed Church. Our dating when at home was limited to three nights in two weeks: two nights attending Rev. Hoeksema's Bible class and the one Sunday night when I was not out of town. Later she often accompanied me when I went out to preach in the Grand Rapids area. The rest of the time we had to depend on correspondence.

Neal Hanko and Jennie Griffioen in their dating years

At the end of my six weeks' stay in Waupun, Walter Griffioen and his girlfriend, Minnie, took my girlfriend, Jennie, to Waupun by car, so that we four could travel home together. We came home by going over the Straits of Mackinac and arrived back in time for the last year of seminary to begin.

During the last year of seminary none of the students were compelled to go out to spend a period of time in the churches, but we all could make full use of the opportunities to prepare to enter the ministry. We did make our visits to Waupun, South Holland, and Oak Lawn, but apart from that we could devote our time to our studies and making sermons.

Around Christmas 1928 Jennie and I became engaged. My fiancée came from a large family. As a result of the caste system in the Netherlands, her mother, Alida, who belonged to the upper class, did no housework. When the children were small, the family had a maid, but when Jennie, who was the oldest daughter in the family, was finished with school, she took over in the family.

That meant making meals for thirteen people, getting some of them
off to work in the morning, cleaning the huge house, and doing the
laundry, besides all the other necessary chores of a large family. She was
often so tired at the end of the day
that she fell asleep on the bed without undressing. The younger sisters
often thought of her as their mother,
since she assumed the responsibility
of caring for their needs. I think that
undermined her health, along with a

Arie and Alida Griffioen,
Jennie's parents, in later years

form of rheumatic fever that she had at age twelve, which affected
her heart. Jennie looked forward with relief to leaving home and
marrying.

Jennie had been working at home for room and board, but
she gained permission from her parents to go out a few days a
week to make money for the necessities involved in getting married. She obtained a job doing housework on the east end of
Grand Rapids, so that she was able to accumulate a little money
for things for her future home.

June 1929 came all too soon as far as I was concerned. That
was the time for the classical examination, which was held in
First church.[3] Each of the six students—Leonard Vermeer, John
De Jong, Andrew Cammenga, Richard Veldman, Bernard Kok,
and I—was allowed twenty minutes for his sermon. That was
hardly sufficient to get into the subject, so that one of the elders
remarked afterward, "If I had to judge you on those sermons, not
one would pass the exam." Rev. Vos and Rev. Verhil also took part
in examining us in subjects assigned to them.

---

3 The classical exams were comparable to the present-day synodical exams,
   for as yet there was no synod.

The first seminary graduation class (1929): back left to right: R. Veldman, C. Hanko, L. Vermeer; front left to right: B. Kok, J. De Jong, A. Cammenga

Rev. Hanko's classical diploma

All six of us were made candidates, and all of us eagerly awaited the anticipated calls. Rev. Hoeksema was spending the summer in the Netherlands and would not return home until the middle of September.

I distinctly remember the evening Rev. Hoeksema called me on the phone. He appeared to be as excited as I was. He said, "Neal, you have the call to Hull!" Then he asked me to call John De Jong to inform him that he had the call to Doon, and to call Andrew Cammenga to inform him that he had the call to Rock Valley.

The summer of 1929 turned out to be very busy. Jennie and I had to make wedding arrangements, purchase furniture, schedule our move to Hull, and I had to prepare for the examinations that would be held in the auditorium of First church.[4]

Since the churches were eager to have their ministers ordained into office so that the catechism classes could get started, everything was arranged to take place as soon as possible after Rev. Hoeksema's return from the Netherlands. Thus the examinations were scheduled for September 18.

Wedding photo of Cornelius Hanko and Jennie Griffioen (September 19, 1929)

I admit that we six did not pass the exam *magna cum laude*. The lower section of the auditorium was filled with people who had high expectations of the first students who had completed the course in our seminary. But there was too much of the unexpected in the exams. For one thing, Professor Ophoff decided at the last minute to examine us on a different subject than that for which we had prepared. Besides, the professors sat in the balcony, and the students sat on the platform on the floor below. The questions and answers did not always carry through clearly. Especially the polemics exam

---

4   The examination was comparable to the present-day classical exam.

(today's apologetics) was quite a failure. But the six men were declared eligible for the gospel ministry.

On the nineteenth of September Jennie and I were married. We paid twenty-eight dollars to the caterer for the food at the reception.

On the twentieth both Andrew Cammenga and Richard Veldman spoke their marriage vows.

The following Monday, John De Jong entered the married state. That same Monday, September 23, 1929, Jennie and I and Andrew Cammenga and his wife boarded the train for Iowa.

Chapter 13

HULL, IOWA

Rev. and Mrs. Hanko arrived in Hull ready and eager to take up their work there. They were newly married, and Rev. Hanko was ready to be ordained.

M y new wife and I arrived in Hull, Iowa, on Tuesday morning, September 24, 1929. Rev. Verhil met us at the train station. The same evening Rev. Verhil preached the sermon and ordained me as minister of the gospel in Hull Protestant Reformed Church. The congregation was invited to come into the basement to make acquaintance with the new minister and his wife, but no one appeared except Ed Vander Werff and his family. The wounds made by the trouble with Ben Danhof were still too raw for the people to become enthusiastic about a new minister.

Rev. William Verhil

The Hull congregation began with thirty-nine families under Ben Danhof. When I arrived, there were only twelve families who remained faithful to the truth. Some who had left were very bitter toward us. There was a feeling of discouragement among the remaining members. A mere handful was left with the debt of the church and parsonage. There had even developed a spirit of distrust, as if they wondered whether or not their fellow members would remain faithful. It was a question of survival.

Hull church building and parsonage

Rev. C. Hanko, age twenty-five,
in his study in Hull

The auditorium that seated about one hundred fifty to two hundred people was considered much too large for such a small crowd. On Sunday the congregation met in the basement, and before the service the consistory met in the furnace room.

The following Wednesday afternoon Andrew Cammenga was ordained in Rock Valley, and in an evening service John De Jong was ordained in Doon. All of that had to be carried out as rapidly as possible, because Rev. Verhil and Rev. Vos had to return to Michigan to attend the fall semester of the seminary. On their way home they had to stop in Pella, Iowa, to ordain Leonard Vermeer into the ministry.

They had to ordain Andrew Cammenga and John De Jong while rain came down in torrents. Cars got stuck in the mud between Doon and Sioux Center, so that Rev. Vos and Rev. Verhil got their Prince Alberts literally covered with mud.[1] When they arrived in Pella the next day, their suits went to the cleaners while they got some sorely needed sleep.

So a new life began for my wife and me in our new home in Hull. We were both filled with excitement, especially waiting for the van from Grand Rapids that would bring most of our possessions. The van with a trailer was delayed by engine trouble in the hills around Dubuque, Iowa, so that it did not arrive until three days later on Friday afternoon. Mr. Mulder and Mr. Korhorn from First church, who moved our belongings, unpacked our part of the load that same day. On Saturday they unpacked in Rock Valley and in Doon. Since they could not get back home before Sunday as planned, they stayed with us in the parsonage. Mr. Mulder, who was a tall man, wore one of my suits with part of his arms hanging out. Mr. Korhorn, who was a short man, wore another of my suits with his hands hidden in the sleeves. But we managed. Monday they were on their way back home.

I was soon faced with a death in the congregation. Grandpa Brunsting was failing rapidly. Before the week was over, I had officiated my first funeral.

---

1   In distinction from a cutaway coat, a Prince Albert was a coat with square-cut tails.

Life was pleasant there in Hull. Our married life was like a continuous honeymoon. We had started a new home in what was practically a new house with eight large rooms and new furniture. We were undergoing a new experience of married life, as well as serving in the ministry. Our associates in the ministry were just a phone call away, and once a week we ventured out in our brand-new 1929 Chevrolet (purchased for 560 dollars with money borrowed from my father) to visit one or the other in Doon or Rock Valley.

Rev. Hanko and Rev. Cammenga in the Hull parsonage. Their friendship ended in the schism of 1953.

The new married experience created problems for my wife, who had been accustomed to preparing meals for as many as fifteen people every day. The first pan of soup proved to be far too much for two people. There were always plenty of leftover potatoes for frying the next day. Besides, we arrived in the Midwest in the fall of the year without any canned goods to carry us through the winter. We attempted to buy carrots, beans, and other vegetables, but we soon discovered that the only fresh vegetable available was cabbage. Eating cabbage every day did not sound very appealing, and canned vegetables from the store were expensive. But we did manage to get through that first winter with plenty to eat.

Our water supply came from the cistern, but the water was filtered before it was drawn out. Our washing machine was hand operated, which gave me an opportunity to spend Monday mornings in the basement pumping the machine. It was only after a few years that we accumulated enough money to buy our first electric washing machine.

There was plenty to occupy my time in the parsonage. Suddenly I was confronted, for example, with sick visiting. The great-great-grandmother (Delia Gritters) of Prof. Barry Gritters was still living. She was in her eighties and needed regular visits. Her son Egbert (or Ebbe) served in the consistory. Egbert's son Ben lived for a time in Hull, and I baptized one of his boys. Later the boy, named Edwin, moved to California. When I was later pastor in Redlands, California, I had Edwin in my congregation. And in Hudsonville, shortly before retiring, I had Shirley Vander Kolk, a daughter of Edwin, in my congregation. I baptized her baby boy, named Brian. I pastored six generations of the Gritter family. What evidence of God's covenantal faithfulness!

But there were also other chores in Hull. There were fairly good-sized catechism classes and societies; there were consistory meetings and, last but not least, two sermons every Sunday. They kept coming around every week. Making sermons seemed like such a tremendous task that often after the Sunday afternoon service, I found myself in the study preparing for the next Sabbath that always followed the previous one so rapidly.

Although the congregation tended to remain aloof and was reluctant to show any great warmth, there was a bond of love that developed among us. Especially the young people were very happy to have a young minister who came down to their level, so that they enjoyed nothing better than being invited to the parsonage for an evening of fellowship or going out on a picnic with us.

One exciting event that took place after a picnic comes to mind. We made it a practice to stay together on the way back from picnics and to take each person home as we returned to Hull. When we drove up into the Blankespoor's yard, we found the kitchen light lit. That was especially strange because the parents had gone away and the children had left during daylight. Rather than having the three young folks who lived there venture into the house, we decided to ride into town, pick up the policeman, and take him back with us to the house. When we approached the house, he too was afraid to enter. He took his big rifle in hand, shot a bullet into the ground, and waited for something to happen. When no one came out of the house, he ventured in and discovered that someone had been there, raided the refrigerator, and then left without taking anything else.

The first page of one of Rev. Hanko's Dutch sermons on John 12:27

The congregation grew steadily. Every summer the congregation held worship services in the auditorium, and in the fall, to save fuel, the congregation worshiped in the basement. Before long the basement was packed to capacity. The last person drew his chair through the door with him. Later the congregation decided to hold the worship services upstairs year round.

The early members took new courage as the congregation grew. They saw hope for the future, and the financial burden was lessening. Yet the wolf was still at the door. The banker threatened time and again to foreclose if the interest on the mortgage was not paid. There were eight note-signers in the congregation who feared that one or more of them might lose his property through a church foreclosure.

A few voices were heard from those who desired an English service. Only one elder, Mr. Vander Werff, had ears for those requests. He began to work for an English service, to the point that the consistory agreed that if he would attend, he and a few others could have an English service on Sunday evenings. That would be a third service. The other elders assured us that they would not be there and that English services would not last.

An evening service in English was started. The young people came and wondered if they could understand an English service since they had never heard one. But that service was cake and ice cream for them. They relished a service in their own language. Slowly the parents came, and soon an English service was held once a month in the morning.

The congregation in Sioux Center was very upset. The church had been organized for the very purpose of maintaining Dutch preaching. The members even insisted that since the preaching was in Dutch, the catechism classes had to be taught in Dutch also, even though the children all spoke English. There was even talk of a protest from Sioux Center against Hull at classis, but the consistory must have realized how futile that would be, since all the churches in the East already had English worship services.

During those first five years three children came to brighten the parsonage. A little more than a year after we were married, Herman was born on October 10, 1930. What an excitement that created! The other two ministers' wives were also pregnant at the same time. Mrs. John De Jong was determined to keep her pregnancy secret. She thought she had kept her secret so well that nobody knew she was expecting. But the Friday evening after Herman was born I had to go to Sioux Center. When I could not restrain myself from telling the people there the good news of Herman's birth, they remarked that they thought it was Mrs. De Jong who had given birth.

We had not tried to keep Jennie's pregnancy a secret, because she was not well during the pregnancy due to her bad heart. She was in bed the first five to six weeks of the pregnancy. The congregation lived in expectation as much as we did. Therefore, when I called Mrs. Ed Vander Werff, who had already heard on the telephone party line the news of Herman's birth, she was kind enough to ask, "And how is the new father?" There was at least one person who understood the trauma of a father, especially when the baby is born at home.

A new baby not only tells you when you may eat and sleep and controls whatever you do, but it is also the center of attention. Life at home revolved around the little one. Our neighbor, Mrs. Wintermantel, was a great help. She would get up early and finish her own work and then come over to help us. She had given birth to a baby boy named Myron with an open back and a water head, whom she nurtured along until he became a normal, healthy child with only a slight stagger. In time Herman and Myron were good friends.

Going for the mail was a daily ritual in our small town. I often enjoyed taking Herm along in a cart or a sled. One winter day I started out and soon realized that the temperature was around zero. I ran as fast as I could, but the poor kid was really chilled by the time we arrived back home. We had to learn to look at the thermometer before venturing out, especially on a cold day.

When Herm was almost a year old, my parents came to see us. They came with another couple. All four of our guests saw that Herm was beginning to stand by the furniture and move about from one place to another. They wanted to see him walk alone before they left, but he failed to do so. They were only a few miles down the road when he started walking from one place to another entirely on his own.

Pa and Ma Griffioen, with Alex, Nell, Marie, and Martha also came to visit us. That was a new experience for them, and the kids had a good time. Later brother John Griffioen came to stay with us for a while and sister Ada was at our home for quite a length of time.

Sixteen months after Herm was born, Fred joined our family. It was in the latter part of January, just at the time the January thaw brought mild weather. Every night of that week the doctor had been warned that he might have to come over in the dead of the night, yet each night went by and nothing happened. There was special concern at that time because Jennie had spent the last six weeks in bed with a urinary problem.

Saturday evening I alerted the doctor again. Shortly afterward I told him to come. Evidently he was not in a great hurry, since he had been alerted so often. When he decided to come, his car had a flat tire. In the meantime, the baby, who weighed less than five pounds, decided to wait no longer and made his appearance unassisted. Since that was a new experience for me, I dashed over to the neighbor, Mrs. Wintermantel, who was always more than willing to help. She came about the same time the doctor arrived. The matter was placed in capable hands. I still wonder whether I had stopped shaking by the time I climbed to the pulpit Sunday morning.

The next week the winter once more settled upon us with all its force. The temperature dropped to thirty degrees below zero and remained there for some time. With a new, tiny baby in the house, the coal furnace had to be stoked even during the night. Even so, the cold penetrated ever deeper into the walls of the house, until we finally had all the rooms shut off except the kitchen and the bedroom. But the poor child was still cold, especially at night. So during the day we placed warm water bottles around him, and during the night we took him into our bed.

Fred grew rapidly. In fact, he had a voracious appetite, which resulted in an attack of colic. The poor, little fellow would pull up his legs with cramps so that we had to walk the floor with him day and night. We felt as if we had completely worn out the carpets in the living room and dining room. The doctor assured us that in six months the problem would be over. He was right. It was quite a relief to see Fred a much happier baby.

Back: Fred, Rev. Hanko, Jennie; middle: Herman and Jantje Hanko, front: Herm

The two boys got along well, as little brothers do. Herm had a fuzzy bunny that kept him content day and night. Fred had his thumb. Wherever Herm went, the bunny went. He would go to play with Myron Wintermantel, the neighbor boy, and his companion went along. After a while the bunny was getting pretty shaggy, but that seemed to make no difference. One fateful day he dragged his treasure through the mud. It came home a soggy, hopeless mess, so we had to throw it away. We wondered what would happen when darkness settled on the manse. But Herm seemed to realize that he had better not complain because bygones were bygones.

Often during our meals Herm and Fred would fight together in their own unique ways, so my wife decided to sit between them. That did help, but they still could not resist leaning forward and growling at each other. When Herm was away, Fred was lost. We took a picture of him, lying sound asleep on the dining room floor in the middle of the day. What else was there to do when his brother was not around?

In August 1934 Elaine joined us. Although my wife had problems with the first two pregnancies because of her heart condition, that pregnancy went along very smoothly.

We had been able to travel to Grand Rapids for a vacation that summer. When we arrived back home another experience awaited us. A seminary student had been preaching in Orange City, Iowa, and staying with one of the families of the congregation. The family had a blind daughter, and the student told the parents, very naively, that he thought he was in love with their daughter. The result was that he was sent to our home to be placed under our care. We told him that it was a temporary arrangement, but he took no heed. The time for the congregational picnic came around, and my wife decided that it was a matter of expediency to stay at home, for she was nearing the end of her third pregnancy. The seminarian felt it was his duty to admonish her, since he thought a minister's wife should participate in the congregational activities. At the picnic I arranged with a family that I would disappear soon after lunch, and that they should take the student home with them. That arrangement was made none too soon, for the next day Elaine came as an addition to the family.

The doctor jokingly said to me, "You want a girl, don't you?"

I assured him that it made absolutely no difference to me. Upon Elaine's arrival the doctor said, "Another boy." And then immediately after, "Oh no! It's a girl." When I smiled he said, "See, I knew you wanted a girl." It was true enough that a girl was most welcome after two boys. Our family had grown to five members.

Rev. Hanko, Fred, Herm, Elaine, and Jennie

Back: Jennie, Rev. Hanko; front: Herm, Elaine, and Fred

An elderly couple lived in a small house in Sioux Center, Iowa. Their home was very small, consisting of only two rooms, a living room and a small bedroom. A lean-to with a sloped roof served as the kitchen. They had no central heating, no gas, and no running water or other modern conveniences. They had no automobile, but they needed none. The church was only a block or two from their home, and they were only a short distance from the stores on the main street of the town. They knew no luxuries but felt no need for them. They had lived together for many years, so that they thought alike and almost looked alike; at least they both wore a look of perfect contentment.

He had been a carpet weaver, and he still did a bit of weaving in a small shop behind the house. It was interesting to watch him as he sat at his loom sending the shuttle back and forth between the warp and the woof. First one shuttle, and then another, and still a third went back and forth as he moved the threads up and down with a foot treadle. To me it appeared as if he would end up with a conglomerate of color without any pattern. When I voiced my fears, he only smiled. Soon the finished product came forth with a beautiful design. One could not help but think that God, according to his perfect plan, weaves his pattern in our lives from day to day. "My life in all its perfect plan was ordered ere my days began."[2]

That same man was an elder in the church and took his office very seriously. As the oldest elder at the public worship service, he led the consistory into the auditorium and sat with the other members alongside the pulpit where they could not only plainly see and hear the minister, but also oversee the flock. As an elder's mate, his wife knew how to be "grave, no slanderer, sober, faithful in all things" (1 Tim. 3:11).

I entered their cozy home one evening as they were sitting at opposite ends of the kitchen, where he was reading to her

2 No. 383:2, in *The Psalter*.

from the scriptures and she was listening as her knitting needles clicked rapidly in her hands. As I took a chair, the Bible was laid aside. After a bit of pleasant conversation he gave his wife a knowing look, and she responded with a smile. A few moments later he again looked at her, and again she responded with a smile. Finally he asked, "Wife, aren't you going to make a pot of coffee?" As if taken by surprise, even though she had known all the while, she said, "Oh! Is that what you wanted?"

The time came when her husband left her to enter his eternal home in the heavens. His wife stood at his bedside, well aware that half of her life had been snatched from her. With tears running down her face she said, "God knows best, but it is hard to see it."

Saints on earth are still imperfect. That serious Christian had one weakness; he had a dreadful fear of dying. When he was ill, I visited him and prayed with him, including in my prayer a request that God's kingdom might come, when he would make all things new. After I had finished he asked, "Dare you pray that?" I wondered what he referred to, and he reminded me that I had prayed for the coming of God's kingdom. I informed him that we not only might, but also must pray for that. To which he answered, "But then I must die."

At another occasion he looked rather pale. I asked him if he was not feeling well. He drew me aside and asked anxiously, "You don't think I will die, do you?"

The time came for him to die. The local doctor stopped at my home to tell me that the man had cancer and was going to die. He added, "You know how he always feared death. You had better prepare him for it." To my surprise, God had already done so. When he was told that he had cancer and would not live long, he took it calmly. I never heard a word of complaint or fear of death. "My grace is sufficient for thee: for my strength is made perfect in weakness" (2 Cor. 12:9).

With God's grace in giving us people such as them, our churches prospered and grew.

Chapter 14

SHADOWS

The years in Hull were happy for the young minister and his growing family. But as the author points out, on this side of the grave there is no perfect happiness. Rev. Hanko tells of the griefs that came to the Iowa community in the 1930s. They took many forms, including trouble in the churches, sudden deaths in the congregations, and financial difficulty brought on by the Great Depression.

Sunny days also have their shadows. Life in Hull also had its shadows. In fact, I was in Hull only three weeks, and I had made an enemy.

It came about this way. As a student I had visited with Rev. and Mrs. Verhil when he was minister in Hull. Almost every evening a certain couple came over to spend the evening. Those frequent visits were bad enough, but that man was very abusive. One evening he said to Rev. Verhil, "You are so dumb that I could bend a nail trying to pound it into your head." After they left, I asked Rev. Verhil why he put up with language like that. He said that he was in Hull only for a limited time and did not want to offend the couple. But whoever was his successor should avoid those daily visits at the outset.

When my wife and I were settled in Hull, that same couple came to visit us. Before long he asked me to stop in his shop every morning when I went to fetch the mail, just as Rev. Verhil had done. I figured it was a good time to bring up the subject, so I told him that I would be too busy to stop in every day. Besides,

I did not think it wise to have special friends in the congregation. He stormed away in a fit of rage, leaving me to wonder what might be the outcome.

Soon he and his family sat as far back in the church as possible. Whenever I said something that he did not like, he sighed loudly and shuffled his feet. When he saw that I seemingly paid no attention, he sat in the very first row of seats with his family and did the same thing. On the occasion of a lecture, he and his family stood at the door and waited until I had introduced the speaker and left the platform. Then they came in and took front-row seats. As soon as the lecture was over, they stormed out before I could get to the pulpit to thank the speaker.

Since both the consistory and I ignored him for some time, he decided to ask for his papers, expecting a committee from the consistory. But the consistory decided to send him his papers at once. His reaction was bombastic, but there was nothing he could do about it.

Then his wife, who had not left the church, decided to take up the cudgel for him. She kept a diary of all my actions. It read something like this: "He visits Vander Kooi at least once a week. Why all those visits?" "Today he went through the alley to go to the post office. Why did he do that?"

She refused to have any visit from me. But soon the consistory was compelled to visit her, until she refused those visits also. The outcome was that she was placed under censure. The matter went to classis. Finally, when it was announced that she would be excommunicated, she came to the consistory to read her diary. She read page after page. One of the elders asked me, "Aren't you going to stop her?" I answered, "Why?" To which he replied, "If you won't, I will." And he commanded her to stop.

It is always difficult to read the form of excommunication, but that was especially difficult because it involved me personally. Besides, I could not help but wonder whether she was normal. In fact, years later, she committed suicide.

Another shadow. We arrived in Hull in September 1929. A month later the stock market crashed. Calvin Coolidge had said in 1927, "I do not choose to run in 1928." He saw the crash coming. Uncle Jim Schriemer, who lived in Grand Rapids, had gone to the bank to take out a big loan for building a number of houses. The banker asked him whether he was not making a good living by building one house at a time. Uncle Jim said he was, but he wanted to expand his business. The banker warned him to leave well enough alone. He was glad he did.

The well-known Depression did not set in until the spring of 1930. Money became tight. Work was slackening. Businesses were folding up. Those who still had a heavy mortgage on their farms lost them. Henry Kuiper of Doon lost his house and farm. Many who had only a small debt remaining on their properties lost everything. I never received the salary promised to me. In fact, one year my annual income was down to less than six hundred dollars, even though I had been called on a salary of one thousand five hundred dollars. Months would go by without seeing any income. At one time my financial worth was fifty cents. We learned that it was essential for our existence to do a lot of canning in the late summer and early autumn. We purchased a large canner that held twelve quarts at one time.

Since there was no work, the government introduced the Works Progress Administration,[1] giving some men opportunities to clean up the roads and to do other odd jobs. Every week they received a small pittance from the government and occasionally a handout of food. The farmers still ate well, because they had egg money with which they could buy the necessary groceries. But the ministers lacked that kind of income.

In 1934 came the drought and dust storms. One day we

---

1 The Works Progress Administration was part of President Franklin Roosevelt's New Deal by which he intended to put thousands of Americans back to work.

were coming home from Sheldon when suddenly the sky in the northwest grew threateningly black. Our first reaction was that a severe thunderstorm was approaching. As we neared home a fierce wind came up, and along with it heavy clouds of dust. One could hardly see the road even with the car lights on. That was almost an everyday occurrence. In the morning when we got up little piles of dust were heaped by the doors. The window sills were black with dust. Even our pillows showed exactly where our heads had lain. Every step showed plainly on the wooden floor.

During the service on a Sunday afternoon, the wind was driving tree branches against the roof and sides of the church building. The sky was so black that it was almost like night. When the lights went out in the church, as often happened in windstorms, I could not see the people. The windows stood out in a ghastly gray. The next day the newspaper reported that many people thought the end of the world had come.

Along with the drought came the grasshoppers in South Dakota. Those pests were so thick that fields were covered with them. When the entire crop was devoured, the grasshoppers gnawed on fence posts. But in Sioux County it was the drought that took the crop.

It certainly seemed as if God's judgments were upon the earth. In June Classis West met in Oskaloosa. I took a car full from our area. Toward evening on Thursday, classis had finished, so we decided to ride home yet that night. Soon we ran into torrents of rain. As we approached Orange City, we had a flat tire, so we waited for the rain to let up and then changed the tire. When the tire was changed, we decided to wait until daylight before continuing on our way, because the roads were bad. Soon after daylight near Orange City we came upon a bad washout, which we might not have noticed in the dark. That night eight inches of rain fell in that entire area. The "million dollar corner" near Hawarden was completely washed out. Parts of wagons hung in trees.

Another shadow. On Memorial Day 1934 the temperature reached 100 degrees. Six of the young people from Rock Valley went to Lake Okoboji for the day. They were all in a boat when one of them, who had come from California, decided to dive off the side of the boat. That scared the girls who were not accustomed to boating. So he tried it again. That time the boat turned over. Henrietta, daughter of John Blankespoor, and her cousin, also a Blankespoor, were drowned. They lived on opposite sides of Rock Valley, one north, the other south. Both funeral processions met on the main street of the town and lined up next to each other by the Reformed church. Since Doon had no minister at the time, I officiated at Henrietta's funeral. A rough estimate was that about eighteen hundred people walked past the two caskets. John Blankespoor suffered from shock for a long time.

In Hull the Ed Dykstra family suffered the loss of a stillborn baby and of a two-year-old daughter within three hours. The baby was buried that same day, and the small daughter, who died from an unrecognized ailment, was buried two days later.

Another shadow. For a long time as the result of backbiting and gossip, fire had been smoldering in one of our neighboring churches, and gradually it involved the whole congregation. The lot fell on me to serve as moderator in that mess. Repeatedly members of the congregation came to the consistory to accuse some other member, with the result that the accused heard about it and brought accusations against the accuser. Often the meetings would carry on long into the night. That went on for some time, until I grew weary of those late hours and told the men that either they adjourn at eleven o'clock or I was going home. The result was that I went home, and after I left decisions were made that required my protest at the next meeting. The situation worsened so badly that it proved nearly impossible to call a congregational meeting. Everyone stood outside but refused to come in, mainly because they wanted to oust one particular elder.

So the classical committee, Rev. Hoeksema, Rev. Ophoff, and

LESS THAN THE LEAST

Rev. Dirk Jonker came from Michigan to settle the matter. They met day after day for almost a week, and stayed with us during that week. The committee called the individuals of the congregation who were most deeply involved and pleaded with them to reconcile with their fellow church members. Only reluctantly were they convinced to do so. One of the elders involved in the trouble reported to Rev. Hoeksema the following day that he had gotten up at five o'clock in the morning, had walked around his whole farm section, and had repeatedly said to himself, "Don't reconcile." Only as he returned to his own driveway did he finally say, "Do it." And he did.

Another individual seemed determined never to confess his wrong. Rev. Hoeksema pointed him to his obligation before his God. Hoeksema warned him of possible discipline. But nothing seemed to move him. Finally Rev. Hoeksema said to him, "Two mountain goats were moving along the side of a precipice when they suddenly met face to face. There was no room to pass. Do you know what they did?" The response was a shake of the head. "The one bent down, and the other jumped over him. Will you bend down?" The answer was a gruff and emphatic, "No." Yet the Lord moved also that stubborn heart to confess.

When all were reconciled with each other, the committee called a public meeting of the entire congregation on Friday evening. Rev. Hoeksema preached a sermon on Philippians 2:1–4: "If there be therefore any consolation in Christ, if any comfort of love, if any fellowship of the Spirit, if any bowels and mercies, fulfill ye my joy, that ye be likeminded, having the same love, being of one accord, of one mind..." He started out by saying that he had discovered that the members of that church were not afraid of anybody: not afraid of the devil, and they even imagined that they were not afraid of God, since they sinned so lightly against him. But he assured them that if God were to step into their midst even for a moment, they would all be filled with terror.

I have heard many sermons, but never one more powerful,

more sincerely spoken, or more effective than that one. The entire congregation was deeply moved; tears were shed, and everyone was more than willing to banish all differences with a determination to start anew in the love of Christ and the power of the Spirit.

In spite of those difficulties, the Iowa churches, including the Hull congregation, enjoyed steady growth.

After spending five years in Hull, I received a call from Oak Lawn, Illinois. In the winter of 1934–35 our way led to Oak Lawn.

The young people came over twice to spend the evening as a farewell. As one of the elders remarked when we were ready to leave Hull, "You came with just the two of you, and you broke out into two bands" (Gen. 32:10).

Chapter 15

AUTOMOBILE AND TRAIN TRAVEL

In this chapter Rev. Hanko takes us back to the days automobile travel was a novelty, a rather unreliable novelty at that. Most Americans relied heavily on train travel, as is herein described.

When I was about eight years old, I had my first automobile ride. One of my uncles had a Studebaker,[1] an open car with carbide lights.[2] He took my mother and me to Hudsonville, Michigan, where some of my mother's family lived. I can well remember that just as we were leaving the city limits on Chicago Drive, my cap blew off, and my uncle had to stop the car to retrieve it. All in all, that was quite an experience.

Shortly after my first ride in 1916, my dad bought his first car, a Model T. It was the first automobile in the neighborhood. It was a pickup truck that could be converted into a runabout by taking off the box.[3] The car had one seat, with the gas tank under the seat. The car had one door, a half door on the passenger's side. It had a brass radiator, and it had to be cranked. In cold weather one of the back wheels had to be jacked up and the car put into gear to give added inertia for starting.

---

1 Studebakers were cars manufactured in the early 1900s in South Bend, Indiana. The manufacturer went out of business in 1966.
2 A carbide light ran off acetylene gas.
3 A runabout was a small, affordable, open car.

The car had a kerosene lamp for a taillight, which usually went out on rough roads. It also had magneto headlights, which would dim very low when the engine idled. Those lights were at their best when the engine was revved. One dark, drizzly night my brother and I were riding east on Lake Drive. Visibility was bad. As we slowed to turn the corner at Diamond Avenue, we suddenly heard a thump. My brother stepped on the brake, and we saw a dark figure arise in front of the car. As this figure came under the street light we saw that it was a woman, who ran away like a hunted deer. She was evidently unhurt but sorely embarrassed. We left our names, address, and license number at the corner drugstore, but never heard any more of it.

One Fourth of July my parents decided to make a trip to Hudsonville. My dad rarely drove and was not the best nor the fastest driver. We left around seven in the morning, went to Fulton Street, and then along Market Street to Chicago Drive. We rode until we came to the grain elevators in Jenison. There we turned left, traveled a certain distance, and then turned right to get to Hudsonville. By the time we arrived it was nine o'clock in the morning. Between three and four in the afternoon we left, arriving home about six o'clock. It had been a long day and a strenuous experience.

A few years later my brother-in-law Otto Vander Woude also had a Model T, with enclosed front and rear seats. One day the car's oil line was clogged, so we took off the pan under the engine, took out the copper oil line, ran a wire through it, and soon had the engine put together and running again.

In 1927 Richard Veldman, Gerrit Vos, and I were in Doon to supply the pulpits in Doon, Hull, and Sioux Center. We went by train to Hull and Sioux Center for Sunday services, but during the week we borrowed a car from one of the farmers. It was usually an extra car the farmer had. One day when Vos was driving his wife, son, and me to Sioux Center, the steering shaft came loose. The car ended up in the ditch. We walked to Sioux Center, and the farmer had to fetch his car while we had to find a way back to Doon.

Richard Veldman, Cornelius Hanko, and Gerrit Vos in Iowa in 1927

The car Seminarian Hanko borrowed in Iowa would not start on this occasion. The stick in his hand was to measure the gas in the tank. His look of frustration implies that there was plenty of gas, and yet the car would not start.

On another occasion Rich Veldman and I went to Sioux Center to attend a consistory meeting. It was about eleven o'clock in the evening when we started for home. Instead of going to Main Street, we stayed on the street of the church and soon settled in the Iowa mud. That was not the first time we had gotten ourselves stuck in the clay, but then we were dressed up and did not feel like digging with our hands in the mud. As we pondered how to get out of that mess, a young fellow returning from his girlfriend's house came past. We asked him to help us, but first he wanted to change his clothes. We thought that was an excuse not to help us, so we settled down to sleep there. But soon he returned with a shovel, dug the car out, and had us on our way to Doon.

A short distance from town we noticed that the radiator had run dry. Rich went into a farmyard, pumped a bucket of water, and began to carry it to the car. The man of the house came out to check on the disturbance, so Rich threw the bucket into the yard and ran back to the car.

On another occasion I was going to Sioux Center to teach catechism. Immediately I discovered that the Model T had neither clutch nor brakes. To start it rolling one had to push it and hop in. To stop it, one ran against the curb or another obstacle. I left the car on Main Street in Sioux Center. But on the way home as the car was climbing a hill, my hat blew off. That meant driving the car to the top of the hill, running back for my hat, and then starting the car by going downhill.

After staying about three months in Doon, Rev. Vos decided that he, his wife, and his son should go home, which meant we had to borrow a car to take them to the Hull railroad station. Having packed his trunk and putting his wife and son in the back seat, Gerrit, Richard, and I took our places in the front seat. All went well, even going downhill, but the problem came when we tried to climb the next hill. Suddenly, with the engine still running, the car refused to budge.

Gerrit stopped a passing motorist and informed him of our difficulty and that he and his family had to catch the train in Hull. The fellow felt sorry for him, so the trunk, Gerrit, his wife, and his son went off with the motorist. Rich and I sat in the car that had refused to run. Giving it another try, we found that it ran perfectly. Instead of turning back, we went to Hull to see Gerrit off on the train. His first thought was that he was seeing ghosts. Then he decided we had pulled a prank on him. He refused to be convinced that after we were relieved of him, his family, and all his possessions the car ran well. When we took the car back to the farmer, we felt obligated to inform him of our experience.

In June 1927, after coming home for exams, Rich Veldman and I returned to Doon for the summer. That time Andrew Cammenga came with us. During our stay we decided to ask Nick

Buyert of Sioux Center for permission to take his car to the Black Hills. He consented.

Andrew Cammenga (driving) and Richard Veldman (back seat)

Monday morning we were off to South Dakota. Before dawn we rode over a skunk, and for a while the smell was almost unbearable. As the day progressed we noticed that the car was heating up. Since it was a borrowed car, we felt that we should have it checked. We stopped at a garage and asked the mechanic if he knew how to prevent the car from overheating. He took a look and told us, "When you get out of town you will see a junkyard. Bring the car there and leave it." That hardly solved our problem, so we drove on.

Late one afternoon of our trip, in torrents of rain, we were approaching Rapid City. When we stopped to ask a passing motorist how much farther we had to go on the muddy road, the other driver asked us how long we had been riding in the mud. By the time we reached Rapid City the car was so hot that we could not shut off the engine. We brought the car to a garage, where the mechanic set it against the wall and revved the engine till it stopped. The next morning the car had to be towed to unlock the back wheels.

Then we were ready to see the park, but the hills were steep, so two of us walked up the hills while the third drove the car. The most hazardous part of the trip was going down the steep hills.

The brake could not slow the car at curves, so the driver was forced to reach out frequently for the emergency brake.

In the park the car had a broken spark plug wire. A piece of fence wire took care of that until we were home again.

We spent one night in a motel that had bedbugs. All three of us were in one bed. The next morning Rich was full of red spots. He had had enough; he wanted to go home.

That day we stood in a railroad station and wondered whether we should avail ourselves of the opportunity to see Denver, since it was likely we would never get there if we did not go then. Our better judgment prevailed, and we started back to Doon, making the trip without further mishap. After we returned home, Mr. Buyert informed us regarding the car's overheating. Before the trip the car had been overhauled, so the pistons were still tight.

By the latter part of August we were thinking of going back home and to seminary. Rev. Vos had accepted the call to Sioux Center and was preparing to go there, but he was waiting for the birth of a baby. We were told to stay until the baby arrived. So patiently we waited it out day by day. Finally the word came that baby Marilyn had arrived, so we could return home and belatedly return to the seminary.

Mr. Cammenga, the father of Andrew, had purchased a new car and drove to Doon to bring us home. Monday morning at four o'clock we started out. The roads were still made of gravel and led us through every town along the route. We reached the first brick road about one hundred miles west of Chicago. It was one lane, which required two wheels off the brick pavement when we met a passing car. We traveled all day and all night and stopped only for gas and a bite to eat. After going through the loop of Chicago we passed through South Chicago, Hammond, Gary, Michigan City, Benton Harbor, and then on through the woods to South Haven, Saugatuck, Holland, and Zeeland, and arrived in Grand Rapids at nine o'clock Tuesday morning. The trip had taken thirty hours. Now the trip is made in twelve to fifteen hours.

In July 1934 my wife and I were expecting our third child. We made the trip to Grand Rapids with our two boys and stayed with my parents. They were glad to have us visit, but were also eager for us to leave. They did not fancy having a baby born in their home.

That was the summer of the big drought when the grasshoppers devoured the entire crop in South Dakota, and the summer of the unforgettable dust storms. It was a hot summer even in Michigan. Therefore, we decided to leave Michigan for Hull at two o'clock in the morning to drive through the cool of the night at least part of the way. By the time we reached Holland, Michigan, we were already turning up the windows. By the time we reached Chicago, we had to turn the heater on in the car as it was overheating. This made me feel miserably sick, so we decided to stop early in the afternoon, sleep through the night, and get an early start the next morning. My wife made the arrangements at a motel somewhere near Dubuque, Iowa. But when the manager saw me staggering out of the car, she decided that the deal was off. She wanted no pregnant woman with a drunken husband in one of her rooms. It took a bit of persuasion to convince her that we would create no inconvenience.

There were also others who had interesting experiences in the automobile. Two men of the consistory of Hull church were appointed to attend the combined consistory meeting in Grand Rapids. They decided to go by car, even though they had never before ventured on a trip as long as that.

They rode along the gravel roads and later in the day came to a detour. Returning from the detour, they found themselves back on the Atlantic-Yellowstone-Pacific Highway and continued on their way. After some time one remarked, "Never before have I seen the sun set in the east." The other agreed, so they decided to stop at a gas station and ask whether they were on the highway to Chicago. They were informed that they were on the highway, but as they were driving off the man at the station called to them "Are you coming from or going to Chicago?" After informing the man that they were on their way to Chicago, they were told that they were going the wrong way. They finally reached Chicago and discovered that the highway led them right through the heart of the city. Cars passed them on both sides. Never had they experienced anything like that. So at the very first opportunity the driver brought the car up on the sidewalk, where he stopped with a sense of relief. He was reminded that he was not in Grand Rapids. They hired a taxi driver to bring them safely though the city and on their way again to their destination.

On another occasion delegates from Doon, Rock Valley, and Sioux Center went by train to Grand Rapids and were returning home. Mr. Tim Kooima from Rock Valley stopped in Chicago to buy a car to drive home. Mr. John Broek of Sioux Center and Mr. Harm Zylstra of Doon went to Union Station to await the train to Rock Valley. While they were waiting, Tim Kooima stopped at the station to offer the men a ride home. Mr. Broek consented, but Mr. Zylstra decided to go home by train. But the train had pulled out without him. He stayed in the station for twenty-four hours waiting for the next train. Because of the milling crowd rushing past, he was very reluctant even to rise from his seat. During the night a policeman thought he was a bum and wanted to send him on his way. But in broken English he said that he had purchased a ticket for the train, and he was allowed to stay. It was Saturday evening before he could board the train, which brought him into Rock Valley on Sunday morning during the church service. Rather than interfere with the service, he waited in a car outside and obtained a ride back home to Doon.

The most common means of travel at that time was by train. Yes, we did go by car when the family traveled, but in those days ministers could travel by train for half price. Therefore, when we traveled alone, we traveled by rail. That was most enjoyable even though we rarely could afford to take a sleeper. It was a trip we looked forward to when the various delegates from the Midwest would travel by train to classis. (At that time, classis was not yet divided into East and West.)

Going to a classical appointment by train was also a pleasure. Because of the Depression the train carried very few passengers. The staff would do almost anything to satisfy those few who still rode in the coaches. On one occasion I went by train to fill a classical appointment in Pella and Oskaloosa. The train that was to take me from Des Moines to Mason City, where I would transfer to the Chicago-Milwaukee line, was an hour late. I told the conductor that since the train was an hour late, I would miss my train in Mason City and would not be able to get home until the next day. After a bit of investigating he came back and asked me whether I was willing to follow orders strictly. I assured him that there was not much I would not do to get home that same day; so the arrangements were made. As we approached the switches in Mason City, the train had to slow to almost a complete stop. I stood, as ordered, on the bottom step of the coach, travel bag in hand, and as the train slowed up I jumped into the ditch. Then, still following orders, I waited until the train was past, only to hear a most welcome voice in the distance, directing me to a waiting taxi. Five minutes before the train was scheduled to depart, we arrived in the Chicago-Milwaukee station.

On another occasion I had two stripped and drawn chickens to take back to Oak Lawn. It was warm in the train, so that I became concerned about my two chickens. I talked to the conductor, who took them to the water cooler, where they stayed on ice until I arrived in Chicago.

At that time Hull was more or less the center of the Protestant Reformed churches in the Midwest. The congregation there had the largest church building, so that lectures, conferences with the German Reformed Church,[4] meetings of classes, and other prominent meetings were held there.

One year comes to mind when a number of delegates from the East were coming by train and were stalled near Spencer, Iowa, because of floods. A few of us got into our cars and drove down to where the train was stalled to pick up the delegates, among whom were Rev. Hoeksema and Rev. Ophoff. That noon we had thirteen people around our dining room table, and we had only one scrawny chicken to serve. Having come from a large family, my wife did not get too excited about those unexpected impositions. She usually had canned meat in the basement that could readily be heated up.

On one occasion Rev. Hoeksema was staying with us when two elderly couples came from Kalamazoo. When one of the ladies heard that Rev. Hoeksema was staying with us, she was determined to stay with us too. When she was told that we had no room, she got herself sick, so that she could not stay "out in the country," but had to stay in town with us. The result was that she stayed in bed all day, and then when we were ready to visit a bit in the evening, she got up, once making the remark, "Oh, Dominie Hoeksema, I could sit up all night and listen to you." He answered, "But I'm going to bed."

Thus, since the nation was increasingly on the move with advancements in travel, we were able to keep in touch with our extended family and other churches in the denomination.

---

4   The German Reformed Church, founded in 1725, is now called the Reformed Church in the United States, not to be confused with the Reformed Church in America.

Chapter 16

OAK LAWN, ILLINOIS

The years in Oak Lawn were difficult for the Hanko family. The whole congregation was feeling the effects of the Depression. Rev. Hanko compares the Oak Lawn congregation to the church in Smyrna, one of the seven churches addressed in the book of Revelation. As the church in Smyrna was spiritually rich in her financial poverty, so was the church in Oak Lawn. Because of that spiritual prosperity, Rev. Hanko enjoyed his labors among them. Yet there was one man (his name is omitted) who caused Rev. Hanko and the congregation great grief. His presence in the church cast a long shadow over all of the pastor's work there. He left the churches shortly before Rev. Hanko left Oak Lawn.

I had been in Hull for five years and wondered whether that was long enough. I actually had no desire to leave. The congregation had grown from twelve families to twenty-five, and peace and harmony prevailed. However, Oak Lawn had been vacant for eight years, not having a minister since its organization. The whole matter of the call weighed quite heavily on me.

Oak Lawn Protestant Reformed Church

While I was considering the call, I received a letter from a man in the Oak Lawn congregation. I supposed that he had written to ask us to come to join them in Oak Lawn. But the opposite was true. He said that the people in Hull appreciated my labors there so much that he felt I should stay. He ended the letter by saying, "Whenever you come through Oak Lawn be sure to stop." Evidently he expected me to decline the call.

After I read the letter, I said to my wife, "We're going to Oak Lawn." She looked at me in amazement and said, "Have you lost your mind? He told us not to come." I assured her that that was the very reason I had decided to go. It seemed to me that there was something radically wrong in a congregation if they would call a minister and then ask him not to accept.

We had the opportunity to hire movers from Orange City, Iowa, who had offered me a very good price. But the consistory of Oak Lawn thought they could do better. Our family was all packed and ready to go, but the mover Oak Lawn had hired did not come. Our coal supply and food were gone, our house was in total disarray, and we hesitated to buy more food because we had

LESS THAN THE LEAST

planned to leave as soon as the movers came. On top of that, Fred showed signs of becoming ill, so we spent the last night in Sioux Center with the Rich Veldman family. The temperature had dropped so low that the car overheated as we approached Sioux Center. The next day we left word with the neighbor in Hull to take charge when the movers came, and we boarded the train to head for Chicago. One of the men from Hull assured us that he would deliver our car to Oak Lawn.

For a total of twenty dollars, the five of us, with eight pieces of luggage, took up the back part of a coach on the Chicago-Milwaukee train to travel to our new home.

After a whole night we arrived in Union Station in Chicago and were met by Dick Kort. He took us to his small house, which already had seven occupants but somehow could accommodate a few more. There we waited for the arrival of our furniture. In the meantime we and others of the congregation worked on cleaning the house that had been rented for us. In the process of cleaning, Mr.____ came in one day and said, "Dominie, will you wash those upstairs windows? I'm afraid I'll break my neck." I could not help but wonder what value he placed on my neck, but having painted houses, climbing a ladder was no problem.

Finally our furniture arrived. My wife could pretty well take things in stride. She never complained about the transfer from Hull to Oak Lawn. But when she saw the cattle truck and our furniture heaped helter-skelter on it, she wept. Our first question to the movers was, "Did you take along the canned goods that were stored at the neighbor's house?" We had a lot of canned goods, and we treasured them dearly in those Depression years. We refused to sign the moving agreement until a clause was added concerning the meat and the other canned goods. The mover had deliberately left the canned goods behind because they were at the neighbor's house. We sat with the mover on the front steps until the necessary calls were made, and ten dollars was taken from the cost of the moving, which amounted to seventy-five dollars.

But that was not the worst. That fellow was no mover. The baby bed came off the cattle truck with a broken leg. The dining room furniture arrived with scratches and cuts ground in by the furniture above it. When everything was unloaded and he was driving off, my wife shouted, "He's taking our blankets!" But there was nothing we could do about it.

Oak Lawn was a typical commuters' town. Many of the men and women worked in Chicago by day and spent their nights and weekends at home. Saturday night was the time to get drunk, so that at five o'clock on Sunday morning, the drunken folks noisily sought their way home. Those who were able worked on their lawns or property on Sunday. We lived as strangers in a little section of the world.

We hear about pea-soup fog in London. I have wondered whether that could be worse than the spring and autumn fogs in Oak Lawn. One night I went by car to teach a catechism class in the church. On the way home the fog was so thick I could hardly see the road. I followed the red light of the car ahead of me, until it suddenly disappeared into the ditch. I felt my way home the rest of the way.

On another occasion I decided that if I would walk in a straight line across the field in the fog, I would come out at Ninety-fifth near Cicero Avenue. But I actually came out on Cicero Avenue, quite a distance from where I should have been. That was not so serious, but coming home was worse. I had all I could do to find Kostner Avenue, the street on which we lived, and then our house.

The worst was the night we came from the Rutgers' house outside of town. At about ten-thirty, three miles from Oak Lawn, we ran into fog. We moved slowly, trying to feel our way. My wife remarked that she was sure she saw lights passing us on our right, which meant that I was in the wrong lane, but the other driver had to be in the wrong lane too. After getting out of the car to investigate and finding that to be true, we proceeded slowly in the proper lane until I had a feeling that we were approaching a crossroad. I parked the car and walked ahead. There I heard voices of men and women asking, "Where am I?" After some delay those cars cleared away and we proceeded to the railroad overpass. There a policeman with a torch led the cars one by one over the overpass. When we finally reached Oak Lawn, I had to get close to the street sign to find out where we were. At one-thirty in the morning we arrived home with a sigh of relief.

Not long after we had settled in our new home, all three of the children came down with whooping cough while we were visiting my parents in Grand Rapids. We took all three of them to the doctor for a shot. The two boys did not object when the doctor gave them their shots. But for their little sister, it was different. They complained bitterly that she also had to be subjected to that ordeal.

Nights seemed to be the worst. If one was not whooping it up, the other was. We walked around with large cloths to catch the vomiting. Fred continued to whoop the whole winter, much to the chagrin of our neighbor. Whenever Fred was in the backyard her kids were hauled into the house. She could not understand that we were so inconsiderate that we allowed him to be outside, a threat to the community.

In January 1935 we moved to Oak Lawn. In March 1936 my father died. We received notice on a Saturday morning that he had pneumonia and was not expected to live. We immediately made arrangements to go to Michigan. On the way wet snow was falling, and our windshield wipers failed to operate, so we tied two strings to them, my wife pulling from one side and I from the other. That same night, toward morning, my father passed away.

Shortly after my father passed away, Mother began to suffer from severe pains in her face, commonly referred to as a tic. The attacks could come at any time, especially when she ate. They were so severe that she ran through the house in agony. There was no known cure or relief, but the osteopath who came once a week could relax her. The attacks lasted for about six years. Since I was on the mission committee and had classical appointments in Michigan, I took as many opportunities as possible to visit her. In fact, she always had my former room ready for me, hoping that I would surprise her.

About a half year before she died in 1941, I received a call to come to her because the pains were incessant. When I talked to the doctor, he said that he could give her morphine to put her out, but he would have to give her so much that she might not wake up again. I talked to her about it and she begged me to go ahead. So we did. She slept for forty-eight hours. Six months later when I received the call that she had passed away in her sleep, I was so thankful that the Lord took her out of her misery that I felt a bit guilty. I felt I should be feeling sad, and I suppose I was. Yet what a relief to think that she was rejoicing before the throne! Prof. Clarence Bouma's wife requested that our children stay with them during the funeral.[1]

Oak Lawn was a devoted congregation, cherishing love for the truth and for their pastor and his family. One could well say of them, "Though you are poor, you are rich," for in material things they were poor, but spiritually they were very rich. It was a pleasure to labor among them.

Oak Lawn church picnic

---

1 Professor Bouma was a relative of the Hanko family and a professor at Calvin seminary.

The fact remained that they were materially poor. In other parts of the nation, the Depression gradually faded out and working conditions improved, but Oak Lawn remained poor. The reason was that almost all the members of the congregation were garden farmers who brought their crops to the city market. During World War II airplanes became the common means of transportation, so that foodstuffs from California could arrive at the Chicago market overnight, long before the local gardeners could bring their goods to market. The result was that when the farmers delivered their crops to market, the markets were already flooded with produce and the prices had dropped tremendously. The Depression simply never left Oak Lawn. But the members of the congregation were willing to give the shirts off their backs for the minister's family, which they virtually did, as will become evident later.

Ladies of Oak Lawn

Eventually the truck farmers had to find another source of income, or move to other areas, as they ultimately did. Later many sought refuge in South Holland, Illinois, and Randolph, Wisconsin, and attended Protestant Reformed churches there.

Oak Lawn Men's Society

The following story illustrates the strong faith of the members in the face of financially difficult times. It was a year of drought, and sprinkling systems were unknown. In July when the fields should have been covered with bright green foliage and a rich yield of ripening crops, there was hardly a sprout to be seen. Even the weeds had difficulty surviving. In that situation one of the members also had the sad experience that his wife was ill and hospitalized for some time. When I visited their home, the oldest daughter, a girl about nine years old, and her little sister were washing the dishes. The other three children were playing in the yard. I walked with the father to the field from which his annual income was expected. What should I say? Before I could utter a word he remarked, "You know, Reverend, God is good. No matter what, God is good." What more need be said?

The people struggled to pay the salary they had promised me. Each week the treasurer came to bring as much money as he had collected. The money was spread on the dining room table, necessary bills for the week were taken out, and what was left was my salary. Often the treasurer remarked, "We'll try to do better next week." We first took out the school tuition because if we failed to pay that on time, we would never catch up. Then the bills were paid. With the rest we had to manage for groceries, clothing, and fuel. We tried to budget, putting money in separate envelopes, but we borrowed so often one from the other that we soon gave up that venture.

One year I did not have enough money to buy a license for the car. South Holland consistory asked me to preach for them, so I told them that I could do that if they would pick me up and bring me back. Frank Van Baren came to get me, and on the way he asked if I was not using the car because the car lacked a license. When I answered in the affirmative, he gave me money to buy a license.

When Christmas came around I made gifts for the children, which they seemed to appreciate as much as a purchased present. My wife bought me a shirt for Christmas, and I bought her a pair of gloves. But the day after Christmas we needed money for groceries, so we decided to return the shirt and the gloves to buy the necessities for meals, but the mutual presents had made everybody happy.

Usually on Saturday we bought a pot roast for a quarter. The meat was sparingly dealt out on Sunday, and the rest was enjoyed on Monday. The rest of the week we made do without meat.

Dick Kort repeatedly helped us to buy fuel for the furnace. On one occasion we went to the car shops to get castoff lumber, long boards that stuck out from the back of the truck. When we went over the railroad track, the whole front end of the truck came off the ground, so I had to stand on the bumper to hold it down.

On another occasion we went to Joliet to fetch some dirty surface coal. In order to do so I had to rob the children's banks of the few dimes and nickels they had saved. But on the way, Dick dented the fender of another car, so that we had to dole out two dollars in nickels to quiet the man. What hurt the most was that the man asked whether we had been playing the slot machines.

Keeping a family clothed was a big job for many people. When a piece of clothing could no longer be used by a member of the family, it was donated to someone who could use it. There was a time when the entire family wore almost nothing but hand-me-downs. Although my father was much shorter than me, I wore his overcoat and shoes after he died.

My Sunday suit was getting very thin, especially in the seat. We felt the need for a new one but could not afford it. At Christmastime we received an envelope from Grand Rapids containing twenty dollars. Later we found out that Gerrit Pipe from Fourth (Southeast) Protestant Reformed Church and his girlfriend decided to give the money to us that they would have spent buying gifts for each other. We actually wept when suddenly we had that much money. After careful consideration we decided to buy a Sunday suit. So we went to a Jew on Fifty-ninth Street, who sold suits that he had picked up at various stores in the city. There we purchased a suit for sixteen dollars. The next Sunday Mrs. Veldman, a sister of Rev. Hoeksema, in her own way made the remark, "That was not a waste of money." She too must have feared that on some Sunday I would come through the seat of my trousers.

The Depression was a difficult time, yet everybody was confronted with the same problem to a greater or lesser degree. We were all in the same boat, so to speak, and made the best of it. There were few complaints. One lesson we learned was to pray for our daily bread. We were much like Israel in the wilderness, having enough for today and waiting upon the Lord for tomorrow.

On top of the financial difficulties was the trouble caused by the same elder who had written to tell me not to take the call to Oak Lawn. I barely had time to make sermons the first half year of my ministry in Oak Lawn. I was too busy trying to straighten out the mess resulting from Oak Lawn's eight years without a minister. Mr. _____ was the center of the difficulties. He could act so pious. He did not want a minister there because then he could read and teach catechism, and he liked that. When I came, things changed.

Before I took the call another minister had said that he was coming to Oak Lawn, and then he declined the call. In his prayer Mr. _____ said, "And forgive the minister who has so treacherously deceived us." A lady came to the consistory and said that if there was a minister who had treacherously deceived them, they ought to do something. That was one of the issues the consistory was dealing with when I arrived. I went to see Mr. _____, and he started confessing far more than he should have. Then we had still more of a mess on our hands.

He came to realize that I was fed up with it. He came to the consistory and said, "The minister needs a raise." The consistory said, "We realize that, but we can't do it." He told them that he would do it alone. So they called a congregational meeting and the proposal went through easily. They were more than willing to give me a raise if it could be done. Before the meeting I had said, "Don't do this." But they said, "You need the raise and Mr. _____ said he could do it." I did not think Mr. _____ would be with us much longer, so I tried to warn the elders. I knew that his big talk of giving me a raise was the precursor to his leaving.

A short time later he came to visit me after his wife had seen to it that my wife was out of the house. He informed me that he was leaving the church. I was not surprised and told him so. He accused me of not trusting him, and I agreed. I said to him, "Last Sunday there was a visitor in church and you told him that you didn't like the sermon, didn't you?" He replied, "How do you know?" I said, "You just told me. And the same was true a couple of weeks ago when there was another visitor in church." Then I admitted that I had been guessing and told him what I knew for fact: he taught catechism once when I was gone, and his instruction bordered on heresy. The Christian Reformed neighbor lady who had been sending her son to our catechism was irate.

In his seminary instruction Rev. Danhof had warned his students that in every congregation they would find at least one man who would make their lives miserable. That proved to be true in Oak Lawn for me. Every time I got a call, Mr. _____ "accepted it" for me. If he had said the opposite, I might have taken the call.

Chapter 17

MOVING

Because the Depression hit the congregation of Oak Lawn so hard, the church did not own a parsonage of its own. The consistory was forced to rent a home for their pastor and his family. Those temporary arrangements proved to be just that—temporary. Thus the Hanko family was required to move many times during their stay in Oak Lawn. The church finally purchased a home the year before Rev. Hanko moved to Manhattan. In this chapter Rev. Hanko describes the various homes and the moves in between.

In the ten years we spent in Oak Lawn, we moved seven times and once found ourselves without a home for several weeks.

The first house the consistory rented for us was in the east part of the town and was surrounded by trees. For a refrigerator the house had a box in the pantry window where food could be kept when the weather was moderate, not too hot and not too cold. The basement stairway came out in the dining room. At the very foot of the steps was the coal pile. It was simply impossible to come out of the basement without carrying coal dust on our feet onto the dining room rug.

One of the rooms upstairs was made into a study, but the study was so cold in the winter that a heater had to be purchased and used to keep the room warm. The big problem was that no sunlight could penetrate through the trees around the house. The result was that all the furniture showed signs of mold, white spots appearing in the varnish.

After a little more than a year we moved to a small house next to the Christian Reformed church. The rooms in that house were small, with the exception of the kitchen. The bedrooms had room for only a bed. Six people could sit in the living room, with nothing but a narrow aisle between them.

The minister of the church next door saw Herm outside one day and asked him whether he was going to be a minister when he grew up. He answered, "No, I'm going to be a deacon." We wondered whether he thought that deacons were better paid. When Herm was old enough he began school in Evergreen Park. The first day he came out of the bus shouting, "I have a nice teacher!" He was all set to go again.

He had already taken a keen interest in reading. It intrigued him that letters made words and words had meaning. At three years of age he had a little cloth book that he knew by heart and could turn the pages exactly when he reached the bottom. More than one person asked, "Can he read?" After he started school, he liked to sound out words on sign boards, utterly pleased to have learned the meaning of another word.

Herm found a new world for himself in school, but Fred was left home with his sister and felt completely lost. There seemed to be nothing for him to do.

I once read a Dutch book called *Children's Sorrows*. It pointed out with examples how minor incidents that seem to us of little importance can mean so much to a child. I recall that on a Christmas day Elaine received a new doll. She was so proud of it that she wanted to take it along to the Christmas program. As we were stepping into the car, she dropped it in the water that ran along the curb. There was no real damage done to her doll, but she felt bad nevertheless.

Once when I was reading the Bible, I came across the name of Levi. I stopped and asked the boys whether they knew who Levi was. Fred answered, "Sure, he is the Jew who sells calves to Mr. Kort." On another occasion the *Church News* had questions for children to answer. One of them was, "Do our churches believe in election?" Herm thought a while, but Fred answered, "Sure, Herm, Dad voted for Wilkie."[1]

It was also in Oak Lawn that Fred was hit by an automobile while crossing the street, but he was not seriously hurt. There Elaine, at the age of about two, had a kidney infection. The doctor exhausted all his means to cure her. Finally he called me into his office and said, "You're going to lose your girl." He knew of only one possible remedy. "Give her a pan of water to play with and encourage her to drink it." So we put a pan of water and a cup in Lans' crib,[2] and she played with water. She also drank plenty, so that it came out almost as fast as it went in. That was the means God used to restore her to health.

After a year or two the owner of that house wanted us out, so I scouted the streets. My daily walk consisted of looking for a house. In the whole town there was only one vacant house, and it had never been finished. It was built of cement blocks, still plainly visible. It had wooden steps in the front and the back. There was no basement, but there was an opening in the back of the house, a crawl space where the oil tank was kept. An oil burner heated the downstairs. The upstairs was unfinished, like an attic, and had no heat. Saturday night came around, and on Monday our time was up for the house we lived in. It was then that the banker came and offered the unfinished house to us, which we took reluctantly, only for want of something better.

The men of the congregation who owned trucks came to move us. Dick Kort had a load of living room furniture on his truck, and Herm and I sat in back, holding lamps and the like. We had warned Kort to go slowly over the railroad tracks, because some of the furniture might fall off. He took us very

---

1 Wendell Wilkie ran as a Republican against Franklin Delano Roosevelt in 1940.
2 The family gave Elaine the nickname Lans.

literally, for when we came to the tracks, the truck hardly moved. Since he was quite deaf, he did not realize that a train was rapidly approaching us at about seventy miles an hour. Herm and I did not know whether we should jump or stay put, but we stayed. The truck was barely over the tracks when the train whistled by. The engineer could only shake his head, and we breathed a prayer of thanksgiving.

The new house needed a lot of cleaning. The previous renters had kept chickens in the attic. The attic had to be cleaned up and made fit for a bedroom for the boys and for a study. A small section at the front of the attic was set off for a study. It had a small potbelly stove to furnish the heat.

Here we learned what pests mosquitoes can be in the summertime. Somehow the pesky critters came through the screens like a plague. One mosquito can pester all night long. So before we went to bed we would round them all up as much as possible on the front room ceiling for one grand slaughter.

Here we also learned about the trials involved in a bad septic tank. Sometimes the odor from that miserable thing was so terrible that one night my mother, who was staying with us, came dashing out of the bedroom with a cry, "No one can stand it in there."

Our Polish neighbor was far from friendly. His house stood not ten feet from ours, separated by a fence and a driveway. When we moved in he welcomed us by saying, "You live on that side of the fence, and I live on this side. We'll both mind our own business." When Walt, my wife's brother, came to Oak Lawn and inquired as to where we lived, he was accompanied by a policeman right up to the door to see whether he was welcome.

Soon an opportunity arose to move to a better house one block east. While the previous house was referred to as the block house, the next house was referred to as the shingle house. It had central heating and many other advantages. The attic was somewhat better than the one in the previous house, and the boys slept in it.

The kids had a lot of room to play at the shingle house. There was a large field next to the house and thick woods behind. The neighbor kids were not the best of companions, but the boys did get along with them. Here at Easter time Elaine was given two newborn ducks, which she fed and cared for. Gradually the ducks grew and wandered around the yard. Before long they were out on the road, so Elaine took them by their necks and led them back home. When they wandered too far, we brought them to a farm, where one was accidentally killed. We ate the other for Thanksgiving dinner.

We lived there when Alice (we called her Allie) was born. Almost from the first day of that fourth pregnancy, my wife was not well. Her heart gave her problems, but there were also other complications. The doctor warned us that the baby would not be born in his office, as was generally the case. For that birth we had to go to the hospital.

When the time came for the birth, we went to the hospital. I was called into the delivery room shortly after Allie was born because my wife had gone into shock. The head nurse attended her without leaving the room from around two o'clock in the morning until about eight in the morning. Since it was a Roman Catholic hospital, the nurse never ceased praying even as she went about her duties. It appeared for some time as if we would lose Jennie, but the Lord spared her for us.

Jennie seemed to be recovering gradually, but on the ninth day she had another attack. At the time we thought it was a heart attack, and it might have been related. Later it was diagnosed as an epileptic seizure.

Complete recovery was slow. Lucy Woudenberg, my sister, came out to help us for a while. The shingle house was in the hands of a real estate agent, who wanted to put us out already before Allie was born but realized that that was impossible. But as soon as my wife was able to get around, he pressured us to find another house.

That led us to a house out on the prairie, right in the center of a section of land that had almost no houses. The owners, the Draismas, had built a house next door and were renting their former house. After some consideration we decided to move out there.

In the prairie house, Allie liked to scoot through the house on a small cart. The basement door did not close readily. It always needed an extra push. One time the door was left slightly ajar, and Allie managed to open it. The next thing, the cart and Allie rolled down the steps and against the basement wall. Thankfully, no serious damage was done.

Here she also learned to walk. She was about two or three years old when on a summer day she was outside and could not be found. All who were home joined in the hunt. Even Mrs. Draisma joined with us in scouting the neighborhood. When she finally went into her house, she found Allie on the kitchen table licking her fingers after sticking them into the sugar bowl.

The Veldman family came by streetcar to church on Sunday. Sometimes they would stop in to visit. The older kids were afraid of Mrs. Veldman, but Allie would go up to her and ask, "Play Old Maid with me, Mrs. Veldman?" She willingly played cards with Allie.

While I was filling a classical appointment in Randolph, a bad storm struck Oak Lawn. Severe lightning split a tree not far from our home on the prairie. Rain came down in torrents and poured in through the doors and windows of the house.

In the winter we could skate all around in the ditches. In the spring, water seeped into the basement of the house, so that I had to care for the furnace by riding in the kids' cart to the furnace through a foot of water.

While we lived on the prairie, it happened that a load of pigs and steers tipped over on 103rd Street, sending the pigs and steers all over the open field. Cowboys came from the slaughter-house to catch them. They had three steers locked in our garage, but the steers forced the doors and burst out. It took all night to round up the wandering steers and pigs.

Here we had all the "modern conveniences" of a farm in the country. A short distance south of the house stood a neat, clean outhouse, out of which the neighbor girl's doll once had to be fetched. In the basement we had a coal stove for heating water for the wash. The water was so hard that it had to be broken with lye before it was fit for washing clothes. On Saturday nights the wash tub came out for the family's baths.

In the springtime the road to Ninety-fifth Street was so muddy that more than one car had to be lifted out of the mud and boards pushed under them to get the cars underway. Even Grandpa Griffioen's big LaSalle settled comfortably in the mud. Sometimes we had to leave our car on the road and walk the last distance to the house.

Mr. Rooda gave us a runt pig. We scoured the neighborhood for planks and two-by-fours to build a pen. The pig grew very well on the refuse from our house and the neighbor's. Mr. Ryan Regnerus butchered the pig for us, and the hams were smoked in Chicago Heights.

The boys found work in the summer for a farmer about a half mile away. Although weeding and hoeing was tedious work, they made a bit of money. Later they worked for a farmer much far-ther away, to whose home they rode their bikes. Today they still look back to the work at the last place as a bit of slavery. They worked sixty hours a week and made ten cents an hour.

It was in Oak Lawn that Lans started kindergarten. The first day she came home with a different attitude from Herm's. When asked about school, her only remark was, "It's alright, but only eight years of that." At first the children all took the Oak Lawn school bus to school. But after a couple of years, the boys walked the one and a half miles to school. Herm was put off the bus for rowdiness, and the bus driver would not let him back on unless the driver talked with me. I thought it better to let Herm walk to learn his lesson. The walks went well, and we saved twenty cents a week on bus costs. A committee from the school board came to plead with us to let the boys ride again because they needed the money. But so did we, and the children continued to walk to school. From my study window I could see them cross the highway to the east. At that time we had no concern for their safety. It often took them a half hour to roam through the open field for a half mile, but we did not mind that.

One day while walking home Fred had his eyes closed while Herm was giving him directions where to go. Mistaking the directions, Fred landed in the ditch that was partially filled with water.

On another occasion the weather turned very cold. At that time Elaine was still riding the bus, so my wife went the half mile down the road to meet her. When she came to her, Lans was calmly sliding on the ice. I went to meet the boys and help them home. They were walking with their backs to the wind. When they saw me they could not possibly figure out why I was there, but I did shield them from the wind through the open field.

Later Evergreen Park School no longer had room for the children from Oak Lawn, so the bus had to take them to Roseland. Some of the children got on the bus at seven in the morning and did not get home until five at night. Our children were some of the last ones to get on. But it was a long, dangerous ride in a packed bus. When the train was approaching in Roseland, the driver still ventured to get through ahead of the train by speeding up the bus, almost bringing the gates down on the bus.

We got along well with our neighbors, the Draisma family. We even had a telephone together, so that when there was a call for them we buzzed, and one or the other came over. Although they were Christian Reformed, they allowed their son John, who was Elaine's age, to come along with us for catechism.

After a few years the Draisma family decided to rent the house they lived in and to return to their former home. That meant that we had to go house hunting again. Then the consistory decided to bring an end to our wanderings by purchasing a house in town.

After some searching, a house was found at a reasonable cost. The house had four large rooms (two with bay windows) downstairs and four rooms upstairs (two with bay windows), with a large tower that extended one story higher. The house also had a fairly large basement with an automatic coal stoker.

The consistory decided to buy the house for six thousand dollars from the elderly woman who lived alone there. Six hundred dollars had to be brought as a down payment, so the consistory went out one day to collect from the members of the congregation. That evening the men came to the parsonage and spread out on the dining room table nickels, dimes, quarters, half dollars, and also paper money. Obviously the cash had come from money saved for doctor bills or from children's banks. It was enough to make a person weep to see how generously out of their poverty the congregation brought up the needed six hundred dollars for the new parsonage.

Our problems were not yet over. When the time came to move, the old lady did not want to get out of her house. We were being pressured by the owners of the house we were living in, and they were being pressured by those who waited to move into their house, all down the line. One day we came home to discover that our neighbors had been forced out and had come to move in with us. That was a bit too much, so we called the men of the congregation to haul out our furniture. It was brought to the church, except for two beds and a kitchen table and chairs, which were brought to a real estate office next to Rutgers' home. The office had previously been a chicken coop and still was not much better, but it did give us a roof over our heads.

Not only were we having trouble finding a settled home, we

were also having trouble finding reliable transportation. On our way back to Oak Lawn in 1938 we were struck by a car near Hudsonville, Michigan. We had a car full, since Aunt Corie and her two children rode back with us. The other car was approaching us in our lane, so I tried desperately to get far enough off the road to avoid it. Just as I thought we had safely passed the car, the driver struck the back part of the Chevy, swung it around, and turned it on its side. No one was seriously hurt, but we were all well shaken up. The police encouraged us to find ways and means to continue on our way home, so we obtained a car from Grandpa Griffioen. We later returned to Michigan, where we bought a Ford V8.

On the way home already it became evident that the Ford had been in an accident, as the front wheel was out of line. That was a minor thing compared to the problem of the water pump howling for lack of oil. The starter failed to work most of the time. No mechanic seemed to be able to find the cause of the trouble. No replacement parts solved the problem. Often we were compelled to push the car onto the road and wait for someone to give the car a push to get it started. Later Pete Reitsma, our brother-in-law, solved this problem with a five-cent washer.

An even more serious problem was the radiator, which often steamed and spouted water like a small geyser. This could happen any time. We might go halfway to Grand Rapids without trouble, and then suddenly the water would spurt out over the car. On a trip to Iowa we had so much trouble that we had to stop in a garage to have the gaskets replaced. We had no trouble until we started back on our way home. On a trip to Waupun, brother-in-law Clyde thought he had fixed the radiator. He had replaced the cap, so that the water no longer spouted out. When we came to Milwaukee on our way home, the engine was so hot that even after a long delay I still cracked both engine heads when I added water.

That in a sense was a low spot in our lives. While we made

our home in a chicken coop, the Ford V8, which gave plenty of trouble as long as we had it, finally gave out completely. John Buiter chopped the broken heads off the engine of the car, brought the radiator away to be boiled out in acid, and did everything possible to make the car serviceable again. We had no car, we had no real home, yet we did have the family complete and well, so we still had reason to give thanks.

A few weeks went by, and the chilly weather of October was crowding in on us. I decided to bring the family to Michigan to live, and I would come to Oak Lawn on the weekends. When I told the real estate man of our plans, he strongly objected. He suggested that I wait until five o'clock. In the meantime, he must have gotten busy. By five in the afternoon he had the papers for the house and had the consent of the old lady to get out. In two days we were busy cleaning the house and preparing to move in.

The house with the tower, as it looked in the 1990s,
the last of many parsonages for the Hanko family in Oak Lawn.

The house with a tower had a special appeal to the kids. When Christmas approached, each one secretly planned to hide his or her presents, purchased for others with a few dimes, in the tower room.

The house had a beautiful hawthorn tree, which attracted many sightseers in the spring. Its huge branches spread horizontally so that the kids could play in it. In the backyard was a cherry tree, which attracted the small wrens that sang their hearts out in the morning. The house also had a chicken coop, in which Mr. Rooda placed seven chickens that were actually the culls from his flock. Only one of them laid an egg a day, but the others made good eating.

But the Lord sent more trials our way. In the spring, just before Easter Sunday, Lans came home with scarlet fever. The accompanying rash was so light that no one noticed. The result, however, was that Allie, Fred, and I all came down with it on Easter Sunday. I did manage to preach but was ready to go to bed soon afterward. Doctor Gasteyer came to check on Allie and immediately asked about the other sick ones in the family. We were quarantined, so Herm had to get out of the house to stay with the Ryan Regnerus family until we were released from quarantine.[3] Many neighbors refused to walk past our house and objected to my wife's coming into the stores. Rev. Ophoff came all the way from Grand Rapids to see us.

Since I had to take time off for recovery, as soon as I was able, I began to paint the house. That was a big undertaking, but I managed to do all of it, except for the tower, for which I needed help. Later I managed to paint the church, which sorely needed a fresh coat of paint.

In the summer my wife had health problems that brought her to the university hospital in Chicago. There she underwent a series of tests and X-rays. Since the Depression was still a problem even for hospitals, we had to pay at every step along the way. Because of my low salary we were paying far less than people with money. The outcome of the tests was that my wife had to

---

3   In those days before the discovery of antibiotics, people with scarlet fever were quarantined.

undergo surgery. At the time I was placed in the waiting room and told that I would be called when the surgery was completed. I went there at eight in the morning, and by two in the afternoon I had heard nothing. Becoming deeply concerned, I looked around for someone to give me a bit of information. I was met by a nurse who was surprised that no one had contacted me, since my wife had been brought down already at eleven-thirty.

It was a long stay in the hospital, for her leg infection demanded a private room, a special nurse around the clock, and doses of penicillin every eight hours. This was a newly discovered drug, very expensive, and had to come from New York. For six weeks my wife was in the hospital, at least four weeks longer than expected. But the head nurse told me at the outset that if I had any financial problem, I should come and see her. When I met her in the hall, I told her that I was coming to see her. She responded, "I should think you would." The outcome was that sixty dollars came in the mail without any name attached, the deacons brought up one hundred fifty dollars, and the hospital settled for three hundred dollars. The Lord certainly provides in time of need. He has never allowed his children to go hungry.

During those weeks Elaine decided to become a sort of convert at the neighborhood mission church. Every morning she would disappear for about an hour. She never wanted to say where she had been. Finally the big night came when the group was giving a public program. Elaine wanted to get dressed up, but my sister Corie, who was staying with us, saw no good reason for that. So in her shabby clothes Elaine again disappeared. She returned with a shepherd she had made with a clothespin and a few other items.

The time had come for Herm's graduation from the elementary school. He needed white pants, but we could not afford to buy any, so we borrowed a pair. To this day I am still a bit ashamed because the pant legs had to be folded up so high that they showed the high cuff even when he wore the pants. But Herm did not seem to mind.

We were nicely settled in the parsonage owned by the church and needed no longer to fear the threat of moving; but in the fall of the year 1944, I received a call from Manhattan, Montana. I had received numerous calls while in Oak Lawn but actually never dared to leave. Every time I had a call, Mr. ___ felt in his heart that I should accept it. Rather than letting him try to run the congregation, I stayed until he left. After he and his family left, I felt free to accept a call to another congregation.

Chapter 18

A TIME
OF GROWTH

In this chapter Rev. Hanko relates some of the history of other Protestant Reformed churches. His original desire had been to be a missionary, so the work he did in organizing some of those churches was especially dear to his heart.

I had some experience in mission work in the Protestant Reformed Churches. I also discovered how difficult and discouraging this work can be, even when working among Reformed people. I was present in Orange City, Iowa, when Rev. Hoeksema spoke a series of lectures, which on the last night drew about five hundred people. At that meeting an announcement was made that an organizational meeting would be held the following night at the home of Mr. and Mrs. Katje. Seven families, mostly elderly couples, were present for organization.

Nevertheless, the period from 1930 to 1939 was one of growth for the denomination. In 1932 Creston was organized on Leonard Street in Grand Rapids. That same year Rev. Hoeksema made a trip to Redlands, California, to organize a congregation there. Another congregation was organized in Los Angeles, which later became Bellflower Protestant Reformed Church. In 1936 a congregation in Grand Haven, Michigan, was organized. In 1937 a congregation in Edgerton, Minnesota, came into existence through the labors of the first denominational missionary,

Rev. Bernard Kok. He labored there and was told that when he had twenty families a congregation could be organized. He had nineteen families, and the mission committee deemed that sufficient and proceeded to organize the congregation. In 1939 he also saw the fruits of his labors in the organization of a church in Manhattan, Montana.

Allow me to mention a bit of history in connection with the organization of a congregation in Redlands. A request had come to Rev. Hoeksema from a few families who were unhappy in the Christian Reformed Church. A lecture was planned, and there was a good turnout. But many who came were very suspicious that the man from the East was just another rabble-rouser who was seeking his own interests. They were present, as it were, with tongue in cheek. Rev. Hoeksema took for his point of approach Isaiah 50:4–5: "The Lord GOD hath given me the tongue of the learned, that I should know how to speak a word in season to him that is weary: he wakeneth morning by morning, he wakeneth my ear to hear as the learned. The Lord GOD hath opened mine ear, and I was not rebellious, neither turned away back."

Particularly one man in the audience thought, "There you have it. He is nothing but a proud self-seeker." Yet as Rev. Hoeksema continued, it became evident that he was expounding the word of God, as referring not to himself but to the promised Christ. That man and many others became extremely interested in forming a congregation, with the result that there is still a flourishing congregation in Redlands today.

In 1940 the Protestant Reformed Churches held their first synod meeting in First church in Grand Rapids. For some time the churches had met in one classis four times a year. Then the churches decided to divide into Classis East, consisting of all the churches east of the Mississippi River, and Classis West, consisting of all the churches west of the Mississippi, and to meet as a synod once a year. That same year the first young people's convention was held in Oak Lawn. Rev. Hoeksema was the main speaker; he continued to serve in that capacity for many years. The following year the Young Men's Society of First church, Grand Rapids, started a radio broadcast over radio station WFUR. Rev. Hoeksema was the radio minister, and even after synod started funding for the *Reformed Witness Hour*, he continued in that capacity for many years. His first radio message was entitled "God Is God." His messages were always thoroughly God-centered.

Synod 1940 held in First Protestant Reformed Church. Seated left to right: Rev. G. M. Ophoff, Rev. M. Gritters, Rev. G. Vos, Rev. P. De Boer, Rev. H. Hoeksema; second row: P. Dykema, N. Yonker, T. Kooima, M. Vander Vennen, J. Cammenga, Rev. L. Vermeer, Rev. W. Verhil, F. LaGrange; third row: J. Brock, Rev. A. Cammenga, M. Flikkema, Rev. C. Hanko, C. Doezema, Rev. J. De Jong, Rev. B. Kok, C. Vander Molen

In the early 1940s efforts were made to organize a congregation in Randolph, Wisconsin. There was one subscriber to the *Standard Bearer* in Randolph. The mission committee asked me to go to Randolph and investigate whether there was any prospect of doing work in the area. That original contact, I think, was

Auke Douma. Upon being contacted he said that he enjoyed the *Standard Bearer*, was very interested in a Protestant Reformed church being established, would do all he could to help, but would never himself join. He attended all of the services, but he never did join. The reasons were that his wife was an invalid who depended on him for transport, and she was opposed to us.

I was instructed by the mission committee not to start services until I had ten or more people. Auke gave me a list of names, and I set about visiting people. I finally managed to get ten people who promised to come.

I looked for a place to worship but was frankly told by everyone in Randolph that there were enough churches and that they did not want any more. I finally went to Vriesland, where I talked with the mayor. The mayor told me the same thing I had heard in Randolph. I said to the mayor, "If I asked for a meeting place to hold a dance, you would find me a place. But when I ask for a place to preach, you refuse." The mayor responded, "That is correct."

I finally found a place. It was a pavilion in the park in Randolph. I held services there and many, many people came. Auke Douma came too, but he said to me, "There is nothing here with which to start a congregation." I asked why, and he said, "They are all people from the Reformed church in town, a church that is vacant, and they are only here out of curiosity. They will never join the Protestant Reformed Churches." And so it turned out.

The fourth Sunday of services, Dewey Alsum came. Auke said to me, "Now you have someone. Go and visit him." So I went to visit him, and Dewey helped me from that time on with names, contacts, and suggestions.

Soon we were able to rent the Congregational church in town, which desperately needed the money and would sometimes ask for an advance payment because of a shortage of cash. On a visit to the Congregational minister with Rev. Hoeksema, we learned that only six or seven people were attending services, although more were supporters. Rev. Hoeksema said to that minister, "Do you know what we do with supporters? We cut them off." "Yes," said the minister, "I heard that you are very strict. But if I would do that, I would not have a congregation left."

The mission committee asked Rev. Hoeksema to preach, lecture, and make contacts in Randolph for three weeks. Since I was in Oak Lawn at the time and had done some work in Randolph, the mission committee suggested that I accompany him.

On a Monday afternoon we started out together for Wisconsin. The trip was very enjoyable, especially because much of the time was spent in animated conversation. I recall that we talked particularly about prayer as intimate covenantal fellowship with God. We agreed that the few words of the Lord's prayer, "Thy will be done," actually express all our needs. If we can pray that in all sincerity, we are assured of perfect peace, come what may. Yet we both felt that that was not enough. After a bit of a pause one of us remarked, "Yet we can and must make all our needs known in prayer and supplication with thanksgiving." Thus the afternoon quickly passed and we arrived in Waupun, Wisconsin.

That night we stayed in a hotel in Waupun. When I bid Rev. Hoeksema good night to go to my room, he said, "But aren't we going to have devotions together?" From then on, whenever possible, we had evening devotions together. Later, to save money we stayed with my wife's relatives in Waupun, who were more than eager to have us lodge with them, and they enjoyed Rev. Hoeksema's company, banter, and hearty guffaws.

Rev. Hoeksema preached on Sundays and gave lectures during the week. The rest of the time we made contacts with many people who showed interest. Many times we were invited to some home for noon dinner or for supper.

A couple who regularly attended our meetings and services and later became members of the congregation invited us for supper. I had always regarded them as elderly and therefore referred to them as "the old Westras." I told Rev. Hoeksema that "the old

Westras" had invited us for supper on a certain evening. While we sat at the table Rev. Hoeksema asked Mr. Westra, "How old are you?" to which he received the answer, "Fifty-seven years." Then turning to Mrs. Westra he said, "And how old are you?" Again the response was, "Fifty-seven years." Rev. Hoeksema was about that same age. He gave me a look with a scowl and afterward said, "I suppose you go around referring to me as 'the old Hoeksema.'"

Each Saturday afternoon Rev. Hoeksema brought me to the train so I could travel to and preach in Oak Lawn on Sunday. As I was ready to step into the train I received the admonition, "You be sure to be back Monday morning. I'll be here waiting for you."

We also had an invitation for noon dinner from one of the farmers. When the time arrived, we drove into the farmyard but noticed that all the curtains were removed from the windows. The house looked like the people were moving out. When we came to the door, we saw the man's wife sitting in the middle of the floor busily packing pots and pans in a box. Rev. Hoeksema remarked, "I thought we were to come here for dinner." The woman responded, "Our minister is just as good as you are." He countered, "I doubt that." But it was useless to waste any more words there, so we quietly withdrew. As we were about to drive off the man came sheepishly out of the barn to tell us that his wife did not want us to come. Rev. Hoeksema responded, "We noticed that." We ate lunch in a restaurant.

The three weeks sped rapidly by and it was time to return to our respective churches. On the return trip, the closer we came to Oak Lawn, the less Rev. Hoeksema spoke. It was obvious that as we were coming closer to home all the work that awaited him in Grand Rapids began to weigh heavily upon his shoulders. When we reached my home, my wife invited him to come in for a cup of coffee, but he refused. Almost without another word he started his car and drove off. My wife said, "How could you spend three weeks with a man as sober as that?" I tried to impress on her that our experiences together were quite different.

By the time I left Oak Lawn in 1945 the Protestant Reformed denomination had grown from three churches to twenty-three. I had always desired to get to know as many of the churches as possible in my ministry, and I took the call to Manhattan, Montana. I preached my farewell sermon in Oak Lawn on January 1, 1945, on Revelation 22:21: "The grace of our Lord Jesus Christ be with you all. Amen." On January 4 our family headed west to Manhattan.

Chapter 19

MANHATTAN, MONTANA

The Hanko family spent three years in Manhattan, from January 1945 to May 1948. Rev. Hanko often spoke of those years as the happiest of his ministry. Looking back on them, he could see how the Lord used that time of peace and plenty to prepare him and his family for the troublesome time of the schism of 1953 in the Protestant Reformed Churches.

Starting out into the unknown was quite a venture. We had heard about Montana, but we had never been anywhere near there. When I accepted the call to Manhattan, the people in the Oak Lawn congregation felt I should not go on the road with the infamous Ford V8, which for years had given us nothing but grief. But that time was still during World War II, and cars were scarce and beyond my financial means. Mrs. Boonsma of South Holland, the mother of Menno Smits, offered her son's car at whatever amount I could pay. We sold the Ford for three hundred dollars and obtained from her a Mercury for six hundred dollars. We had to obtain gas stamps from the government for the trip.[1]

In January 1945 all our household goods were crated and packed in a boxcar to be shipped to Manhattan. We ventured out

---

1   The government was strictly rationing the use of gas due to World War II.

on a bitterly cold day, so cold that all the windows were frosted except for only a small opening in the windshield to see ahead. In fact, when we reached the bridge at the Mississippi River, we passed it and had to turn back.

The Hanko family on the way to Manhattan

We stayed in Hull with the Andrew Cammenga family over Sunday. Monday morning dawned with a raging blizzard. It looked as if we could not get away, but by noon the wind subsided, the sky cleared, and we decided to go on our way. That evening we arrived in Chamberlain, South Dakota. There was some snow blowing over the road, but none that interfered with travel. The motel manager was surprised to see us and warned us that the road west was so completely closed that we could not get away for days and possibly weeks.

The next morning the sun was shining, and we decided to continue on our way. All along the way water poured alongside the road. The sudden thaw had opened the roads in a short time. We were beyond Rapid City, South Dakota, toward sunset, and since the weather was favorable, we decided to go on to Miles City, Montana. That stretch of road was lonelier than we realized. All the way we saw nothing but the white of newly fallen snow and a lone white owl sweeping in front of the car headlights. We were glad to reach Miles City around nine o'clock, and there we spent the night.

Here I will recount one incident in order to show how an ant-hill can become a mountain by gross exaggeration. As we were coming out of the restaurant in some western town, Herm, as kids will do, pushed Fred off the sidewalk. Fred got his foot wet and Herm got a scolding. As the incident was told and retold, it grew and grew, until finally Herm had pushed Fred into the river. Let us heed the warning not to exaggerate!

The next day we started up over a pass, which proved to be slippery because of the snow that had fallen during the night. As we approached a curve in the road, a car came toward us on our side of the road. Obviously the driver could not get his car on the right side, so we had no choice but to drive off the road into a snow bank, with all four wheels off the ground, not far from the edge of a cliff. As I debated what to do, a truck came around the curve. The driver saw our problem, stopped, hooked the car to the back end of his truck, and pulled the car back onto the road. Since no damage was done, we could proceed thankfully on our way.

That evening we followed the consistory-drawn map that showed the route from Belgrade to Churchill and arrived at Henry Van Dyken's home at suppertime. There we had our first taste of venison. For a few days we stayed with Sam Van Dyken and his wife. Since it would take a few weeks for our furniture to arrive, enough furniture was brought into the parsonage that we could stay there. Rev. Martin Gritters came to install me. He preached on Ezekiel 9:11: "And, behold, the man clothed with linen, which had the inkhorn by his side, reported the matter, saying, I have done as thou has commanded me."

When our furniture finally arrived by train, we had to keep the doors of the parsonage open to unload the furniture. Our canary, which had survived the trip west, died from exposure to a draft.

The church building in Churchill

The parsonage in Churchill

Churchill was the loneliest, loveliest spot in America. There were no paved streets, no sidewalks, no streetlights or shops, but only a few houses, two churches, a Christian school, and a cemetery. It was the center of a Dutch community consisting to a great extent of members of the two churches. Although it was often referred to as Manhattan, the town of Manhattan was ten miles away. It was so quiet at night that we sometimes awoke with a start. Imagine coming from the outskirts of Chicago, where the trains whistled past at seventy miles per hour, where traffic could be heard all night long, and where planes flew toward the airport. In Churchill we were living in a quiet valley where the mooing of a cow attracted attention. For anyone coming from the hustle and bustle of a big city, it was quite an adjustment to live in a community where everyone moved at a leisurely pace. We soon learned that the necessity of the slow pace was the high altitude, almost a mile above sea level.

A quick trip to the grocery store in Amsterdam, a nearby town, meant a discussion with the clerk about the weather or some recent happening in the valley. I came to Harry Leep one day when he was harvesting. I asked him, "Busy, Harry?" He replied, "Busy, man! I can't keep two feet on the ground. Let's have a cup of coffee." When we left Montana, we hoped to continue in that slow, steady stride, but we failed.

The Gallatin Valley, in which Churchill is located, is one of the most scenic places in America. The Bridger Mountain Range is to the east, the Spanish Peaks to the south, and the Tobacco Root Mountains to the west. Even the north had mountains. The valley was known as "the Dutch settlement." Wednesday was shopping day in Bozeman for the Dutch in the settlement. Other communities also had their shopping days. If you wanted to meet someone from the valley in Bozeman, you stood at the five and dime store, and soon you would be drinking a cup of coffee with someone in the store.

As long as we were in Montana we never wearied of the beautiful mountains and the dazzling sunsets. Even the sunrises were interesting because we had to look to the western peaks to see that the sun had risen. All day long the appearance of the mountains changed, since the sun cast various shadows on the mountainsides. The views from the study window and the kitchen window were most inspiring.

In the winter when the entire area was covered with white snow, it appeared as if a trip to the highest peak was only a half hour's walk away. But one had better not try it. At night the big sky was arrayed with millions of stars, like Abraham's seed, the church. The largest stars seemed just beyond our reach.

The setting sun was the most spectacular sight of all. Often the whole sky would be a brilliant display of pink and lavender as the shadows gradually climbed the Bridger and night began to fall. We were often amazed at the dazzling splendor of the setting sun and could only cry out, "My God, how great and glorious thou art!" Is that not the experience of the believer as his life's day on earth draws to a close?

The winters were long in the high altitude. About the middle of September we received the first snowfall. The snow was wet and hung heavily on the trees, telling us that summer was past. Gradually the cold air from the north crept in. We experienced many clear, cold days. There were times in January and February when the temperature went down to thirty or forty degrees below zero. In that cold weather there was no wind. It was worse when the temperature was around zero and there was a strong wind. That could be dangerous, because the wind could cause the cold to penetrate one's lungs and cause lethargy or fatal sleepiness.

One night I drove to Bozeman to teach a young people's catechism class. When I stepped out of my car, the wind almost took my breath away. While I was teaching, the temperature dropped to slightly below zero. After the class the people warned me not to venture out to Churchill in that weather, but the family was at home and would soon wonder why I did not return. So I made the trip, but as it were on the wings of prayer.

There were actually two seasons in Montana—a long winter and a short summer. We shoveled snow yet in May. About the second week of June the air was different; summer had come. The days were warm, but the nights were chilly. In fact, a cloudy day was a chilly day. When the clouds hid the sun it was immediately chilly. What compensated for the cold weather were the many bright, clear days with plenty of sunshine.

Those years in Manhattan were possibly the best for my wife.

The house was not too large, the family not too demanding. Peace and quiet reigned in the congregation, and we were treated royally. Financially it seemed as if we had fallen into the lap of luxury, as all the members were doing well. It seems that my wife never felt better than during those years, even though she had to be careful for her heart in the high altitude. She enjoyed having folks stop in for a chat about news in the valley or some happening in the outside world. She also enjoyed various trips we made, taking in all the scenery and attractions of the far West. She made her weekly shopping trips to Bozeman, even stocking up on staple foods in case the winter storms would prevent us from getting out for a week or more. For me it was a period of relaxation before the task that still awaited me.

I was called to Manhattan on a salary of two thousand five hundred dollars and a cow. When I read the call letter, I thought the mention of a cow to be a bit humorous, but it did not take long before we all realized the value of having our own cow. True, we had to learn to milk her and to milk her twice a day, as much as possible at the same time each day. Fred, Elaine, and I learned and took our turns milking, although Fred milked her the most. Elsie, as our cow was called, liked Elaine the best, because the cow had been accustomed to having a small girl milk her. Fred and I would occasionally get a sweep of her wet tail in our faces, but Elaine was spared that experience. The advantage of having our own cow was that we had plenty of milk, all the butter we needed, plenty of buttermilk, and last but not least, a yearling calf for meat, which was stored in a locker in Amsterdam. As long as we stayed in Manhattan, we were always furnished with a cow.

We came to the valley at a very opportune time, a time when the people in the valley were experiencing a transition from the horse to machinery, from binding the wheat in sheaves to the self-propelled combine. Those were prosperous years; the price of wheat was high, and the farmers were taking advantage of it. There, for the first time in our married life, we could afford to buy a refrigerator. We bought it on credit, but some members of the congregation made the final payments.

I should mention the irrigation system. There were dams in the mountains holding back the snow water in the spring and summer. Throughout the valley there were numerous irrigation ditches that brought to the land the sorely needed water. Our garden and lawn, our pasture, and the church lawn were also on the irrigation system. At certain times the superintendent would come and ask whether we wanted water. Thereupon he would inform us that the water would be at our place at six-thirty in the morning. That did not mean a minute before or a minute after, so we had to be prepared. If the proper gullies were not made, the water would flood and drown the entire garden and yard. It took some time to prepare the proper gullies to steer the water first in one direction and then in another, so that everything would get plenty of water without being flooded.

I should also tell about the Chinook, a westerly wind that comes in the winter at any time of the day or night. We could go to bed with the temperature quite low and awaken in the morning to find that a great thaw was taking place. Often we saw the ditches flooded and water running over the road. We had to drive the car through the water, watching carefully for mailboxes on each side of the road and trying to stay on the gravel.

As a family we enjoyed reading a book about some scenic or interesting place in the mountains and then visiting the area. We visited Virginia City, a ghost town full of relics, where the miners had attempted to make their fortunes and where the vigilantes finally had to bring law and order. Some hair-raising tales are told about those places.

Allie started school in Manhattan. The school was just across the street, virtually next door. She soon learned that by raising her hand and wiggling in her seat she could escape a few minutes from the classroom. She did that so often that Fred wondered how it was possible that Allie could be looking into his room time and time again. The teacher called to ask whether she had a problem. From the first day of school Allie disliked it.

Elaine enjoyed the school because she found many friends there. She also had a lamb that had to be fed with a bottle at recess time, at noon, and at night. The boys teased her lamb by holding out their hands to it, but when it came for them, they spread their legs apart and the lamb dashed through in disgust. The lamb liked to chase Allie. Allie soon learned that if she ran up the front porch the lamb would follow but dared not come down. The creature stood there bleating until someone came to help it down.

The lamb also liked to go for my wife and catch her behind the knees to make them buckle. One Saturday evening I was taking a bath when it dawned on me that I had failed to loosen Elsie the cow so that she could go out to the pasture when she had had her fill of hay. I asked Jennie to go and do that little thing for me. When the bath was finished, I went to sit in the living room. It was a while before I realized that my wife had not returned from the cow barn. I looked for my jacket, but she had put that on. Then I looked for my boots. She had them on too. Finally I got to the cow barn to find her inside, patiently or impatiently waiting for someone to come. The lamb was outside the door, ready to buck the door shut every time she tried to open it. She was not exactly happy with the creature.

Before long the lamb knew how to break down the fence and run loose. One night it ran over to the Christian Reformed church where some meeting was to be held. As the people opened the doors of their cars, the lamb dived for them. The minister's son came over to ask if Elaine would please fetch her lamb away from the church. We decided that the time had come to bring the animal to Bozeman.

Young calves also liked to break loose. One day Fred had to chase a calf all over Churchill, from one yard to the next, from one pasture to the other. Those pastures had just been irrigated, which made running after a calf a sloppy task. Mind you, that calf even jumped over a cattle guard.

Each Saturday Elaine went to Bozeman with two girls for music lessons. One Saturday she complained of pain in her side. The result was that instead of taking her music lesson, she ended up in the hospital for an appendix operation.

Fred found his friends in Manhattan. The Van Dyken boys across the road liked adventure. They, along with Fred, made high stilts with which they liked to cross the nearby creek. In the winter he enjoyed snow skiing, which was such a common sport that some boys came to school on their skis behind a car. His closest friend was the son of the Christian Reformed minister. They were always experimenting with something or other.

The Christian school was not all that might have been desired. I could not quite figure out how the young people did so well with the education they received in the school. It seems that parents sent their children only as long as they could not be useful at home. Therefore, there were only two grades in the high school, the ninth and the tenth. The consistory had assured me before I accepted the call that there would soon be eleventh and twelfth grades in the high school. With that in mind I had accepted the call to Manhattan, since Herm was already in high school. I soon discovered that the addition of the eleventh and twelfth grades would not happen in the immediate future.

Herm spent a year with us in Manhattan, and then we faced the question, what next? We asked him what his plans for the future were. If he intended to become a doctor or lawyer, we would keep him home. If he intended to become a minister or teacher, we would send him to Michigan for Christian instruction. He said, "Don't you know that I intend to become a minister?" Although we had never talked about it, Fred piped up, "You thought I would be a minister, but that's not for me. I plan to be a school teacher."

So Herm went off to Michigan in the fall to stay with Uncle

Bern and Aunt Lucy Woudenberg and to attend Grand Rapids Christian High School. Their son Bernie and Herm traveled by bike together to school and to work. In the fall of the next year, Uncle Bern and Aunt Lucy preferred to be relieved of the responsibility of caring for a teenager, so Herm spent the next year with Uncle Pete and Aunt Nell Reitsma. Having to break up the family in that manner was one of the deciding factors in my future decision to leave Manhattan.

The community prospered even though the United States was still involved in World War II. Part of my work was to write regular letters to the five boys from the congregation who were in the service. My wife attended Red Cross meetings and helped pack clothes for relief of families and friends in the Netherlands.

On April 12, 1945, we heard that President Franklin Roosevelt had died. On May 8 we were up at seven in the morning to hear President Truman's message on VE (Victory in Europe) Day. On August 14, 1945, we heard word of Japan's unconditional surrender. The president declared a two-day holiday. The congregation held a special service of thanksgiving on August 15.

Chapter 20

FARMERS
AND FRIENDS

During the years of his ministry Rev. Hanko frequently preached from the book of Ephesians.[1] Perhaps some of those sermons were addressed also to the congregation in Manhattan, which was so very dear to him. When one reads Rev. Hanko's reflections on his time in Manhattan, one cannot help but think of Ephesians 4:16: "From whom the whole body fitly joined together and compacted by that which every joint supplieth, according to the effectual working in the measure of every part, maketh increase of the body unto the edifying of itself in love."

Our family spent three pleasant years in the Manhattan congregation. Almost the entire congregation did everything in its power to make life pleasant for us. Many stopped in to have a cup of coffee with us. Our holidays were all carefully planned so that we never sat home alone. We made trips in the mountains, to Yellowstone National Park and Glacier National Park, and in the meantime also had many visitors.

We had 100 percent attendance in the services and in the catechism classes, and practically 100 percent attendance in all the societies. If one did not attend, he or she heard about it. Everyone, even the young people, was very cooperative. The church was the

---

1 See appendix three for Rev. Hanko's handwritten sermon on Ephesians 3:8–11.

center of activity for them. The young folks liked nothing better than to come to the church and give a program. Those who could sing made up a quartet or trio. One who could play the piano played a piece. Someone else gave a speech on an assigned subject. That went smoothly; no one refused to participate. Then we all ate lunch before going home. A visitor would have thought that the program had been arranged in advance. I challenge any minister to try that in his congregation. The right community is needed for something like that.

We had many visitors stay with us, one of whom was Ed Stouwie from Chicago. He stayed for a lengthy time in Manhattan, and most of that time he lived with us. On one particular Sunday evening he attended our young people's society to discuss the three points of common grace. He was a member of the Christian Reformed Church at that time, but he and his father were sympathetic to the Protestant Reformed Churches.

In the summers both Herm and Fred got a good taste of farming in the West. Herm worked for at least two farmers, the one still quite old fashioned, the other had adopted the new machinery.

When Herm was home with the family during the summer, he worked for Menko Flikkema. Herm once got a baling hook so deeply in his thigh that he had to go to the doctor, who plugged the hole up with seemingly endless strips of cloth to prevent infection. Herm also worked for Dave Schipper, who had a barn full of cats.

Fred had his first working experience with a local who lived in Churchill. Later he worked for Pete Flikkema. During the harvest time Fred was the tractor man, fully responsible for the tractor during that season.

A few summers I also helped Pete Flikkema with the harvesting. I prepared the necessary sermons in advance, and when harvest time came, I spent the week from Monday morning to Saturday evening with the harvesters. We always had a very pleasant time because all the workers were from the church. Menko and Pete Flikkema harvested together. They had three combines and two trucks, with Gerrit Flikkema in charge of the entire crew.

One person who could hardly be forgotten was Henry Ungersma. He was a close neighbor who lived on Church Hill. He might well be referred to as a gentleman farmer. He was a dry land farmer, which means that he had his farm in the hills where irrigation was impossible. As a result he left half the land fallow each year to give the soil time to collect moisture from the rains. He worked the land only twelve weeks of the year. He was in the real sense an outdoor man who enjoyed nothing more than hunting and fishing. Since he lived close by, he often stopped in to take me on one of his activities, either to fish, to practice shooting, to sow grain by airplane in the hills, or just to enjoy the scenery. From a distance he could spot a stag, an elk, an antelope, a moose, or a mountain goat. While I sat looking without seeing anything, he pointed out to me the animals, nicely protected in their natural habitat. When we went fishing, my fishing line and bait dangled in the water while he drew out one fish after another.

It would hardly do not to mention that there was also in Manhattan a man who tried to make life a bit unpleasant in the congregation. As I have mentioned before, Rev. Danhof had warned us as students that in each congregation we could expect at least one troublemaker. There was such a character in Hull, there was also one in Oak Lawn, and that man fit the bill in Manhattan.

Before I was to visit that man for family visitation the first time, the elder asked me whether I had ever become furiously angry on a call. I assured him that I never had experienced that on a pastoral call. He responded, "This time it will happen. It has always happened in the past." Thinking I was well prepared for the worst, we entered the home and proceeded with the visit. It was not long and I lost my temper as a result of that man's constant needling. Afterward the elder said, "I told you so." From that time on, I learned to ignore the man whenever he tried to rouse my temper.

Whenever I preached a sermon on Christian instruction, he would stay away from church for a while because he felt the school was required to bring a bus to his house to fetch his children. When I went to Bozeman to have catechism with the young people there, he refused to send his children, since I could also come to his house. When the entire congregation came to celebrate communion in the morning, he refused to come but came as a lone partaker in the afternoon. We soon discovered that the best way to treat his antics was to ignore them. If he stayed away from church for a while, the consistory did not bother to visit him. Soon he was back in church, and I received a few chickens as a peace offering.

One more character should not be forgotten. Herm worked for him a while in his machine shop, where he made wagon boxes. He had married a woman who was a member of the Black Stockings, a branch of the Mennonites. The Mennonites believed in apostolic succession through a series of bishops from the time of the apostles until today. These Mennonites believed that they received a special gift of the Holy Spirit and could speak in languages they had never learned. They also thought that their children could be baptized only when both parents were members of the Black Stockings.

At the time of their marriage the husband was unconverted, so it made no difference to him that his wife belonged to that sect. Later he was converted under the preaching of Rev. Kok and joined our congregation at the time of its organization. When their first baby was born, the problem of baptism came up. This man insisted on baptizing the baby, while his wife insisted that he should join her group and baptize the baby with her. He had to take the baby from her forcibly for baptism.

When I came to Manhattan, they had had their second baby. No one dared to mention the subject of baptism. I talked with him, and he suggested that I talk with his wife. I did, but it proved to be a one-sided conversation. She did not say a word, but when

175

I insisted that the baby had to be baptized, that she could not do it, and that therefore she should leave the baptism of the child to her husband, she left the room and went into their bedroom. Then the issue became one of endurance. Who would hold out the longest? After some time she came to look around the corner of the door to see whether I had left. I took that opportunity to tell her that on the next Sunday the baby would be baptized and she should not interfere, for that would bring trouble.

There was quite the suspense that next Sunday. Would he come? Would he come without a struggle? What a relief to see him come into the church with the baby nicely dressed. It was much more of a relief to hear that his wife had offered no resistance. What is interesting to note is that my wife became quite friendly with her as Jennie took sewing lessons from her. That did much to clear the atmosphere and give the woman a better impression of our churches.

I must tell of a little incident that happened in our home. In that part of the country it was customary that a salesman who happened to stop in around noon would be invited for dinner. One noon we invited a salesman to eat with us. My wife had placed a pan of buttermilk broth (*soepen brei*) on the table for dessert. The salesman took some potatoes and, thinking the buttermilk pap was gravy, poured a good dose of it on his spuds. My wife told him that the broth was dessert and that she would get him another plate, but he assured her that he liked his potatoes that way. The kids kept stealing glances at him and barely held back a snicker or two as the salesman ate the sour pap and potatoes.

In 1947 Professor Schilder made a second visit to America.[2]

---

2 Professor Klaas Schilder was a member of the *Gereformeerde Kerken* in the Netherlands. He opposed Abraham Kuyper's view of the covenant and was deposed in 1944 by the Synod of Sneek-Utrecht while in hiding from the Nazis. He had been in a concentration camp because he was one of the few who dared publicly to criticize Hitler and the Nazis. The synod deposed him without ever giving him a hearing. He then established the liberated churches, called *De Gereformeerde Kerken onderhouding Artikel 31* (The

During his first trip to the United States in 1939, he had stayed with our family for a little while in Oak Lawn. In the fall of 1947 he stayed with us for a whole week. Almost from the time he arrived we discussed and disagreed on the covenant and the baptism of infants. Later Mr. and Mrs. Van Spronsen spent a month with us.[3] She was much more ready to adjust to our way of living than he was. Again the different views of the covenant were discussed.

Rev. and Mrs. Hoeksema along with their children, Lois, Homer, and Gertrude visited us for a few days. A group from the church decided to take them and us to Yellowstone National Park. They took along roasted chicken, a carton of boiled eggs, and many other delicacies. Lois, Homer, and Gertrude wanted to see snow. Little did they realize that farther into the park they would see more snow than they cared to see. When they saw the first small heap of muddy snow, they had a snowball fight and got themselves pretty dirty.

Visit to Yellowstone National Park; left to right: Rev. Hoeksema, Homer Hoeksema, Elaine Hanko, Fred Hanko, Jennie Hanko, Gertrude Jonker, Lois Hoeksema

Reformed churches maintaining article 31). He led the liberated churches until his death in 1952. These churches were and are sister churches of the Canadian Reformed and American Reformed churches. Schilder gave us endless grief by introducing into our churches the idea of a conditional covenant, which was the major factor in the schism of 1953.

3   Mr. and Mrs. Van Spronsen were a couple from the Netherlands and members of the liberated Reformed churches who toured various Protestant Reformed churches in the late 1940s.

We had gone through the entire park without seeing a single bear, even though at that time the bears lumbered along the roadside, looking for handouts. People did feed the bears in spite of the many signs along the way that read "Do not feed the bears." Just as we were to leave the park we saw a bear. Rev. Hoeksema stopped his car and fed the bear a cookie. It so happened that a ranger saw him, came to his car, and reprimanded him. The incident might have passed unnoticed, except that the previous Sunday Rev. Hoeksema had preached in our congregation about keeping God's law and how readily we transgress it. He had used the example of the farm laborers in the Netherlands, who stood along the wall in the church under the sign that read "Do not spit tobacco juice on the floor." Reverend remarked that they stood under the sign and still spat on the floor. When we stopped for lunch no one said anything about the experience with the bear until suddenly one of the men spoke up, "Yes, under the sign and spitting on the floor." Even Rev. Hoeksema, though a bit embarrassed, joined in the laughter.

In 1947 Rev. Hoeksema was on his way to Montana to preach for me when he had a stroke in Sioux Falls, South Dakota. When he began to recover, his right side was lame and his speech was slurred. To all appearances his preaching and teaching had come to a sudden stop. Yet the Lord gave a slow but remarkable recovery, so that he could be active in the churches yet for a number of years. Some of the resonance of his voice was lost, but his voice was almost as powerful as before. He walked with a cane and had limited use of his right arm and hand.

Elaine finished the eighth grade in Manhattan Christian School and received a diploma. Fred was ready to enter the eleventh grade and would have to go to Michigan to continue his Christian education. In May 1948, after taking state exams, he graduated from the tenth grade in the high school. He and the Christian Reformed minister's son were the highest in the class.

But the people in Michigan had no desire to continue bearing the responsibility for our sons. It was at that crucial time, on January 28, 1948, that a call letter came from First church in Grand Rapids. I dreaded the thought of leaving Manhattan, as well as of assuming all the work involved in a congregation of five hundred families, even though the congregation would have three ministers. Nor did it appeal to me to work along with two other ministers in the same congregation.

Rev. De Wolf informed me that if I decided to come, he would give me his cooperation. Nevertheless he left the impression that he did not want a third minister in First church. After I received the call to First church in 1947, Rev. Hoeksema had written me in 1947 of his desire that I come. He did not want to influence me but wanted me to realize that another man was needed in First church, and he would like to see me come. That was almost a challenge.[4]

So reluctantly but nevertheless convinced that the call was of the Lord, I accepted the call to First church, informing them that I would come at the end of the catechism season in May. That gave the congregation an opportunity to find a house and to prepare it for our coming.

The congregation in Manhattan was very sad, if not a bit angry. Rev. De Wolf had left Manhattan for First church after only a brief stay, and we were leaving after only slightly more than three years. But the people bid us farewell with God's blessing.

When the time came for us to leave, we auctioned some of the furniture. The consistory of First church had sent two thousand dollars for moving expenses and left it up to us how we wanted to transport our belongings. I shipped the books by mail and some of the furniture by rail. The rest we sold.

Reluctantly we left behind the congregation and environment

---

4   See appendix one for Hoeksema's letter from Bellflower, California, to Rev. Hanko.

that we had so greatly enjoyed. Elaine was very reluctant to leave and promised her girlfriends, "I'll be back."

When we left on May 17, 1948, I was deeply concerned about my wife. I feared that on the trip to Michigan she would have a heart attack. Each night I checked for an emergency doctor, but she made the trip well. Arriving in Michigan she seemed happy to be with her family, whom she had not seen, except for an occasional visit, for nineteen years.

Chapter 21

FIRST PROTESTANT REFORMED CHURCH— 1948 TO 1953

The first five years spent in First Protestant Reformed Church of Grand Rapids were years of adjustment for the Hanko family. They had to adjust to city living, a busier lifestyle, and a far larger and busier congregation. Nevertheless, those years would have been enjoyable if not for the trouble that was brewing in the churches at that time.

The time came in late May 1948 that we had to bid goodbye to the congregation of Manhattan and take up lodging on Bates Street in Grand Rapids. The consistory of First church had sent me money for moving and suggested that I might want to dispose of much of my furniture that had been moved so often. Charles and William Doezema at Mastercraft Furniture in Grand Rapids, Michigan, helped us buy new furniture at greatly reduced prices.

The house on Bates Street was very commodious and pleasant, but I missed the view of the mountains that I had enjoyed from the study window in Montana. Yet I could enjoy the whole row of windows on the south side of the house over the porch. Besides the study there were three good-sized bedrooms upstairs and one downstairs. The living room with a fireplace, dining room, and a den were downstairs. Both floors had a full bath. The kitchen, with a small breakfast nook, was possibly the most pleasant of all. The house had been completely cleaned and redecorated, which made it very easy for us to get settled.

The parsonage at 1221 Bates Street that the Hanko family used while Rev. Hanko was minister in First Protestant Reformed Church.

Soon after we arrived, there was a welcome program, my installation, my inaugural sermon, and the matter of getting acquainted in a new environment. I had grown up in First church, but while I was absent for the nineteen years of my previous ministry, a new generation had arisen.

First Protestant Reformed Church in Grand Rapids, Michigan

The consistory of First Protestant Reformed Church in 1948;
Rev. Hanko (right) and Rev. De Wolf (left) sit front and center.
Rev. Hoeksema is absent.

My wife did not fancy becoming a part of a large congregation of over five hundred families, but she enjoyed having our family together again without the threat of the children's leaving home to attend school. Also her relatives were nearby. She seemed to adjust quite well; however, we had a busy life, which soon took its toll.

After each Sunday morning service while the kids were in Sunday school, my wife's sister Nell and her husband Pete Reitsma came over for coffee. It did not take long before Herm made friends with young men of the church who visited together in their various homes from week to week. Fred also fit in quite readily.

Elaine had made friends in the Manhattan congregation and felt at home there. She had to make another adjustment from attending a small school in Montana to a much larger Christian school in Grand Rapids. But she found friends in Grand Rapids, and Jean Faber (now Mrs. Jason Kortering) became one of her closest friends. Elaine graduated from the eighth grade in

Manhattan and graduated again from the ninth grade in Baxter Christian School in Grand Rapids. Thereupon she went to Grand Rapids Christian High School. Although she had decided not to attend college, she took the college preparatory course as the best course offered there. In her last year she received all *A's* so she did not have to take the examinations. She also wrote a paper on nursing, on which the teacher made the comment that she would make a good nurse. But Elaine had no desire to take up more schooling. She obtained a job with Alice Kooienga at Southwest Ice and Fuel Company, where she was trained for office work.

In the same year that Elaine graduated from Baxter school, Herm graduated from Grand Rapids Christian High School. I was impressed when the class came into the auditorium of Fountain Street Church singing, "Holy, holy, holy!" Herm started Calvin College in the fall in preparation for the ministry.

In his spare time Herm worked for Veldman's Grocery, where Fred worked later. Herm also worked for Raleigh Vander Ploeg, who sold vegetables. Later Herm spent a summer working in cement.

Allie went to Baxter Christian School. There were two disadvantages there for her. There were far more children in Baxter school than in the school in Manhattan. Besides, there were many steps inside the school and out. Allie dreaded the thought of going to school. Sometimes the teacher called to ask whether Allie was sick, because she was not in school. One time I went out to look for her and found her sitting on the curb of Fuller Avenue. One noon I drove to the school at the time the classes would be coming out. I waited until I saw Allie. Then I noticed that when she tried to walk down the steps, the boys pushed her so that she would fall. Tenaciously she clung to the railing, waiting for the boys to leave. Kids can be so very cruel.[1]

---

1 Alyce, or Allie as the family called her, was brain damaged at birth, which left her handicapped. Part of her handicap was a spastic condition that made it difficult for her to keep her balance while walking.

Things did not go well at all while she was in Baxter, so it was a great relief when Adams Street Protestant Reformed Christian School opened in September 1950. Allie had Mrs. Slomp for a teacher. She had years of experience with children, and all went well. I had told her when Allie entered her class that if she had difficulty to send Allie home at noon. Mrs. Slomp was certain that there would be no problem, and there was none.

Mrs. Slomp seemed to think that we did not know how to handle Allie. She mentioned occasionally that she would like to have Allie stay with her in her home, so when we decided to go to Florida in January 1953, we suggested that Allie stay with Mrs. Slomp. She agreed to that, but the very first evening Mrs. Slomp brought Allie back to our house on Bates Street to be with her siblings. She admitted that she knew how to be a teacher but not a mother.

After Allie finished Mrs. Slomp's class, we decided to send her to Children's Retreat.[2] At eighteen years of age she went into a supervised workshop for a few years.

On Labor Day 1948, we took a short vacation to Green Lake with Corie and Otto Vander Woude, my sister and her husband. There Jennie had an epileptic seizure. A doctor who was vacationing there thought it was a heart attack and sent her to St. Mary's Hospital. It was only later that Dr. Avery discovered her problem.

In the summer of 1950 we were invited to spend four weeks in Bellflower, California, while Rev. Lambert Doezema was on vacation.[3] My wife, Fred, Elaine, and I traveled there by car. The people had rented an apartment for us and had it well supplied with food. We were treated royally and taken to various scenic places. There we met Mr. and Mrs. De Groot. She was formerly

---

2   Children's Retreat was a branch of Pine Rest Christian Hospital that educated handicapped children.

3   Rev. Doezema later left the Protestant Reformed denomination in 1953, as did most of the Bellflower congregation.

Dorothy Jansma from our Hull congregation. We found them to be a very congenial couple with whom we spent considerable time. A few times we went to the ocean with their family to ride the waves.

My wife had a spell early in the morning toward the end of our stay in Bellflower. Whenever she had a spell it was usually in the early morning hours. Once we were back home and another spell occurred, we called Dr. Avery, who sat by her for two hours, watching her reactions. Then he came and told me that he wanted her in the hospital for a brain scan. For a while she continued to have occasional spells, but when the Dilantin, a seizure medication, took effect, her problem was solved. She took the medication the rest of her life.

Rev. Hanko and Rev. Homer Hoeksema at the 1950 young people's convention

In the summer of 1951 I spent considerable time working among the liberated in Canada, first in the Hamilton area and later in the Chatham area. A Protestant Reformed church was organized in Hamilton and one in Chatham. When those churches felt they did not need the Protestant Reformed Churches and could be on their own, they left the denomination. The people differed significantly with the Protestant Reformed doctrine of the covenant.

It soon became evident that there was a lot of work to be done in First Protestant Reformed Church. There was always a large number of sick and shut-ins who had to be visited at regular intervals—some almost every day, some once a week, some every two weeks, and many once a month. Since that was one task that had been sorely neglected in the past, the consistory insisted that a complete record be kept of every visit and that the visits be regularly reported on the weekly bulletin.

The most difficult visits were to those people in mental institutions who could not respond. Whatever message I brought to them I had to prepare in advance so that I did not appear to hesitate, wondering what to say. Among those calls were also the wildly confused patients, whom I tried to reach with the word of God and penetrate into the darkness of their confusion to awaken evidence of the grace of God. I was convinced that the Holy Spirit operated also in those saints, and responses could be obtained with a bit of effort. That proved to be true in all cases except one person who left the impression that there was no spiritual life present.

In August just before going on vacation Rev. De Wolf and I were handed a stack of cards for family visitation. That first year we made the majority of family visits. The elders took the rest. That meant sandwiching those calls between sick visits, catechism classes, society meetings, and other activities. Since that involved using every spare moment from September until April to fit in the family visits, the consistory decided to reduce the number of calls for Rev. De Wolf and me, so that we each had a significantly lighter load. It would have been nice if a minister could have visited every family in the congregation once every three years, but that would have taxed us beyond capacity. Under the new system each family had visitation from a minister once every four to five years. Families had visits from elders in the other years.

To tell the truth, when I accepted the call to First, those sick calls and numerous family visitations troubled me the most.

I feared that they would become very wearisome. True, during the first summer the sick visits were very depressing. I seemed to carry all the problems of the sick with me day and night. But after the other activities were underway, I began to enjoy that part of the work even more than the rest. Preaching for such a huge audience never had a special appeal. The people seemed too distant from me. After the schism of 1953 preaching was easier.

The congregation before the split was much too large and cumbersome, even for three ministers.[4] Rev. Hoeksema took the pulpit on Sunday mornings. The Dutch services in the afternoons and the evening services were shared by Rev. De Wolf and me. We shared the wedding and funeral services, each taking every other one. The age groups in the catechism classes were split in two, but that still left classes of forty and fifty.

Besides the routine work in the congregation, there were also many family problems that had to be solved. Often on Sunday or late at night, I would be called out for some family trouble.

One night especially stands out in my memory. A lady called to say that her husband had left the house to commit suicide. I went to the home and then accompanied her to Reeds Lake, where she thought he had gone. We arrived there and saw him in a boat on the lake. After a bit he came to shore and said that he did not want to talk to that "so-and-so," referring to his wife, but he would talk to me if I joined him in the boat. I knew that he was drunk, but I ventured into the boat anyway. His wife took their car home, and I sat out on the lake in the dead of night trying to talk some sense into a half-drunken man. About midnight he suggested that it would be no effort at all for him to dump the boat. I assured him that I did not doubt that. But I added, "I know where I am going, but where are you going?" The Lord marvelously preserved us, for the man rowed to shore and went home with almost nothing more to say.

---

4 The 1953 church directory lists 437 families and 147 individuals.

Another incident worth mentioning involved a lady who was not a member of the Protestant Reformed Churches, but whom I was asked to visit in Pine Rest. She was there for the third time because of her suicidal tendencies.

When I approached her carrying my Bible, she told me that the doctors did not allow reading the Bible to the patients. I told her that the doctors could not give me orders. She should listen, and if the Bible spoke about her, she should nod, and if not, she could shake her head, meaning no. I read Psalm 77. By the time I had reached the third verse, "I remembered God, and was troubled: I complained, and my spirit was overwhelmed," she was nodding and soon after said, "That's me." When I finished reading, the dam broke. She poured out her soul about the sins she had committed since leaving home as a girl of seventeen. I visited her as long as she stayed in the hospital.

It was some time later on a Tuesday morning that she called and said that she was ready to end her own life. I would find the back door open. I told her to wait at least until I got there. When I arrived, I saw that her kitchen was set up so that she could put her head in the oven, turn on the gas, and die. She was in the living room. I asked her, "Where would you be now if you had carried through?" Coldly she answered, "In hell." After I talked and prayed with her, she agreed to clean up the things in the kitchen. A few years later I happened to meet her; she was a changed woman who assured me that she had found peace with God.

At the close of each society season there were so many banquets and parties that I would surely have developed an ulcer if I did not already have one. The ulcer problem, which had been there since my student days, worsened steadily. One time when my wife and I were ready to leave for Randolph for a preaching assignment I could feel the ulcer break. I hoped that the bleeding would not be too bad and decided to go anyway. That was very foolish, for when we arrived in Waupun I was bleeding so badly that I had to give up the idea of preaching the next Sunday. Herm came to drive us home.

Then there was the unforgettable Thanksgiving Day in 1950 when Jennie was in the hospital on account of her heart. I had started bleeding a few days before Thanksgiving. The day before Thanksgiving I was walking from Butterworth Hospital when I felt the blood spurting from the ulcer. By the time I came home I felt weak enough to lie down. It was a good thing that I did not have to preach the next day. During the night I began to vomit blood, so that on Thanksgiving morning I was taken by ambulance to Blodgett Hospital. When my wife heard that I was hospitalized, she came to see me and then decided to go home. I had three days that I barely knew I was alive, since Dr. Avery kept me on the brink of consciousness.

At the first council meeting held after my arrival in First church, it became evident that trouble was brewing in the congregation. There was a strange tension caused mainly by the deacons, which was hard to analyze but could be very keenly felt.

At the first consistory meeting that I led shortly after my arrival, the matter of a different home for Rev. Hoeksema was brought up. I had to appoint a committee to visit Rev. Hoeksema to ask him whether he would be willing to move to a different home. The reason was that Rev. De Wolf wanted to live in the parsonage next to the church. Naively, I chose two men, Mr. Jim Kok and Mr. Gerard Koster, who had always been good friends of Rev. Hoeksema. Afterward I was told that I could not have made a worse choice, because those were two of the worst opponents of Rev. Hoeksema.

The matter of getting the senior pastor out of his house never succeeded. An option was placed on the house on the southeast corner of Fuller Avenue and Bates Street. That was a small house with no space for any minister's library, much less for Rev. Hoeksema's library. He turned that down flat. So did De Wolf and I. Suggestions were made to build a house for Rev. and Mrs.

Hoeksema, but when he described the size of the library he wanted, the committee realized that they would never be able to sell a house of that sort. Finally the entire matter was dropped, but the tension between Rev. De Wolf and Rev. Hoeksema only intensified.

Before one of the early consistory meetings I received a call from the clerk, requesting that I come to his office to discuss the agenda for the evening. I did that, but on my second visit to his office before a consistory meeting, I discovered that matters on the agenda were discussed, motions were suggested, and some of the consistory members were encouraged to make those motions. All of that was done while a highly influential man from the congregation, a supporter of Rev. De Wolf, was present, even though he was not a consistory member. After that I refused to take part in those highly irregular conferences.

Two young men, Henry De Raad and Henry De Bolster, fresh from the liberated churches in the Netherlands, joined our congregation and attended our seminary. It was not long before they had the brazen audacity to file a protest with the consistory against Rev. Hoeksema and me, objecting to our preaching. Of course, they got nowhere, but it was evident from which direction the wind was blowing.

In January 1953 Ed Kooienga called on a Monday and told me to ask the consistory for a ten-day vacation so that we could accompany him and his wife to Florida. They would be leaving the next day. The first order of business that night was my request for a break, which was readily granted. The consistory realized that we were under tremendous pressure and that a rest would be beneficial. So at recess I called home and told my wife to get ready to go.

It was a very pleasant and relaxing trip. We had gone with the Kooiengas more often on their boat on Lake Michigan. Sometimes on Wednesday afternoons we turned our backs on the work and went off to rest in the boat. We would have supper together there and then return home. Now we were in for a bigger trip.

We saw Cypress Gardens and spent some time there. Our original destination was St. Petersburg, where we spent a few days. On Saturday we took the ferry across to Bradenton, where we attended the chapel on Sunday. The visiting minister was an acquaintance from the Midwest. When he met me after the service, he asked whether we intended to attend the evening service. We told him that we did. That evening he preached a sermon on 1 Timothy 2 in connection with the inauguration of President Eisenhower that week. He did well on the first part of the text, but he made the phrase "who will have all men to be saved" in verse 4 refer to all men without exception. As he preached he looked at me every so often that it became embarrassing. After the service a man asked whether I was Protestant Reformed. I told him I was. He said, "I thought so. The preacher was afraid of you." If universalism was the preacher's conviction, why did he not come with full force to show me that I was wrong?

On our way home we went by way of Miami, St. Augustine, and through the cotton fields and estates of Georgia. We arrived home on Saturday but discovered that De Wolf was very unhappy about my absence. He refused to take his turn preaching the next morning, so I had to work into the night to prepare to preach twice that Sunday. That was just one more indication of the ill wind that was blowing through the congregation and the churches in 1953.

Chapter 22

PROFESSOR SCHILDER COMES TO AMERICA

Prof. Klaas Schilder of the Netherlands was unjustly cast out from his church over various doctrinal differences, just as Rev. Hoeksema had been cast out from his church. The two men formed a bond because of that common ground. When Schilder came to the United States, the rest of the Protestant Reformed churches also received him as a friend and a brother, even though he differed with those churches on the doctrine of the covenant. The friendship later soured, but it was too late to save the churches a great deal of grief.

In 1939 Professor Schilder of the Netherlands was invited by William B. Eerdmans, founder of the well-known Eerdmans Publishing Company and a prominent member of the Christian Reformed Church, to come to the United States. An extensive schedule had been arranged for a preaching and speaking tour through the country.

For some time discussions had been carried on in the Netherlands by means of pamphlets and brochures on such subjects as self-examination, the two natures of Christ, the covenant, and common grace. On the last two subjects, common grace and the covenant, Prof. Valentine Hepp of the Free University of Amsterdam, who represented the segment of the followers of Abraham Kuyper, and Professor Schilder of Kampen Theological School,

Klaas Schilder

who represented the segment that followed the *Afscheiding* of 1834, were engaged in a discussion.

When some of the professors of Calvin seminary became aware of Schilder's coming, they were afraid that sleeping dogs would be aroused, especially regarding the subject of common grace. They published a notice in the church papers the *Banner* and *De Wachter* warning the churches not to allow Schilder on their pulpits.[1]

The result was that when the professor arrived in the United States, he discovered that most of his scheduled appointments had been canceled. Somewhat in disgust, somewhat in frustration, he called on Rev. Hoeksema to have a talk with him, since Hoeksema also did not agree with Kuyper's doctrine of common grace. The result was that a conference of area Protestant Reformed ministers was held in Rev. Hoeksema's living room. The men spent a very pleasant evening exchanging experiences in the conflict our churches had gone through in America and the struggle that was going on in the Netherlands. Soon a number of speaking engagements were arranged by our various churches.

Thus it came about quite unexpectedly that Schilder came into contact with all of the Protestant Reformed ministers and congregations. He was a congenial person and pleasant to have in our homes. We all enjoyed his visits, and the members of our congregations were also impressed by his speeches. True, he had a speech impediment, which, along with his speaking in Dutch,

---

1 *De Wachter* (The watchman) was the official Dutch denominational paper of the Christian Reformed Church.

made it a bit difficult to follow him, but it was refreshing to hear him. He was well received.

Rev. Hoeksema was no less attracted to the professor. It should be understood that in a sense Rev. Hoeksema was a loner. That was partly due to his character, his determination to be well-prepared for any important event, and his peculiar position in defense of the truth. He was virtually a lone warrior, and he was very much aware of it. At times he would complain, "I'm all alone. I have no intimate friend, none whatsoever." His closest colleague was Rev. Ophoff. Rev. Hoeksema loved him dearly, admired him for his faithful and determined stand for the truth, and would defend him when anyone tried to say anything against him. Yet Rev. Ophoff was younger than he and did not think himself equal to his colleague. All the other ministers were younger, with the possible exception of Rev. Vos, but he also was Hoeksema's former student.

Schilder was attracted to Rev. Hoeksema, who in turn was drawn to a man who was well versed in doctrine and had much in common with him, even when it came to the conflict in which Schilder was engaged in the Netherlands. There were some fundamental differences between them regarding God's covenant, but they fell into the background while other vital interests were discussed.

Those differences on the covenant were hardly referred to in Schilder's first visit. He regarded the covenant as a framework, a sphere in which God gathers his church in the line of successive generations of believers. He held that all baptized children of believing parents are included in the covenant and receive the covenantal promise, "I will be thy God." But it is a conditional promise. If a baptized child dies before he comes to the years of discretion, he is saved on the basis of the promise. Covenantal parents often stated in the obituary of one of their children, "Our comfort rests in God's promise." But having come to years of discretion, the child must embrace the promise and give expression to this by making public confession of his faith. If after due admonition he refuses to do so, he is regarded as a covenant-breaker. The promise still stands, but if he dies without embracing the promise, he is lost forever.

The liberated often give this example in their defense of their covenantal view. One tells his son that if he gets good grades in school, he will receive a bicycle. That, of course, is a conditional promise.

Another example the liberated use is of a check or promissory note that reads something like this: "Jehovah promises to pay to John or Mary the sum of eternal life." This check is signed by God at baptism. As long as the check is not cashed, it is only a sheet of paper; but when it is cashed it retains its full value. The value depends on the party who cashes the check.

When the objection is raised that this makes God's promise dependent on man and leads to Arminianism in the covenant, the answer is given, "But God must give the grace to accept the promise."

As I see it, the differences regarding the covenant are the following:

Gereformeerde Kerken: the covenant is a contract between God and all baptized children consisting of an offer of salvation, a demand to believe and to repent, and a threat or warning to those who do not embrace the offer.

The liberated: the covenant is a framework in which God works salvation. This consists of a promise of eternal life, a condition of faith, and a warning to covenant-breakers.

Protestant Reformed: the covenant is a relationship of friendship between God and his elect people in Christ. Baptism is a means of grace that seals the word, which is a savor of life unto life or a savor of death unto death.

Schilder spoke to a large audience in First church in Grand Rapids, which had a seating capacity of over 1,200 persons. The auditorium was packed; all available space was taken. People had to sit on the platform, and some listened by means of loudspeakers in the basement.

Schilder felt that there was a possibility that the breach between the Protestant Reformed Churches and the Christian Reformed Church could be healed, if only there could be an open discussion. So a conference was arranged in the Pantlind Hotel of Grand Rapids to which all the ministers of our denomination and all the ministers of the Christian Reformed Church in the area were invited.[2] Our ministers came out in goodly number, but there were only a few Christian Reformed ministers. The meeting was opened and the question arose regarding how to proceed. Rev. Hoeksema suggested that he had prepared a paper that he would like to read, which would set some guidelines. A committee was appointed to decide whether or not his paper should be read.

When it was finally decided that it should be allowed, Rev. Hoeksema read his paper, which addressed the question whether a reunion of the two denominations was desirable and profitable.[3] He explained that if reunion were to be attempted, common grace should be discussed. A silence followed. Dr. Schilder urged the Christian Reformed ministers to respond, but the silence hung heavily in the air. A few voices of warning were raised that they would be opening a can of worms, or something similar to that. No matter how much Schilder pleaded with the Christian Reformed ministers, they refused to speak for or against what Hoeksema had read. Finally, the suggestion was made to adjourn and to give the Christian Reformed ministers time to prepare an answer and bring it to another meeting. That meeting never happened.

2 The Pantlind Hotel is now called the Amway Grand Plaza Hotel.
3 The paper Rev. Hoeksema wrote was later translated by Rev. H. Veldman and published in a pamphlet entitled *Reunion with the Christian Reformed and Protestant Reformed Churches: Is It Demanded, Possible, Desired?* The pamphlet is now included in Hoeksema and Danhof, *The Rock Whence We Are Hewn*, 435–71.

In 1939 World War II broke out and all communication with the Netherlands broke off, especially after the Germans invaded the Lowlands. Nothing was heard of Schilder nor about him, except that Rev. Hoeksema received a card on which was written, "Our friend is Acts 16:23."[4] That message could mean just one thing. Schilder, who had strongly opposed the Nazis, even comparing them to the antichrist, was incarcerated by the Germans. Later we learned that he had been released but that he had gone underground to escape further persecution by the Nazis. While he was underground the Synod of Sneek-Utrecht of 1944 deposed him from office in the Reformed Church of the Netherlands. Schilder became the leader of the Reformed Church (liberated).

At the Protestant Reformed synodical meeting of 1947, Schilder's name was brought up again. Some correspondence had been restored after the war, and Rev. Hoeksema, eager to meet his friend again, made a motion on the floor of synod that the Protestant Reformed Churches invite Schilder to speak for us. An objection was raised that we did not agree with him on his view of the covenant, but Rev. Hoeksema said that he had full confidence in our men that they could certainly hold their ground if the matter of the covenant was brought up.

Schilder came, visited, and spoke in all of our churches. He was even given permission to preach in some of our pulpits. He had gone through some bitter experiences during the invasion of the Nazis in the Netherlands, and in many ways he enjoyed our way of life. On one occasion he was asked just before sitting down for a meal, "Are you hungry, Professor?" He responded, "No, I have never been hungry again, not after being in the concentration camp." He even talked of coming again, the Lord willing, at which time he would like to learn to drive an automobile.

---

4 Acts 16:23 reads, "And when they had laid many stripes upon them, they cast them into prison, charging the jailer to keep them safely."

I was still in Manhattan at the time of his second visit in 1947. He came and spoke for the congregation there. In one of our conversations he said, "I despise your covenant view." I said to him, "That's mutual." I figured that the ministers and members of the Protestant Reformed Churches would never get along with him for any length of time. Yet it appeared that the ministers of Classis West were especially impressed by his friendliness and his intelligence. One of them remarked that it grieved him to see that a greater light than Rev. Hoeksema had risen among us while the latter was still living.

A conference was held in First church, which a number of Protestant Reformed ministers attended. The subject of the covenant was brought up on that occasion, but Rev. Hoeksema was still recovering from the stroke he had experienced in June, which hindered him greatly in speaking.

Schilder conference in 1947

Professor Schilder did not seem to think that the Protestant Reformed opposition to his covenantal view would deter immigrants from his churches from joining the Protestant Reformed Churches. Rev. Hoeksema and Professor Schilder addressed each other as Herman and Klaas. When the latter was ready to return to his homeland, Rev. Hoeksema and his wife accompanied Schilder to New York.

But all that changed soon afterward. When Professor Schilder was back in the Netherlands, he wrote an article in *De Reformatie* in which he expressed his agreement with Prof. William Heyns regarding the covenant,[5] a view that Rev. Hoeksema in previous years had strongly condemned as Arminianism injected into the covenant. You can find Hoeksema's disagreement with Heyns discussed in the book *Believers and Their Seed.*[6]

For various reasons some Protestant Reformed ministers felt very strongly drawn to Professor Schilder and his conditional promise in the covenant. There was a growing resentment against Rev. Hoeksema and his leadership. Some, while realizing that his advice on many matters was needed, took offense that he usually took the leadership in discussions and that his opinions were rarely challenged. Some even secretly considered him a dictator.

Although Rev. Hoeksema had suffered a severe stroke in June 1947, he had recovered sufficiently that he could carry on his work in the churches. He preached once a Sunday, expounding the truth of the Heidelberg Catechism. He also continued to write in the *Standard Bearer* and performed many of his former duties. God had remarkably restored him.

There was unrest and dissatisfaction among many of our ministers. They were unhappy about the lack of growth in the congregations and were eager to have their flocks increase in numbers. They took offense from much that Rev. Hoeksema wrote, particularly when he spoke of being *distinctively Reformed*. That term no longer appealed to them. They resented his leadership and desired to assert themselves in many ways.

There was also a spirit of complacency among the members of the churches, an attitude of having attained with nothing more for which to strive. Among others there was discontent. The preaching was too doctrinal, the sermons too long, the society

---

5   *De Reformatie* (The reformation) was the paper of the liberated churches.
6   Hoeksema, *Believers and Their Seed*, 1–14.

meetings too dry. They wanted more life, more entertainment, and more relaxing companionship.

As a result many ministers were avoiding doctrine in their preaching. They chose texts and prepared sermons that were more practical, more appealing, yet at the same time lacking in distinctiveness. One could not say that the sermons contained heresy, but neither were they positively Reformed in content. That lack of distinctiveness in the preaching led to the stifling of many efforts toward starting Protestant Reformed Christian schools.

There was also a desire among some to assert one's self and be independent. The synod had adopted catechism books to be used in our churches, but one minister made his own catechism books. In Michigan we had our weekly church paper called *Church News*, which was sent throughout the churches. The Midwest started a magazine called *Concordia*. In Michigan we had the *Reformed Witness Hour* broadcast on stations throughout the United States; the Midwest began the *Sovereign Grace Hour* broadcast.

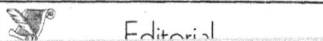

First issue of the *Concordia*

In First church the supporters of Rev. De Wolf tried to isolate a part of the congregation that they thought was theirs. There was a time too when they talked about withdrawing peaceably. They had a proposal to start a new congregation, but the consistory was afraid if it allowed them to withdraw, they would form a congregation that was not Reformed and nothing could be done about it.

In 1948 two of our ministers visited the Netherlands and met with the contact committee of the liberated churches. The ministers informed the committee that Dutch immigrants were welcome in the Protestant Reformed Churches because we had no official stand on the doctrine of the covenant. Thus the liberated view of the covenant would be accepted in the churches. It was true that the churches never had officially adopted the covenantal view developed by Rev. Hoeksema, but it was also true that his view of the covenant is based on the fundamental truth of the sovereignty of God. This means that there is no room in our doctrinal stand for a conditional promise in the covenant. As a result of the statement of those two ministers, a professor in the Netherlands wrote to the immigrants in Chatham and Hamilton, Canada, that they should join the Protestant Reformed denomination because they would be allowed to maintain their covenantal view.

I labored among the Canadian churches during one summer. The Dutch folks there were very willing to receive visitors who spoke Dutch because they felt like strangers in a new country. They also freely talked about their liberated views, which weighed heavily on them because of their recent struggles in their homeland. I was welcome in all their homes, was served many cups of tea, and had no difficulty in stirring up discussions about our differences regarding the covenant.

It rather surprised me, and yet I accepted it as being sincerely meant, that when a certain man went out with me to meet new immigrants he would say, "You know, we are now Protestant

Reformed. In our covenantal view we completely lost sight of predestination. The Protestant Reformed ministers have opened our eyes to that fact, so that now we also embrace God's sovereign predestination." On another occasion another man spoke about the true church. They had so strongly maintained that the liberated churches were the only true church. But then he said that the Protestant Reformed Churches were the true church in America. I asked him what he would do regarding joining a true church, if he were to return to the Netherlands. He informed me that then he would be compelled to organize a Protestant Reformed church in his homeland.

I made one interesting visit to a new immigrant, a woman, who said as soon as I introduced myself, "You speak a good Dutch, but you were not born in the Netherlands." She invited me in but immediately demanded an answer to three questions. "Did the Christian Reformed Church refuse their pulpits to Dr. Schilder?" "Did the Protestant Reformed Churches open their pulpits to him?" "Do the Protestant Reformed Churches disagree with him on the covenant?" When I answered each question in the affirmative, she said, "You are an honest man. I'll serve you a cup of tea." It appeared as if she had spoken to some people who had not been honest with her.

In the meantime the mission committee was confronted with requests from many of the immigrants from the liberated churches to become members of the Protestant Reformed Churches. It was also evident that the liberated stood firmly on their idea of the covenant and the conditional promise to all baptized children. Therefore the mission committee presented a request to the synod of 1950 to make a declaration that would define in no uncertain terms our convictions regarding common grace, the general and well-meant offer of salvation, and God's covenant. As was later clearly expressed in the document, it was intended to assist in mission labors.

The synod of 1950 drew up and provisionally accepted the

Declaration of Principles with only one dissenting vote. The Declaration was to be presented to the churches for approbation. Our missionary declared that he could work with it, although he later opposed it. The one person who voted against it felt very strongly about it, even to the extent that immediately after the session he said to some of his colleagues, "Now you have put a noose around your necks, and they are going to hang you."

Some of our other ministers opposed it as a fourth creed in addition to the other three creeds and complained that they were being restricted in their preaching. They began to preach the error of conditions unto salvation.

At the 1951 synod the Declaration of Principles was ratified by the churches by a very narrow margin. At that time we had twenty-five churches and twenty-eight ministers.

I was present when Rev. Herman Veldman was chosen to be minister of the Hamilton congregation from a duo that also included Rev. John Heys. Judging by the conversations I overheard, I thought Rev. Heys would receive the call. Some seemed very vehement about not calling Rev. Veldman. Yet when the votes were counted, Rev. Veldman was chosen. He labored there a year, and by that time it became evident that Hamilton wanted to break away from the Protestant Reformed Churches. Many troubles arose there.

Rev. John Blankespoor and I had been appointed as church visitors that year. As we were traveling to Hamilton, John asked, "What will you report to classis if we find that Rev. Veldman is responsible for the trouble there?" I assured him that we would report exactly according to our findings.

The Hamilton consistory was fully prepared for our coming. The consistory had evidently decided to be very frank and open to the church visitors. I led the meeting, and soon an elder, the man who said they had become Protestant Reformed, read a paper in which he strongly defended the liberated view of the covenant over against our view. When he finished, I asked him,

PROFESSOR SCHILDER COMES TO AMERICA

"When were you lying? Did you lie when you went out with me and said that the people had become Protestant Reformed? Or are you lying now?" He boldly answered, "Then, of course." Another elder also had a paper he wanted to read. It was another long document in defense of the liberated doctrine of the covenant. When he finished, I reminded him of what he had said about the true church. He heartily agreed but admitted that he had never meant what he said.

Finally, after it had grown late, I asked the consistory, "Is Rev. Veldman to blame for the disagreement here?" I received the answer, "Actually, not at all. He told us in advance that he would preach most emphatically the truth of the covenant as he believed it. He gave it to us double barrel, but we could have expected that." Obviously they had deceived the Protestant Reformed Churches because they wanted to use them until they were able to organize a congregation that maintained the liberated view. Not Rev. Veldman but the Declaration of Principles had soured them.

There was also a strong reaction against the Declaration of Principles in the liberated churches in the Netherlands. Much to Rev. Hoeksema's dismay, Professor Schilder immediately and publicly declared that his friendship with Hoeksema had come to an end.

Various ministers from our churches began to defend conditional theology, stating that scripture taught conditions unto salvation. An article appeared in *Concordia* that defended a teaching of conditions in scripture. Ultimately an article appeared that defended faith as a condition unto salvation. The writer had not only completely ignored the teachings of scripture that faith is a gift of God's grace, but also ignored the Reformed confessions, particularly the Canons of Dordt, which state that

faith is...to be considered as the gift of God, not on account of its being offered by God to man, to be accepted or rejected at his pleasure, but because it is in reality conferred, breathed, and infused into him; nor even because God bestows the power or ability to believe, and then expects that man should, by the exercise of his own free will, consent to the terms of salvation, and actually believe in Christ; but because he who works in man both to will and to do, and indeed all things in all, produces both the will to believe and the act of believing also.[7]

A serious conflict had arisen within the Protestant Reformed Churches.

---

7 Canons of Dordt 3–4.14, in Philip Schaff, ed., *The Creeds of Christendom with a History and Critical Notes,* 6th ed., 3 vols. (New York: Harper and Row, 1931; repr., Grand Rapids, MI: Baker Books, 2007), 3:591.

Chapter 23

THE SCHISM
OF 1953

The year 1953 was a trying one for the Protestant Reformed Churches and its members. The cost of schism is high. Rev. Hanko paid with his own health. The stress of dealing with a divided consistory and congregation took its toll. His son remembers that after consistory meetings his father sat up late at night, munching on soda crackers to calm his churning stomach. Was the cost too high? Rev. Hanko answers that question with a resounding, "No!" After the split the churches could confess with Job, "But he knoweth the way that I take: when he hath tried me, I shall come forth as gold" (Job 23:10).

During those years, there was plenty of unrest within our churches. Rev. Andrew Petter began writing about conditions in the church papers. On Tuesday afternoons De Wolf and I walked after catechism to discuss the affairs of the week. I mentioned Petter's articles, to which De Wolf responded, "I can agree with him as long as he does not make faith a condition." Soon an article did appear with the heading "Faith a Condition."

One Tuesday morning our missionary called to assure me that he was so happy, especially after working with the liberated in Canada, that he was Protestant Reformed. I told him that I was glad to hear that and that he should inform our people of that. He was under a cloud of suspicion for his lack of distinctiveness.

Evidently what he was looking for was an opportunity to preach on the pulpit in First church. I was aware of that, so on Thursday morning I offered him the Sunday morning pulpit with the understanding that he would preach a strong, doctrinally distinctive sermon, assuring the people of his faithfulness to our churches. Instead, he preached a wishy-washy sermon that could have been preached from almost any pulpit. He made no statement that could be called heretical, but the whole sermon was so completely man-centered that it could hardly be considered a defense of the Reformed truth as taught in the scriptures.

I was upset, but no more so than the consistory. The next evening at the consistory meeting there were numerous complaints about that type of sermon being preached by our missionary. The consistory decided to make copies from the tape, to study the sermon, and to bring up the matter again at the next meeting. Thereupon we decided to call him into the meeting and admonish him regarding that type of preaching, which certainly did not represent us well on the mission field. He came to the meeting. At first he revealed a bit of bluster, but he finally listened without comment to what the elders had to say. Evidently he was glad that we were not making a greater issue of his sermon.

Somewhere around January 1953 one of our ministers called and wanted to visit me. Soon we were in a heated argument, since he was flinging charges at our churches. We had changed, not he. Finally I suggested to him, "Why don't you leave? Get out, and leave us with peace." He got up, took the doorknob in his hand, and said, "We'll split first!" With that he stormed out, but he revealed that destroying the Protestant Reformed Churches was foremost in his mind. He had gone through the denomination (and we were paying him for it) spreading all sorts of propaganda against our doctrine, our people, and our ministers, especially Rev. Hoeksema and Ophoff.

Consistory of First Protestant Reformed Church before the schism of 1953; front row far left: Rev. Ophoff; center: Rev. Hoeksema (left), Rev. De Wolf (right)

About that time Adams Street Protestant Reformed Christian School opened, in spite of the open opposition of De Wolf and his friends. Once the school opened, he reluctantly encouraged everyone to support the school, since it was there anyway.

De Wolf came to me one Thursday morning and said, "Do you suppose I could say something like this off our pulpit?" The statement he mentioned reeked of conditional theology. I told him that the statement was not Reformed. He claimed he could say it and remain Reformed, whch showed that his statements were deliberately planned.

On April 15, 1951, Rev. Hubert De Wolf preached a sermon on Luke 16:29: "Abraham saith unto him, They have Moses and the prophets; let them hear them." In the course of the sermon he accused some of the members of the congregation of being proud of being Protestant Reformed. He said that wearing "Protestant

Rev. Hubert De Wolf

Reformed" on their coat lapels would not bring them to heaven. It was in that connection that he added, "But I assure you that God promises every one of you that if you believe you will be saved." That statement bore all the semblance of a general, well-meant promise to all who hear the gospel. Besides, it spoke of faith as a condition to salvation.

After his infamous sermon Rev. De Wolf reportedly said to one man, "Well, I said it." "Yes," said the man, "but it took you long enough."

I must admit that I was deeply grieved by that sermon. When I came home, I said to a group of young men gathered with our boys in the living room, "It seems to me that Rev. De Wolf is going to leave us." No more was said, but the next day Rev. Hoeksema, who was not at that evening service, called me and asked about the sermon. I told him as reservedly as possible what I thought of it. On Tuesday Rev. De Wolf called me and asked, "What makes you think that I intend to leave?" I answered, "After the sermon of Sunday evening I cannot imagine that you want to stay." He replied, "Well, I have no intention of leaving."

At the next consistory meeting there were at least two protests against De Wolf's sermon. Rev. Hoeksema appointed a committee to study the protests and to supply the consistory with an answer, but he added that the committee should not be too ready to condemn Rev. De Wolf, because the matter might not be as serious as it appeared to be. Obviously he wanted to protect his colleague as much as possible.

Since there was a division in the consistory regarding De Wolf's statement, the case dragged on for some time. The elders were plainly taking sides for or against the pastor. Finally, when those in favor of Rev. De Wolf were in the majority, they decided to drop the entire matter.

Although that was improper, since the case should have been settled one way or another, there was a sense of relief that maybe peace had been restored. The last Sunday in August 1952 Rev. De Wolf preached a sermon that was thoroughly Reformed. Rev. Hoeksema was so pleased that he made a point of commending the Reverend on it and added, "Keep it up, Hubie."

Two weeks later, on September 14, Rev. De Wolf made his second statement that created offense in the congregation. He spoke on Matthew 18:3: "Verily I say unto you, Except ye be converted, and become as little children, ye shall not enter into the kingdom of heaven." In the course of the sermon, he stated that conversion is a prerequisite for entering into the kingdom.

By that statement he again introduced the idea of conditions that man must fulfill, making conversion a prerequisite to enter the kingdom. Scripture plainly teaches that God converts the wayward sinner. God certainly does not bind himself to prerequisites. If he did, it could mean only that it is necessary for us to convert ourselves.

Someone may ask, but does not God call to repentance? Did Paul not say to the Philippian jailer, "Believe on the Lord Jesus Christ, and thou shalt be saved, and thy house" (Acts 16:31)? True. But when God calls to repentance and faith, he is actually arousing in our consciousness his own work of grace (Eph. 2:8–9). We read that Jesus said to the father of the demoniac son, "If thou canst believe..." (Mark 9:23–24). The man replied, evidently in amazement, "Lord, I believe; help thou mine unbelief."

I insert here that on that same Sunday evening another minister told his congregation in Holland, "This is my stand on the issue of conditions: When God speaks about his people he speaks unconditionally, when he speaks to his people he always speaks conditionally." During the week, I offered to show him passages of scripture that showed that God spoke to his people unconditionally, but he refused to discuss it with me.

Now Rev. Hoeksema and the consistory had had their fill.

They realized how deceptively Rev. De Wolf was working to win over as many people as possible in the congregation. New charges were made, and the entire case was once more opened. Not a Sunday went by that De Wolf did not try to create sympathy by choosing psalter numbers that stressed how much he had to suffer as a martyr for the cause.

That controversy in First church came to a head in the spring of 1953 at Classis East, where a minority report was adopted, composed by two elders, in which they recommended that Rev. De Wolf should publicly retract those two statements as heretical, regardless of what interpretation might be given to them.

The matter was clarified when Rev. Rich Veldman tried to defend De Wolf on the floor of Classis East by showing how his statements could be interpreted in a Reformed manner. I was ready to jump up and say, "But De Wolf does not mean that." However, De Wolf himself stood up and said, "Rev. Veldman knows very well that's not what I mean."

Rev. De Wolf delayed as long as possible with making an apology. On June 21, 1953, he made an apology that actually laid the blame on those who regarded the statements as heretical. They should have known better.

Jennie wrote in her diary for that Sunday and Monday, "Rev. De Wolf preached and I made up my mind that it was going to be the last time if he did not change. He created quite a stir and a lot of people thought he apologized...Neal very tired and worn out."

"Monday—Did the washing and did not even get through before dinner because the telephone rang all the time. At night they had consistory meeting and they had a bad time I guess. Neal felt terrible when he got home at about 1:30 a.m. I guess the split has really come and De Wolf refuses to retract the statements he made. So once more there is a division in our churches. Just what will happen time will tell. But it surely is the truth that will stand."

With a close vote and with the reluctant agreement of the

consistory of Fourth (Southeast) church, Rev. De Wolf was suspended from office and those of the consistory who agreed
with him were deposed. Although De Wolf was suspended, not
everyone agreed that he should be deposed. Yet his censure was
important for our existence as churches. While we may have
remained a Protestant Reformed denomination, we would have
lost all we gained in 1924.[1]

Consistory of First Protestant Reformed Church after the schism in 1953;
center front left to right: Rev. Hanko, Rev. Hoeksema, Rev. Ophoff

You may wonder why after the deposition we left the church
building to meet in the auditorium of Grand Rapids Christian High School on the corner of Franklin Street and Madison
Avenue. The De Wolf faction notified the consistory that they
intended to hold services in the auditorium of First church the
coming Sunday. The consistory discussed whether to insist on

1 For the rest of the facts concerning the appeal to Classis East and its
   decision and the deposition of De Wolf and those of the consistory who
   supported him, see David J. Engelsma, *Battle for Sovereign Grace in the
   Covenant: The Decclaration of Principles* (Jenison, MI: Reformed Free Publishing Association, 2013), 103–20, 192–93.

our right to meet there but decided against it. Our insistence on meeting in the church building would have stirred up more trouble. Besides, we were confident that all those who loved and had so consistently fought for the truth in the past would be willing to meet elsewhere until the matter of the church property was settled.

An announcement was made in the *Grand Rapids Press* that First Protestant Reformed Church would hold its services at the regular time in the Christian high school auditorium on the corner of Franklin Street and Madison Avenue. Everyone wondered how many would be at the services on Sunday. One man warned his children that they must not be disappointed if there were only a few. To his surprise as he approached the school, he saw numerous cars parked in the area and told his children, "Hurry or we won't get a seat." There were many members present. The auditorium was filled. True, to our sorrow many familiar faces of those whom we would have liked to see there were missing, but everyone felt a sense of relief that once more the struggle was over and peace was restored.[2]

---

2 Feelings still ran high even among those who remained with the Protestant Reformed Churches. In October 1954 Rev. Hanko received a call from one of our churches. One of the members wrote him the following letter, from which I have omitted the names:

Dear Rev.,
According to your letter, which was read in our church last Sunday, you said we should be free to write you if it would help you in making your decision. I would like to inform you that you received 22 of the 41 votes that were cast, and the main reason you got so many was because _____ [a strong opponent of De Wolf] was also on the trio. There is a faithful element left in this church that consider _____ a detriment to the church if he were here. Who we would like on the trio the consistory does not see fit to put on. The only minister we care to hear and the only one that preaches the gospel of Christ instead of hollering about conditions is _____ [a minister who supported Rev. De Wolf and later left the churches]. We have heard plenty of hollering here in the last years about conditions and that also in an entirely different viewpoint than what the De Wolf faction presents them. Hoping that you find it impossible to accept this call.

As in 1924, Rev. Hoeksema chose for his text that morning John 6:67: "Then Jesus said unto the twelve, Will ye also go away?" Once again we were reminded that we should continue to stand for the truth, for God's blessing rests only on those who are faithful even unto death.

The temporary loss of property had one big advantage. There were many in the large congregation of First church who were mere hangers-on, driftwood, as it were. They would remain with the church edifice no matter who took over. We were delivered from them, for it took determination to break away and meet in another place.

We wrote the De Wolf faction and asked if we could come to some amicable settlement. To that they responded that they would receive no correspondence from us unless we addressed them as the First Protestant Reformed Church of Grand Rapids, Michigan. That was more than we could grant. Our name meant more to us than all the property. That name not only designated us as the defenders of the truth for which the property was dedicated, but it also involved all the other churches who remained faithful with us. For our own sake, but also for the sake of the other churches, we had to defend our name as First Protestant Reformed Church of Grand Rapids, Michigan. This is also in harmony with article 28 of the church order, which says, "The consistory shall take care that the churches, for the possession of their property and the peace and order of their meetings, can claim the protection of the authorities; it should be well understood, however, that for the sake of peace and material possession they may never suffer the royal government of Christ over His church to be in the least infringed upon."[3]

When the matter of the property went to court, it was immediately evident to the judge which side was in the right, as he said

---

3 Church Order 28, in *The Confessions and the Church Order of the Protestant Reformed Churches* (Grandville, MI: Protestant Reformed Churches in America, 2005), 389.

to us in private, "This young whippersnapper wants to take the church away from you." The judge maintained, as did later the Supreme Court of Michigan, that the property had been dedicated to the Protestant Reformed truth.

Classis East met in September with two sets of delegates from First church. The classis had to face the question of which delegates would be recognized: those of the faction that De Wolf and his elder represented or those represented by me and my elder. Without much hesitation the latter were recognized as the proper delegates. De Wolf and his elder left the meeting, and those who sided with him also left.

Classis West met and, with the exception of Rev. Homer Hoeksema and his elder, decided to refuse to recognize the deposition of De Wolf and his supporters.

The Protestant Reformed Churches were sorely decimated. Some congregations, namely Bellflower, Manhattan, Orange City, Oskaloosa, Rock Valley, and Sioux Center, faded out completely. Others lost many members and struggled to survive. The denomination also lost seventeen ministers. First church was reduced to about forty percent of its former membership.

The question arises whether the controversy was necessary. To that there is only one answer. That so many left the denomination shows that they did not love the truth of God's sovereign grace sufficiently to fight for or even to die for it. I grant you that a number of them were misled, even deceived into leaving, as is evident from the return to the denomination of some. But those who were well aware of the issues involved are responsible for forsaking the truth of God's sovereign grace, whatever their motives may have been.

One may ask, "Could the split have been avoided? To that there is again but one answer, "No." Although many may have had personal grudges or left for other personal reasons, they were obviously not content among us. Defending the truth always demands sacrifice. He who will be Jesus' disciple must take up his cross and follow him. He who loves father or mother, sister or brother more than him is not worthy of him.

Did they leave because they agreed with the covenantal view of the liberated rather than with our view? Obviously that was not always the case. Almost immediately most of them turned their backs on Professor Schilder and joined the Christian Reformed Church. De Wolf and his followers continued under the name Orthodox Protestant Reformed, but in 1961 they too joined the Christian Reformed Church.

The Lord had spared and restored Rev. Hoeksema sufficiently to face that last struggle for the truth. One is reminded of the words of the patriarch Jacob concerning his son Joseph in Genesis 49:23–24: "The archers have sorely grieved him, and shot at him, and hated him: but his bow abode in strength, and the arms of his hands were made strong by the hands of the mighty God of Jacob."

Have the Protestant Reformed Churches and her members profited from the split? We certainly have, especially from the aspect that the truth of God's sovereign grace has been preserved among us. You can be sure that if we had continued without the purifying fires of 1953, today the churches either would no longer exist or would have no right of existence, because for the sake of peace we would have sacrificed the heritage God has entrusted to us.

There was also progress in our churches. This is particularly true regarding the beautiful truth of God's covenant as we confess it, the relationship between God and his people as a fellowship of friendship in which he is our sovereign friend and we are his peculiar possession and friend-servants.

We see, possibly more clearly than ever, that there are no conditions in God's covenant, no, not in the old dispensation and not in the new. God had privileged the church of the old dispensation to know him and to address him as Jehovah, the sovereign, eternally unchangeable, covenantal God. That name strongly emphasized the sovereign Friend / friend-servant relationship between God and Israel. God gave Israel his name Jehovah even while Israel was still under the bondage of the law. When Jesus came, he taught his disciples, among many other things: "After this manner therefore pray ye: Our Father which art in heaven" (Matt. 6:9). Imagine the surprise of those men who had been taught from infancy to address God as Jehovah. It must have taken some time before they could fathom that new address in their prayers. In fact, it took until Pentecost, when the Spirit of the glorified Christ was poured out in the church. This is the Spirit of adoption, who cries within the heart of the elect Jew, "Abba," and in the heart of the chosen Gentile, "Father." Together they could address God as "Abba, Father" (Gal. 4:6). Since we are adopted as sons and daughters in God's house and are heirs of everlasting salvation, God testifies by his Spirit in our hearts that we have the right to know him and call him our Father in Christ Jesus, our Savior and Lord.

This precious truth of the covenant seals to our hearts the one and only comfort for body and soul, in life and in death, that I am not my own. I belong to my faithful Savior Jesus Christ as part of the family of the living, covenantal God and as an heir of life eternal with him in glory. I will see him in all the riches of his holiness in Christ Jesus, will know him perfectly, and will delight in his praises forever and ever! Completely, with my whole being, I will live solely to his glory! God is GOD! Soli Deo gloria!

Chapter 24

FIRST PROTESTANT REFORMED CHURCH —1953 TO 1964

As the story continues in this chapter, the reader will get a sense that as the pastor's family had come to maturity, so had the churches. The churches started their first foreign mission field on the island of Jamaica. And while the churches mourned the deaths of their two leaders, Rev. Hoeksema and Rev. Ophoff, as related in this chapter, they were able to continue their work of being salt and light.

Throughout the entire conflict of the last few years our family stood firm and united. For that I could be very thankful. The struggle was very painful, since my closest friends had turned against us. Thus it was comforting and encouraging that at home we had peace and harmony. My wife left the meeting of the Adams School Mothers' Club when the De Wolf faction tried to take over. A number of women followed her and immediately reorganized as the true continuation of the Mothers' Club. Later the opposition pulled out of the grade school as one man, hoping thereby to make it impossible for the school to continue. But in spite of them the work carried on. There were fewer students but better harmony.

The question came up concerning the *Beacon Lights*, the magazine for Protestant Reformed youth, which had not been published since the split. Two committee members came to me and asked my opinion about starting *Beacon Lights* again. I asked them, "Do you have any money?" They admitted they had none, but they were determined to go out and seek donations. As soon as there was enough money for publishing an issue, they went to print. Soon *Beacon Lights* was coming to our homes right on schedule.

In August 1953 the young people's convention was hosted by First church. The chosen theme was "The Armor of God." On Tuesday afternoon of convention week Elaine and Jean Faber sat all afternoon on the church lawn waiting for delegates to register. No one came. It appeared as if there would be no convention. Yet the evening meeting was well attended. The delegates had waited until the evening to find out about their lodging. All went well until the banquet night. The committee figured the meal for the delegates and a few others. But many of the De Wolf group stormed in and acted as if they belonged there. The committee went out scouting for food, and all ended quite well.

The Hanko family in the Bates Street parsonage;
front left to right: Jennie, Rev. Hanko, Allie; back: Fred, Elaine, Wilma, Herman

Herm entered the seminary in the fall of 1952 under Rev. Herman Hoeksema and Rev. George Ophoff. In May 1953 Herm married Wilma Knoper. Theirs was the last wedding ceremony in First church before we temporarily lost the property.

Little did Herm realize that because of the shortage of ministers after 1953 he would soon be out preaching in the churches. The next year he was sent to Edgerton, Minnesota, to work there. Herm and Wilma were blessed with their first child, Ronald Herman, on August 30, 1954.

Fred had been going to Calvin College for the past three years but was weary of the erroneous teachings. In the fall of 1953 he had an opportunity to start teaching in a Christian school in Kalamazoo, which kept him occupied for the next two years.

In May 1955 Elaine went with the Pastoor family to Europe for twelve weeks. They took an ocean liner across the Atlantic. She and Thelma Pastoor enjoyed the leisurely trip both ways. They spent about three weeks in the Netherlands and then traveled south into France, Switzerland, and Germany.

On August 11, 1955, son Fred and Ruth Miersma were joined in the bond of holy matrimony and took up residence in an upstairs apartment on Franklin Street. Fred took up teaching in Adams school. In 1957 Fred and Ruth purchased a house on Adams Street, not far from the school.

At the June 1955 synod, Herm was made a candidate for the ministry. I remember the occasion very vividly, because I was so deeply impressed, even a bit shaken by the fact that he also would spend his life in the ministry in our churches. I felt somewhat as David did when he heard that Solomon would succeed him on the throne and said, "Who am I, O LORD God, and what is mine house, that thou hast brought me hitherto?" (1 Chron. 17:16).

Herm received and accepted a call to Hope Protestant Reformed Church in Walker, Michigan, and soon he and his family were settled there.

Nineteen fifty-six was the year a tornado swept through

Hudsonville and Standale. Herm and Wilma came to our house on Bates Street. I was in the building of First church. Although I knew that a storm had passed through between seven and eight o'clock, I was not aware of the severity of it, nor of the damage that it had done, until I came home at ten. Herm and Wilma had tried to get back to their home, the parsonage of Hope church on Wilson Avenue near Standale, but were barred by the National Guard. Especially in Hudsonville and in Standale, there was considerable damage and also a number of deaths. The day after the tornado, April 4, 1956, Wilma gave birth to their second son, Cornelius.

In August Allie, Jennie, and I accompanied Herm, Wilma, and Ron to Michigan's Upper Peninsula. Since Neal was a small baby, he was left behind with relatives. Herm preached in Grand Haven, Michigan, on Sunday. Monday we started out with a rented trailer to Northern Michigan. It was a relaxing, pleasant week of sightseeing, but there was one big drawback—it rained every day we were up there. The rain was not so bad for us, but it was far worse for families in tents with little kids. Can you imagine keeping kids in a small tent rainy day after rainy day? The novelty of such an experience soon wears thin. Little Ron kept us entertained on that trip. At Tahquamenon Falls his little feet moved in the direction of every puddle of water along the way.

In August 1957 we went with the Pastoor family to a couple of secluded cabins on Traverse Bay, which was an ideal place to relax. Actually we were not far from the main road, but a very narrow, winding trail through a dense woods led down to the cabins at the water's edge, giving us a feeling of seclusion.

We continued to go to that cabin for a few years. Usually Don and Jess Rietema accompanied the Pastoor family and stayed with them in their cabin. We had some very pleasant times together there. The first week the men would do a lot of fishing, as if our lives depended on it. The second week I would begin to relax. After getting up in the morning, we would have breakfast, and I would sit down to read. Soon I was sleeping. At noon we would have lunch, and again I would take a long nap. In the late afternoon and evening we visited, but we went early to bed.

One year Herm and Wilma, Fred and Ruth, and their kids stayed in tents near Lake Michigan. But that was a rainy week, so they packed up their wet belongings and came to our cabin. The Pastoor family was going home Saturday, so we rented their cabin for a week, and all of us stayed there. As I recall, it was a chilly week. It was cold on the lake fishing, and fishing was not too good. We felt comfortable near the heater.

One year while we were at the cabin my wife had a problem with her heart. She was filling with fluid and was very uncomfortable. Thursday we decided to go home. I called Dr. Avery and he came at once. Friday he came again. I asked him whether I should get help in the house for the meals. He answered, "Today we do nothing. Tomorrow we will see again." He had tried to relieve her of the fluid but failed. Saturday he came back and was much relieved because she had gotten rid of a lot of fluid and felt much more comfortable.

My stomach ulcer was still plaguing me, so my doctor planned stomach surgery for the summer of 1958. Dr. Carpenter was recommended, and he took away about seventy percent of my stomach. Before the surgery he reminded me that we were in the hands of the Almighty, and afterward when I wanted to thank him, he said, "Don't thank me, thank our God." He was a Lutheran but seemed to be very sincere about his religion.

I had expected that after the surgery, from which it took about six weeks to recover, I would henceforth be a semi-invalid. The opposite was true. I never felt better, and I could eat food that I had not been able to eat before.

On January 10, 1958, Elaine married Richard Bos. Fred and Ruth had moved to Adams Street, so Rich and Elaine moved into their house on Franklin. Elaine had a small home wedding, including only the family and a few of our closest friends. She did not want an ostentatious display in public. We were confronted with the problem of where we should draw the line if we began inviting the congregation. To this day I am still sorry that she did not have a bigger wedding. She is our only daughter who married, and we should have given her a better send-off. But it was a nice wedding. Ed Kooienga had arranged to furnish the music. Rich and Elaine came down the stairs and spoke their vows in front of the fireplace in the living room. Grandpa Griffioen wore a tie that had been in style many years ago.

Our summer vacations shifted from Grand Traverse Bay to the cottage of Clyde and Reka in Waupun, Wisconsin.[1] Reka always welcomed our coming, and Clyde was a pleasant fishing companion. Although we explored other fishing lakes, we were always directed back to that little lake where Clyde had his cottage. For me and Clyde it was an annual event to float down one of the rivers in the area. About seven o'clock in the morning the women took us to a place where we launched the boat. At three o'clock in the afternoon the women picked us up some miles down the river. We did very little fishing, but we had a good time just drifting along as the river twisted and turned through fields and hills.

We also stayed at Fox Lake, near Randolph, Wisconsin. There we were entertained at night by the crickets.

In the summer of 1962 we went to Loveland for a few weeks. Don and Jess Rietema went along. They had hardly ever, if ever, been out of Michigan. They enjoyed seeing the open prairie and the herds of cattle.

We returned by way of the Black Hills. Both Don and Jess enjoyed the high rocky cliffs, the faces of Mount Rushmore, and the scenery in general. We sat by the lake to eat lunch. Then the time had come for us to point the car in the direction of Michigan.

In 1963 Herm accepted a call to Doon, Iowa. There the

---

1 Clyde and Reka were Mrs. Hanko's brother-in-law and sister.

Hanko boys had a good taste of farm life in the Midwest. They enjoyed the open country and the trips to the Rock River. Whatever else they experienced, they would not forget the years spent in the little town of Doon. Two years later, in 1965, Herm accepted the call to be professor in the seminary and took up residence first in our old house on Bates Street and later in Walker, Michigan.

In 1963 my wife and I went to Jamaica. The previous year, Mr. Harry Zwak and Mr. Henry Meulenberg, both of whom still have descendants in the churches, had gone and come back with a favorable report. Next Mr. and Mrs. Meulenberg and Jennie and I were sent to investigate the field.

The work in Jamaica had a rather interesting beginning. In the late 1950s and early 1960s, the Protestant Reformed Churches had a broadcast to England over Trans World Radio from Monaco. The program came on at ten-thirty on Sunday morning, following the Billy Graham program. Although the program was directed toward England, it could be picked up in Germany and even beyond to Curacao and Tasmania down under. The broadcast brought a response of about seventy-five pieces of mail per year.

Among those letters was one from a Jamaican, who for some reason was in England and had picked up our message. He wanted to know more about our confessions, so I sent him a psalter. He responded that he wanted me to come to England. Since that was impossible, the mission committee offered to him that the churches would pay for his trip to Michigan when he returned to Jamaica. As a result of that contact we received a list of the membership of twenty-one congregations in Jamaica, with the request that we assume responsibility for them.

We wrote Rev. Frame, who was mentioned as minister of First Hill Church. He responded that if we believed in holiness, we should come. If not, we could forget it. Little did we realize that by holiness he meant Pentecostalism.

It was a rare experience to visit the island of Jamaica. I had felt for some time that our churches should reach out in a mission project, yet little did I think that a door would be opened for us in such a strange way in Jamaica. A small house had been rented for us in the town of Luca. Mrs. Frame and another woman were our cooks and housekeepers. They arrived at five o'clock in the morning and often stayed until eleven at night. We practically pushed them to their homes because we wanted a few moments alone to discuss the experiences of the day. Our beds were old and narrow but serviceable. The bugs came through the open windows, the watchdog barked most of the night, a donkey brayed just outside our room, and a rooster crowed at dawn. Our meals were skimpy, but they served their purpose.

The Sunday services lasted a long time. With Rev. Frame taking the lead and Mrs. Frame in charge of the singing, we could have gone on indefinitely. The enthusiasm was most encouraging.

Although we made the town of Luca our headquarters, we rented a car and tried as much as possible to visit the twenty-one "churches" that had so unceremoniously been made our responsibility. Our first visit was to "Rev." Thompson, who was also at the airport to meet us. We soon discovered that he had a small group of women in his "church" and that they also practiced voodoo. But what turned us off completely was his suggestion that if we would give him twenty-five thousand dollars, he would bring us most of the people in town. I told him he was too mercenary for us to deal with him. The sad part was that he also had rented an apartment for us, and we had to tell the landlady that he had not been authorized to do that.

We thought we could make a schedule and by strictly following it we could visit four or five churches in one day. Our first appointment was with Rev. Davis at nine o'clock in the morning. We arrived a bit early, but he already had his congregation assembled and the children enthusiastically singing. Their shoes were nicely lined up under their chairs. The singing went on and on. Finally, about ten o'clock he reached into his briefcase, pulled out an alarm clock, and after studying it carefully decided that it was nine o'clock. Then, evidently to show his great talent, he stood ranting and raving for a while. After that I spoke, explaining to them the purpose of our mission. Since our schedule was already ruined, we allowed two young men to give us a duet on their instruments. I recorded the music, and to their utter amazement, if not fear, I played it back for them. From that time on I had repeated requests for the box that spoke.

We decided that the best way to work was to plan only Sunday services. We would arrive at a certain church and give some of the women and children instructions to beat their drums. That was the signal to come to the tabernacle. In about an hour the other women had put on white dresses, the men had cleaned up a bit, and giving the drummers time to change their clothes, we soon had a service started. Our speeches and sermons were greeted with "Amens" and "Hallelujahs," which we hoped was an indication that they were listening.

We went back to Luca. One morning Mrs. Meulenberg got up and noticed red spots on her arms and legs. She had noticed a few before, but never that bad. She asked Mrs. Frame what she thought about them and received the simple answer, "Bedbugs." For a little while we had a revolution going. All three of my companions were ready to pack up and go to a motel. When I saw how serious they were, I issued an ultimatum. "You can all go, but I have work to do here. I want to know these people, and to know them, I have to live with them." That was that. We all stayed.

One Thursday we decided to go to Kingston. We wanted to see whether we could obtain a certificate for Rev. Frame that would give him the right to perform weddings. That he greatly desired, and we thought we would do him that favor. We stayed in what might be called a bed and breakfast, two upstairs rooms with a bath, that is, a spray over a tub. When we decided to retire the landlady said, "I have two dogs and two night boys, but lock your doors and windows."

We had planned to return to Luca on Friday but were held up by all kinds of technicalities. We were sent to one place where the doorkeeper wanted to know our business. Politely we were referred to "second floor, third door." There we once more explained our business. The man listened attentively and decided that we were in the wrong place. We should go so many blocks west, and so many blocks south, and there someone could help us. That went on and on, while we perspired along the way. Finally we met a woman of Spanish background. She listened to our tale of woe and told us to give her an hour to work on our problems. When we returned she had everything worked out for us.

In the meantime the people in Luca thought we had fallen among thieves and robbers and would never return. Needless to say, they were glad to see us back.

Rev. Frame planned a Sunday night service on the soccer grounds in the town. The Bishop (that is how he referred to me) would speak. We had quite a crowd. The interesting part was that I had often wondered if something like that would be possible. Now I was confronted with it. I spoke on Matthew 11:28: "Come unto me, all ye that labour and are heavy laden, and I will give you rest" and explained to them that a white man is just as black inside as anyone of the colored race. There seemed to have been quite a reaction in the town, but we met none of the reactionaries in the Sunday services.

All too soon our time was up. The morning of our departure dawned. We had failed to report to the airport to check our tickets for our return, so our seats were canceled. However, there was a British plane leaving in an hour. We dashed off to the motel and packed our baggage by throwing everything in willy-nilly. Then we had to get rid of our car and report at the plane. The plane was waiting for us, so we hastily stepped aboard and soon were going almost straight up into the sky. At customs I warned the inspector that our luggage was a mess, but he opened my suit-case, picked up socks and underwear that had tumbled out, hastily slammed it shut, and refused to open the rest.

A new field had opened, and the pictures of our trip to Jamaica attracted much interest in the Grand Rapids area. Mr. and Mrs. Meulenberg, my wife, and I also traveled by train to Protestant Reformed churches in the West to show the pictures. On the way to Loveland, Redlands, and Lynden we stopped in Doon and saw Herm's family. On the way to Lynden Jennie developed a cyst in her large bowel. She suffered great agony in San Francisco and in Lynden. We went to a doctor in Sumas who advised us to return home as soon as possible. We arrived home late on a Thursday evening. The next morning I called Ferguson Hospital. By two o'clock in the afternoon, my wife was in surgery.

The years of hard work, long hours, and bitter struggles were taking their toll on us, and much more so on Rev. Hoeksema. Especially the latest strife within the church had been extremely painful and difficult. He remarked at one time that the schism of 1953 was in some ways worse than the conflict of 1924 because the conflict in 1953 was brought about by men whom he had trained, whom he had trusted, and who turned against him and were out to destroy the church.

He no longer walked with a cane, but he was not as quick on his feet as before the stroke. His arm and hand were impaired so that his son Homer had to help him by typing his articles for the *Standard Bearer*. His voice had lost some of its resonance but was still strong. His cheerfulness that brought a pleasant smile to his face had faded and his former hearty laughter was no longer heard. It was evident to all of us that our pastor was aging. That was especially true when he first came to the pulpit on Sunday morning. Yet as he carried on in the service, he seemed to gain energy, and when he was preaching he seemed younger, once more filled with enthusiasm and zeal for the word. He always enjoyed preaching, possibly more than anything else.

His mind was still clear. Some in the audience feared that he might be unable to carry on through the entire service or that he might become confused; yet that never happened. In one instance he stated that he wanted to point out six facts. Some in the congregation wondered if he would be able to remember them and keep them in logical order. Yet step by step he continued through the six points without hesitation.

He continued to write in the *Standard Bearer* and also continued to teach in the seminary. Sometimes he had only one student, but he diligently taught and enjoyed the work.

He and I continued to enjoy a good working relationship. On Thursday I called him up for the sermon information for the bulletin, and he would say, "Well, you know what I'm going to preach on. Just make a theme and divisions." So I would, and he would usually use that too, except once he got on the pulpit and said, "Now the bulletin has this theme, but I changed it." Knowing he was preaching on the catechism and knowing his makeup, I could formulate his theme and points. I knew too what line we were on, whether he was emphasizing the covenant or justification, and I drew up the theme and divisions accordingly. The arrangement usually went well.

Some of the older ministers would offer their sermon outlines to the younger ministers, especially for busy times. Rev. Hoeksema did the same for me, but I refused. I knew from the start that would never work. I had to preach my own sermons my own way.

The opposition in the Christian Reformed Church had not lessened. We had an occasion to meet with four professors of Calvin seminary to discuss a small matter. On the way to the meeting Rev. Hoeksema remarked that he dreaded meeting those men. The business was transacted in short order, and we were ready to leave when one of the men invited us to have coffee with them. Rev. Hoeksema declined, but I suggested that we stay. We no more than sat down and all four of them accused Hoeksma of teaching a parallel predestination, that is, even as God chooses his elect purely by grace and in no way because of their works, so God also sovereignly reprobates the wicked, regardless of their evil deeds.

We asked them to prove that Hoeksema taught that. With an almost sarcastic smile one of them remarked that it was virtually self-evident. We insisted that they prove that that was his teaching, but they brushed all further discussion on the subject aside. We left there more than a bit unhappy.

A quotation from *Reformed Dogmatics* will show that a parallel predestination was by no means the conviction and teaching of our pastor. "Reprobation is the eternal and sovereign decree of God to determine some men to be vessels of wrath fitted unto destruction in the way of sin, as manifestation of his justice and to serve the purpose of the realization of his elect church."[2]

In the summer of 1958 Rev. Ophoff, the trusted colleague of Rev. Hoeksema who had resolutely supported him through all the struggles, suffered a stroke while on his way home from a trip to Canada. He and his wife stayed at a hospital in Toledo, Ohio, until he was able to make the trip home. Since Rev. Hoeksema desired to see him as soon as possible, we visited him in the hospital in Toledo, where we had the opportunity to talk with him, encourage him, and pray with him.

Mrs. Ophoff was a remarkable woman, a faithful wife and a kind, understanding mother. When they returned home, she took excellent care of her husband, even to the extent that she virtually collapsed under the burden. Rev. Ophoff never fully recovered. At times he felt a sense of guilt, wondering whether he had done the right thing by staying up those long nights to prepare articles for the *Standard Bearer* or lessons for the seminary. Yet at that time he had no choice, for the work awaited him.

He was gradually failing, but he never faltered in his

---

2 Herman Hoeksema, *Reformed Dogmatics*, 2nd edition (Grandville, MI: Reformed Free Publishing Association, 2004), 1:231.

assurance of God's promises that cannot fail. He remained a staunch defender of the truth he loved as long as he lived. He was taken home on June 12, 1962, at the age of seventy-one years, there to hear, "Well done, good and faithful servant, enter thou into the joy of thy Lord." When he departed, Mrs. Ophoff was in a rest home and hardly realized what had happened. Yet when she saw him in the funeral parlor, a single tear fell upon her cheek. Rev. Hoeksema preached the funeral sermon on Psalm 73:24: "Thou shalt guide me with thy counsel, and afterward receive me to glory." We all missed him.

In the early 1960s Mrs. Hoeksema's health began to fail. She had been a loyal help to her husband throughout all the years of their marital union. She also knew how to rear and guide her family, especially in times of storm and stress. Her husband depended on her sound judgment of people's characters more than most people realized. He did not appreciate simpering people or sugar-mouthed individuals, but he readily accepted and trusted a person at face value. He could not imagine that anyone would be dishonest or deceitful, since he himself was straightforward and said exactly what he thought, even at times quite bluntly.

It was a pleasure to visit Mrs. Hoeksema during the time of her failing strength. I was always greatly impressed by her deep spirituality and confident hope. On September 23, 1963, the Lord reached out to take her into the rest that remains for the people of God. Rev. Hoeksema sorely missed her. An important part of his life was taken from him, leaving a great void that could not be filled.

Gradually he was forced to give up his preaching, instructing in the seminary, and contributing to the *Standard Bearer*. He had always hoped to die in the harness, that is, to be taken away in the midst of his labors, but the Lord had something better in store for him. He had time for quiet reflection and fellowship with his Lord. He experienced possibly more than ever that through prayer and meditation God shares his own communal life with his saints in intimate covenantal fellowship. He could say with the sweet singer of old, "Yea, the secret of Jehovah / Is with those who fear His Name; / With His friends in tender mercy / He His covenant will maintain. / With a confidence complete, / toward the Lord my eyes are turning; / From the net He'll pluck my feet; / He will not despise my yearning."[3]

He had seen the churches recover from the shock of 1953 and in his own family experienced God's promise realized, "I will be a God unto thee, and to thy seed after thee" (Gen. 17:7). He was full of days and was ready to enter into the eternal rest. His departure was on September 2, 1965. He could say with the apostle Paul, "I have fought a good fight, I have finished my course, I have kept the faith: henceforth there is laid up for me a crown of righteousness, which the Lord, the righteous judge, shall give me at that day: and not to me only, but unto all them also that love his appearing" (2 Tim. 4:7–8).

His son Prof. Homer C. Hoeksema, who succeeded him as editor of the *Standard Bearer*, wrote:

My copy for this issue was not all ready yet when the tidings came early this morning, September 2, that the Lord had granted my beloved father the desire of his heart, that he would be delivered from this life, which is nothing but a continual death, into the glory of the inheritance incorruptible, and undefiled, and that fadeth never away.

His departure, though painful for and mourned by his dear ones and by all of us who came to know him as pastor, teacher, and friend, was not unexpected. For several months already the Lord had removed him from his active labors in our churches, and particularly in his beloved First Church. Besides, he himself had expressed

---

3 No. 415:7, in *The Psalter*.

the wish, when he was losing his ability to communicate a couple of months ago, that "I hope it won't be long." And now the Lord has delivered him. Last Sunday we at First Church prayed that when we could no longer reach him, the Lord might reach him with his Spirit and grace to comfort him. Well, the Lord certainly answered that prayer. He reached him and called him home.[4]

With the passing of those two giant defenders of the truth, another era of our history had come to a close. They had passed on the sword of the Spirit to the next generations. Also to those generations comes the word of the Lord: "Be strong in the Lord, and in the power of his might!" (Eph. 6:10). "Be ye stedfast, unmoveable, always abounding in the work of the Lord, forasmuch as ye know that your labour is not in vain in the Lord" (1 Cor. 15:58).

---

4 Homer Hoeksema, "Rev. Herman Hoeksema 1886–1965," *Standard Bearer* 41, no. 21 (September 15, 1965): 484–85.

Chapter 25

REDLANDS, CALIFORNIA— 1964 TO 1971

Hope Protestant Reformed Church of Redlands, California, warmly welcomed the Hanko family in 1964. The congregation's care of them became even more evident when Mrs. Hanko suffered a debilitating stroke a few months after their arrival. The congregation's fellowship and love sustained the family during that trying time.

I n 1964 at the age of fifty-seven, I felt that the time had come to make a change. I had received a call from our church in Redlands, California, for the second time since I had been in First church.[1] A smaller congregation would be less work and less tension, also for my wife. We thought we might be able to do a bit more traveling and thus have more contact with the other churches.

It seemed after our trip to Jamaica that it was comparatively easy to break with First church, where we had spent sixteen years, and go to Redlands. Since we had a large house on Bates Street and were informed that the house in Redlands was small, we had to dispose of everything that we could not use there.

On June 29, 1964, Allie, Jennie, and I pulled out, leaving

---

1 See appendix four for the call letter from Hope Protestant Reformed Church in Redlands, California.

behind the families of Fred and Ruth and Rich and Elaine. We stopped in Doon, where Herm was minister, and spent a little time with his family, then continued to California.

Already when we were coming down the Cajon Pass we saw and smelled the filthy, yellow smog that hung over the valley. How different that was from the 1950s, when looking down on Redlands from the hills, the whole area with all its color and flowers looked almost like the garden of Eden. And now, smog.

Herm flew to the airport in Los Angeles and then took a helicopter to San Bernardino so that he could install me. He preached on 1 Corinthians 9:16 with the theme "The Preacher's Necessity." I preached my inaugural sermon on Ephesians 6 with the theme "The Request for Intercessory Prayer."

We received a hearty welcome, but for the first six weeks I wondered whether I could take the change in climate. Every morning I woke up with a headache. When we made a trip to the mountains to escape the smog, the situation upon our return was even worse. But we did adjust, and we learned to live with smog. The warmth and friendliness of the members of the congregation made up for any breathing problems that we might have had.

Sunday mornings after the service we were invited with the whole Feenstra family to the home of Thys and Jeanette. Sunday evenings we were invited to the Gritters, the Gaastras, the Van Uffelens, the Van Voorthuysens, or the Van Meeterens. My wife was urged to become a Sunday school teacher, which she also enjoyed.

But the strain of the past years had taken its toll. My wife had been repeatedly in Blodgett Hospital during our stay in Michigan. She had had her varicose veins removed; she had suffered occasional kidney infections; and from time to time her heart had made breathing difficult. She also had occasional seizures, for which she took Dilantin. Very often she complained of tiredness, yet she had forced herself to carry on.

Looking back, one wonders how much of a strain the 1953

controversy was on her. Always in the past, as well as during the difficult time in Redlands, she had shown her confidence in me and my decisions. I recall riding along a slippery road in Godfrey Canyon in Montana one night. Suddenly we met a sharp turn over the railroad tracks. Because it came so unexpectedly and because it was so slippery, I said, "I can't make it." She responded, "Oh, yes, you can." And we did. Her confidence in me meant a great deal to me in our life together.

Sometimes I wonder what would have happened in the days before 1953 if she and the family had not stood so firmly with me. I would never have joined the opposition, and the burden would have been unbearable. Throughout the controversy we had peace and harmony at home, but the strain of those years was not good for her already poor health.

When we left Grand Rapids, Dr. Avery said that he would not allow us to choose a doctor in Redlands, but that he would have one ready to take care of us. He chose Dr. Fallows, who was very ready to come over any time we needed him.

About six months after we came to Redlands, one would say just enough time for the congregation to get to know her, my wife had a stroke. How suddenly, even in a split second, all our hopes and plans were shattered. The stroke occurred on Tuesday morning, the first week of the new year. We had finished breakfast, and I had suggested that we do a bit of shopping for the consistory visit scheduled for that evening.

My wife went to the bedroom to get ready to go. I sat in the breakfast nook waiting for her to return. It seemed that she was staying away a long time, so I got up to see what was delaying her. She lay unconscious on the floor by the bedroom window. I thought it was a heart attack and called the doctor to inform him. He came immediately. He took one look and informed me that it was a stroke. Already then her left arm was limp. We laid her on the bed and waited for the ambulance. I followed with my car as they took her to the San Bernardino Catholic Hospital.

It is difficult to describe the next four weeks. Jennie returned to consciousness but could not talk. We tried to have her write, but that also was impossible. From day to day we saw no change. The hospital gave us no information. To all appearances she either would not live long or would remain a total invalid. It was only after the twenty-third day that she seemed to rally and show improvement.

Herm and Wilma came out at once. Wilma took over in the home and Herm preached for me. Charlie and Sena Van Dyken, my sister and her husband, also came for a short visit.

After Herm and Wilma left, Ruth came with two of her children, Carrie and Freddie, to spend some time with us. After Ruth left, Elaine came with her two youngest. After a few weeks Rich came with the two older kids. At a time like that one realizes in a very special way how wonderful it is to have children who are willing to step in and help in time of need. The very fact that they were there made the load so much easier to bear. That meant so much to my wife and me, and also to Allie.

After twenty-eight days Jennie was ready to come home. One can imagine what an adjustment that took for her, who had always been so very active. The forced inactivity was a severe trial for her during the entire nine years that she was still with us, yet she rarely complained. She had to sit and watch us and be content with nothing more than her daily exercises. For some time we went to therapy, which gave her so much improvement that she could walk with a cane.

The congregation was very understanding and helpful. More than one person expressed their appreciation for getting to know her as she was before the stroke. Many offered their services. Thys and Jeanette brought over a wheelchair. Don Feenstra, son of Thys and Jeanette, would stop in on his way from work, sit down in a chair right by the door, chat a little while, and then go on. Sometimes he would call that he had corn or some other vegetable fresh from the garden.

My wife took physical therapy from a woman who was a Seventh Day Adventist. She also took speech therapy at Redlands University. Little Barb Van Voorthuysen, daughter of Everett and Audrey, would sit by her and try to help her. She would say, "Say Barbie," and my wife would try to say it. At first Jennie could say nothing but "pretty" whenever she tried to talk. Later she was able to use a few words, but actually her ability to speak and write never came back. She had a keen memory, knew exactly what was going on, but could not express herself.[2] The fact that she was impaired on her left side was a trial, but it was far worse that she could not communicate.

Rev. and Mrs. Hanko visiting their son Herm and his family in Doon, Iowa, in 1964 after her stroke.

We communicated with her by signs and by trying to figure out what she meant. That was difficult, because sometimes it would be so simple and so obvious. We would be sweating and struggling and trying to guess, but we were nowhere near figuring out what she was trying to say. Sometimes she got the impression we did not want to understand. I could understand that too, because it was so obvious when it finally did come out what she meant.[3]

---

2   This inability to communicate is called aphasia.

3   A letter Rev. Hanko wrote to his son in September of 1963 reads as follows: "Mom is very discouraged. Often she cries, often she expresses her eagerness to die, often she feels that she is nothing but a burden to all of us. At times she is cheerful, at times she puts forth a new valiant effort, but she would like very much to withdraw herself from company—because as she says, she can't talk anyway. It certainly takes a lot of grace to bear such a cross. Gradually she feels that she will never talk again, never use her hand again, never be of any good to any of us. And that makes it so very hard. But she does know, and I'm sure she rests in the fact that God's way is always good."

After we were in Redlands a few years I had surgery for a hernia and prostate problems. Once again Herm and Wilma willingly came out to be with us, Herm to fill the pulpit in my absence and Wilma to help in the home. Herm was then teaching in the seminary and was no longer in Doon, Iowa. The family lived in the First church parsonage on Bates Street until their house was built near Hope church.

I had gotten the hernia when we were packing books in Michigan to send them by mail to Redlands. We placed all the books in the same size boxes. Each box weighed about seventy pounds. While I was carrying a box to a truck, I felt the hernia break through. As time went on it became increasingly worse, especially while I stood to preach. The time had come to do something about it. The doctor was sure that it was also the right time to take care of the prostate, although I had sensed no problem there. Some years later, while in Bradenton, Florida, I was advised to have my prostate checked. I was told that the doctor in Redlands had done a good job.

I was in a semi-private room in the hospital in Redlands. Next to me was a man with a very bad heart, but he refused to remain in bed. He was always roaming about the room, even at night, cautiously looking for the nurse to be sure to be back in bed when she came into the room. One day he went out on the porch. There he had a heart attack and was bellowing like a bull. The nurses got him back in his bed, but no one was eager to give him CPR. He did come to after a bit. The head nurse said to him, "Heaven doesn't want you, hell isn't ready for you, and we have to put up with you." A few days later he was sent home.

A skeptic arrived as my next roommate. Earlier he had refused to be in the same room with a minister. The head nurse told him that there was no private room available for him and that he should be content and wait for a room where he was. Reluctantly he consented, but he never said much. He did have to listen to those who came to read to me from the Bible or from some religious literature. One day after someone left, he remarked, "Dry as dirt, but keep it up." After a few days a private room was available, but when they told him he could move he said, "Don't take me away from my buddy. I want to stay here." He was moved to a private room, but later he sent me a subscription to a San Bernardino daily newspaper. What could have gone on in that mind?

I made my regular visits to Classis West and to the annual meeting of synod. The only synod meeting I missed was in 1965, the year my wife had the stroke.

From 1967 to 1969 I stayed with Fred and Ruth whenever classis met in the Midwest. They had moved from Michigan to Doon, where Fred taught. They later returned to Michigan, where Fred taught in Hope school.

I recall particularly one winter in Doon when the snow was piled fifteen to eighteen feet along the roads. When the wind blew the roads were closed by drifts. Those storms seemed to always come on Thursdays, which caused school to close for the rest of the week.

I also recall one winter when I stayed with Rev. Jason Kortering in Hull, Iowa. On a Sunday afternoon an elder came into the consistory room and said, "We are due for a heavy snow storm. The geese came to my farm, ate their fill, and headed south." That evening we called the airport and were told that all planes were on schedule. The next morning Rev. Kortering started out with me to Sioux Falls, South Dakota, while the snow was steadily falling. At Rock Rapids we called the airport again and were informed, "All planes are on schedule." When we came to Sioux Falls it was snowing so hard and the snow was so deep that we could not even reach the terminal. I stayed over in Sioux Falls, while it took Rev. Kortering three hours to get home again.

Then there was the time that I never made it to Iowa. When I arrived in Denver for a layover, I was informed that the airport in Sioux Falls was fogged in. I called Bill Griess from our Loveland church, took him and his wife out for dinner, and stayed there for the night. The next day the airport was still fogged in, so I returned to Redlands. Mission not accomplished.[4]

On another occasion classis met in South Holland, Illinois. Thys Feenstra and I arrived by plane over Chicago but could not land because of a tornado sweeping through the south side. Our plane went to Kansas City, where we had supper. At four in the morning we arrived in Chicago, where members of South Holland were patiently waiting. After an hour or two of sleep we went to classis. That evening we finished about ten o'clock. We had to help the two delegates from Lynden meet up with their wives, who had gone to Grand Rapids, so Thys and I drove the men to Grand Rapids, arriving there about five o'clock in the morning. I slept a few hours but got up in time to see the grandkids off to school. That afternoon we managed to get a plane to Denver, but in Denver we had to wait until midnight before we could get a plane to San Bernardino. Another night without sleep. Jennie had stayed by Mrs. John Van Uffelen while I was gone, so I picked her up and then went to bed. Thys discovered that Jeanette had gone to Oceanside in southern California. He drove out there, but when he arrived he was so tired that he fell asleep in his chair with a cup of coffee in his hand.

When we went to synod by car, we usually went with the three of us—Jennie, Allie, and I. When we went by plane, my wife and I would go. Her wheelchair went with us. We usually stayed with Rich and Elaine as long as synod met. It could be quite warm in Michigan at the time of synod, but we always enjoyed the visit.

Every year we made a trip to Lynden, Washington, either for church visitation or for pulpit exchange or for both. On those trips we saw much of the northern California coast, the Oregon coast, Crater Lake, and parts of Washington. My wife enjoyed

---

4 These anecdotes are from events that took place during visits to the Midwest for meetings of Classis West.

traveling, especially with the Feenstras. Jeanette understood her fully. They would sit in the back seat and point to some landmark or just smile knowingly at one another.

I always enjoyed going to Lynden. Although I never was minister there, that congregation was always close to my heart. We saw the people when the congregation was still a small, struggling group without a minister and hardly able to survive. Every time they received a decline to a call, their hopes would once more be shattered. On one occasion of our visit they were about to give up. When I read another decline, they were so disappointed that they sat and wept. They were not able to sing throughout the service. Afterward one said, "We worked so hard to keep our children in the church, and now no minister wants to come here." Eventually Rev. Bernard Woudenberg did take the call and did a lot to build up that congregation. Today they have their own church edifice and are well established.

While I was in Redlands I had an occasional classical appointment in one of the churches of Classis West. While I was away my wife stayed with Thys and Jeanette Feenstra or with George and Epka Joostens. The Joostens were very good to her and treated her with utmost care and concern.

I recall one appointment in Aberdeen, South Dakota. I was so weary then that I wrote to Rich and Elaine that I was coming to their house a week before I filled the appointment. I wanted no one to know that I was there, because I wanted to rest. As soon as the plane was airborne I fell asleep and did not wake up until we arrived in Chicago. That week of rest did me a lot of good. After my stay with Rich and Elaine I stayed two weeks with Mr. Hauck in Aberdeen.

When I came to Redlands, there were not many young people, but there was a younger generation gradually growing up. As soon as it was feasible, I took seven young people by Greyhound bus to the young people's convention in Grand Rapids. That was a healthy experience for them, for they realized that there were many more young people in other churches who were Protestant Reformed. Some of the girls have made their permanent homes in Grand Rapids.

I enjoyed my ministry in Redlands, and for the most part it was also well received. Not too long after I left, a school was started and is still doing well today.

After seven years the time had come to make a change. We went to Redlands in June 1964 and left there in October 1971. I had received a call from Southwest the year before. I had had the letter of acceptance in my pocket, but circumstances made me decide to tear up the letter and write a decline. A year later I felt free to go to Hudsonville.[5]

Throughout the years, some of the old pillars of the Redlands church have entered into the rest. I am thinking of the Gaastras, the senior Van Voorthuysens, the Van Meeterens, the Vander Veens, and the Van Uffelens. One generation comes and another goes, and God's covenant continues from age to age the same.

---

5 See appendix five for the call letter from Hudsonville Protestant Reformed Church.

Chapter 26

HUDSONVILLE PROTESTANT REFORMED CHURCH—1971 TO 1978

The years 1971 to 1978 saw Rev. Hanko do a great deal of traveling on behalf of the churches. The denomination also celebrated its fiftieth anniversary during those years. While Rev. Hanko does not mention the occasion in his memoirs, it must have been a joyful one for him, but his joy was surely tempered by the grief of losing his dear wife, whose death is recounted in this chapter.

Thys and Jeanette Feenstra rode with us from Redlands to Hudsonville, giving us the advantage of not having to travel alone and giving them the opportunity to visit their family in Michigan. Not long after we arrived in Hudsonville our furniture also arrived. Then it was a matter of unpacking and getting settled. Once more the whole family was together in the Grand Rapids area, including Herm and Fred and their families.

It was especially nice for my wife to be near the grandchildren and to see them again. She knew that she would not have many more years with us, and she was glad to have that short time with the family. No noise was too great for her as long as the grandchildren were having a good time.

Shortly after coming to Hudsonville, two young men of the congregation were killed in separate accidents. I officiated at both funerals.

I also was called back to Redlands for two funerals there. I had very few funerals during my stay in Redlands, but Mrs. Ade Van Meeteren, mother of Chuck Van Meeteren and grandmother of Mrs. Don De Vries, died and I went to officiate at her funeral. It was interesting to stay in the home of the deceased and see how the most intimate acquaintances came to the home to meet the family. It seems to me that that is so much nicer than going through the difficult period of endless visitors at the funeral home, often those who are virtual strangers to the family. What also appealed to me was that the whole congregation, including the men, came out for the funeral service, which was at eleven o'clock in the morning. Afterward lunch was served at the home of the deceased, and everyone was expected to be there.

A lot of our people were moving into the Hudsonville and Jenison areas, so the congregation grew steadily. The work was enjoyable there and the consistory was most cooperative. One could never escape the fact that Rev. Gerrit Vos had spent some years in the Hudsonville congregation and had definitely put a lasting stamp on it. Throughout the years, even to this day, the older people liked to speak of something that Rev. Vos said or did.

In 1972 I was given permission to go to Jamaica to encourage and help Rev. Lubbers in his labors there. On my way out there I intended to take the Jamaican plane from Chicago to Montego Bay. The plane started out about ten o'clock in the morning, but we were hardly airborne before an engine gave out. The pilot landed rather abruptly. The man sitting next to me said, "They almost killed us." I answered, "It wasn't that bad." In the terminal that man stayed close to me, possibly thinking that "in unity there is strength." When I went for lunch, he went along. About two o'clock a call came over the intercom that the Jamaican passengers should go to the Delta desk. Soon after we arrived there, we were informed that there would be no room for us on that flight. The man responded, "That's twice."

Between three and four o'clock we boarded a flight to Jamaica.

But we were no more than airborne and the announcement came over the intercom, "This plane will not stop in Atlanta, as intended, but at Jacksonville." My new friend responded, "That's three times. I'm going back to Chicago." I asked him whether he did not have a God in whom he put his trust. I told him that if God wanted me to go to Jamaica I would get there, no matter what. He said, "Never mind. Don't start that kind of talk." From that time on he was silent, but at Jacksonville he disappeared, and I continued on my way without him.

Rev. Lubbers was looking forward to my coming and was sadly disappointed when I did not arrive as scheduled without an explanation of my delay. I had requested that he be paged at the airport, but he never heard it. Since I did not know my exact destination, I was not allowed to leave the airport, but I called a taxi driver who agreed to take me to a hotel in the city. The next morning I visited the post office to get the Lubbers' address. They knew only the general direction. We headed that way, and when we got close, we stopped at a store. I walked in and called, "Does anybody here know Rev. Lubbers?" A lady in the store who was also a neighbor of the Lubbers told the taxi driver how to find the residence. How surprised Rev. and Mrs. Lubbers were to see me! If I had suddenly dropped out of the sky, they could not have been more elated. Rena was raking the lawn. She dropped the rake, did not even greet me, but ran into the house crying, "George, George, Case is here!" Soon we were busy visiting the various churches, as well as teaching his students.

One Sunday evening we were coming home from a church service when the engine of our car began sputtering. Every time we climbed a hill the sputtering increased. Going downhill we had no trouble. That part of the island was not very safe, especially not for white folks who had money on them. So we sputtered along, breathing a prayer that we might make the next grade. We were thankful when we arrived home again.

I should tell about an interesting experience in one of Rev.

Eliot's churches.[1] The church was on the eastern section of the island. To get there we had to get off the main road and ride five miles along an almost impassable road full of deep ruts. Every time we dropped into a rut we wondered whether we would pull out. After that there was a forty-five-minute climb to the church. A young woman, eight months pregnant, a Miss Hill, took it upon herself to lead us to our destination. She climbed easily along those rocks. When we arrived, the church mother set out two chairs for us and told the women to keep away from us. When all was arranged in the tabernacle, the mother came out and said to the women, "Come, come." So the women went in. It was evident that that mother was going to be sure she had charge of the situation, so I told Rev. Lubbers to go to the pulpit at once and conduct a formal service.

The reason we had come was that Rev. Eliot had complained that the group did not want him to preach for them anymore. We were there to investigate what the problem really was. A thunderstorm came up out of the sea. Immediately the mother ordered me away from the open window and moved my briefcase closer in as well. She wanted to remain in authority in her church. She also requested that we ordain two men who in her estimation had come to "the state of grace." That we refused to do.

It took a lot of questioning. We even called aside Rev. Eliot with some of the men of the group. Finally the information seeped out that Rev. Eliot was chasing away the young people of the church. It took a bit for Rev. Eliot to admit why that charge was brought against him, but finally it came out that the group had love feasts at which everyone enjoyed curried chicken and joined in a lot of singing. Emotions rose as the tempo increased, until two of the opposite sex would wander off to the tabernacle or to the manse or to the woods to engage in sexual improprieties.

---

1   Rev. Eliot was a minister in the Jamaican churches.

That we strongly condemned, agreeing with Rev. Eliot that those things ought not be. We insisted that either they had to be willing to have Rev. Lubbers come there at regular intervals, or we would shake their dust from our feet. After a few days we were informed that they preferred the latter. No more was heard from them.

On the last Sunday I was in Jamaica we both preached in the Waterworks congregation, Rev. Lubbers in the morning and I in the afternoon. There was a couple with three children who had walked three miles to church in the morning and three miles back home. We told them that we would pick them up for the afternoon service, but by the time we arrived at their home they had long ago left for church. During the service we had a severe electrical storm, and I had to quit preaching for a while. We all huddled in the center of the building and sang psalter numbers. When the storm was over, the elder reminded the congregation of what I had already said, repeating it almost verbatim, and even adding parts of Rev. Lubbers' sermon of the morning. After the service we offered to take the family with three children home, but we had water in our gas tank, so they were forced to walk home.

Some of the older folks in Jamaica were taught the five points of Calvinism. When one woman was asked what Calvinism meant to her, she was able to respond, although she had little or no formal education, "I am nothing but a poor, lost sinner. God always loved me as one of his sheep. Christ died for his sheep, so also for me. He gave me faith, so that now I believe in him. He will always care for me, protect, and watch over me as one of his sheep." In her own way she did include all five points. Not a bad way to know Calvinism.

For two and a half years my wife enjoyed her new surroundings in Hudsonville, but gradually the full reality dawned on her that no amount of exercise could change her condition. More and more she became discouraged with the effort, but we felt that as long as she was trying she would not give up completely.

Going to church was difficult for her, especially because the crowds bothered her, and she could not communicate. She did attend the adult Bible class until the very end. On the last evening that she attended she suggested that we sing psalter number 17. One of the last two Sundays she attended church, she complained, "I can hardly do it anymore." We also realized that it was getting very hard for her but did not want to discourage her from going.

On Thursday evening, March 6, 1973, she complained that she was terribly sick. I tried to get a local doctor, but none was available. It became evident that she might soon lose consciousness, so we called the ambulance, which took her to Blodgett Hospital. Dr. Avery was there waiting for her. He gave a complete report of her case history to the resident doctor without any notes before him. I was amazed in what detail he reported on all that had happened since he first saw her in 1948. Afterward he said to me, "I made one mistake. I said that you had gone to Wisconsin. I meant California."

On Friday evening he told me that my wife's heart was so severely damaged that she could not possibly recover. A year before that, he had called me into his office to show me X-rays of her heart. At that time he had said, "Have you ever seen a heart as large as that? That is going to give us trouble."

I urged Dr. Avery, if there was no possibility of recovery, to make the end as easy for her as possible. I did not want him to hook my wife up with all kinds of artificial means of survival, if it was hopeless anyway. During the night from Friday to Saturday the nurses started her heart again. Again I urged the doctor not to add any unnecessary suffering. He gave the order to the nurses to let her rest as quietly as possible. That same evening she left us to enter her heavenly home.

The next few days were almost like a nightmare. It was nice that people came and expressed their condolences, but that was so wearisome that I gave a sigh of relief when it was all over.

What I did appreciate was that the night my wife died, the family went to the home of Fred and Ruth, where we sang psalter numbers. I also appreciated that on Sunday morning Professor Hoeksema preached on Hebrews 4:15–16: "For we have not an high priest which cannot be touched with the feeling of our infirmities; but was in all points tempted like as we are, yet without sin. Let us therefore come boldly unto the throne of grace, that we may obtain mercy, and find grace to help in time of need." That sermon was very comforting. I also was glad that after the funeral we could be together as a family in the basement of Hudsonville church, where the ladies served us supper.

My wife was sixty years old when she died. She had had a hard life. Since she was twelve years old she had had a weak heart, but she was still required to do much of the work in caring for a family of thirteen. Married life was not always easy either. There was not only our growing family, but also the near-poverty conditions in the early years of our marriage. Besides, a certain extra responsibility rests on the shoulders of a *Juffrouw*, or minister's wife.

So Allie and I were left with just the two of us, but the Lord has always provided, even in an amazing way. For a few years, Ann Griffioen came in one day a week to clean the house. Allie had a babysitting job in a home where the mother had died and left the husband with three children. Later she worked a year and a half in the kitchen of Brookcrest Nursing Home washing dishes. After that she had another job of babysitting for a lady who worked and needed someone to watch the little ones.

In the summer of 1974 I was asked to make another trip to Jamaica, that time with Rev. John Heys. Because that was so soon after my wife's death, Allie accompanied me.

When we left I picked up my tickets, assuming that Allie's was included with mine. When we arrived at Kent County Airport, I had no tickets for Allie. I could get tickets to Chicago, but not beyond. When we took our seats in the plane, a man came to sit across from us who said that he had overheard us at the airport. He wanted to pay for Allie's ticket to Jamaica. I told him that that would not be necessary, since I was meeting Rev. and Mrs. Heys in Chicago, who would help me pay for the ticket if I lacked the money. Upon our arrival in Chicago, the man accompanied us out of the plane and down the concourse, insisting that he was going to buy a ticket for Allie. Since I did not know what he was up to or why he was willing to buy her a ticket, I insisted that it was not necessary. But he kept following us. Finally I stopped and told him that we were not going on until he left us. Rev. Heys helped me buy a ticket for the rest of the trip.

FELLOWSHIP HALL CHURCH

One of Rev. Hanko's trips to Jamaica

We met Rev. and Mrs. Heys in Chicago, since they had gone there earlier to see her mother. Rev. Heys requested and received from the airline a pass to sit in the cockpit of the plane on the trip to the island, so he sat in the cockpit from Chicago to the Bahamas, and I sat in the cockpit from the Bahamas to Jamaica. The captain kindly explained the various instruments to me while in flight and told me to watch when we were making our descent.

We rented a motel room and a car at Montego Bay. We were supplied with two maids who made the meals and cleaned the rooms. Soon we were under way visiting the churches.

Allie Hanko and Rev. and Mrs. Heys make their way to Sunday worship.

One task that was entrusted to us was the ordination of Kenneth Brown and Leonard Williams as ministers in the Jamaican churches. Rev. Heys made a trip to Shrewsbury to pick up five women, relatives of Brown, who was to be ordained in Fort Williams. Rev. Frame read the installation form. At the close of the service various people stepped forward to make a speech of congratulations. Especially the women from Shrewsbury became very emotional and began singing and swaying. In fact, they almost pushed Mrs. Heys and Allie out of the tabernacle, so that Allie grabbed hold of Mrs. Heys. We decided that that was enough, so we told Rev. Frame to end with the benediction. He called the people to order and pronounced the benediction, and then Rev. Heys and I left. How long the ceremony lasted in the tabernacle we never found out.

One Sunday Rev. Heys and I decided to join a service that was being conducted by Alvin Beckford. We quietly took our places in the back seat. He was preaching on the same text that I had used for the installation of Rev. Brown. We both were amazed how well he had remembered my sermon and did not mind at all that he was repeating it. It showed that the Jamaicans for the most part could not read well, but they had learned to listen and to retain what they heard.

Rev. Heys and I also supervised the ordination of Leonard Williams in Belmont by the sea. The congregation had a very poor tabernacle, consisting of nothing more than a few posts with palm branches for covering. Since it was raining, the water was dripping down our backs. I suggested to an elder that we have another meeting place, and he offered his home. As we walked to his home we walked through the weeds, getting our suits wet and muddy. There the living room was set up for the service. Rev. Eliot requested that Leonard get down on his knees next to the table. Throughout the reading of the form, Leonard was there behind the table. When Rev. Eliot came to the point of asking the questions, he leaned over to Leonard, who lifted his head to answer. That continued with all the questions. Finally, he was allowed to get up and sit on a chair.

Later Alvin Beckford was ordained in Cave Mountain, and Trevor Nish in Lacovia, but we did not participate in those ordinations.

During our stay on the island we had two funerals. One day we were informed that Kenneth Brown's sister, who lived in the United States, had been beheaded and that her body was being shipped to her mother's home. The funeral was planned for a Sunday, so Rev. Heys and I agreed to take the service if they could have it at seven o'clock in the morning. They agreed to that. After the service the casket was placed on a pickup truck and taken somewhere to the hills where it was buried.

One Sunday morning while Rev. Heys was preaching in Waterworks, a man was called out of church. He came back, took his seat, and sat through the service. After the service, he asked if Rev. Heys would take the funeral for his seven-year-old boy. Rev. Heys looked at him in amazement. "Yes," he said, "I was informed during the service that my boy who was in the hospital had died." The next day Rev. Heys and I went to conduct the funeral. We found that the casket was not yet ready. The ladies in the church had washed the body, and others were making the casket. About three in the afternoon they were ready for the service. We went up an incline and set the casket on a chair, and the father stood by the casket. Rev. Heys preached the funeral sermon. That man's wife was with the women who stood to the side, availing themselves of every opportunity to sing.

Then we went to the top of the hill where a grave had been dug. I conducted the committal service. The father wanted to say a few words, but the neighbors thought it was growing late and started shoveling in the dirt. I took the man by the arm and walked down the hill with him. I said to him, "You have not cried since your boy died, have you?" He shook his head. I asked him, "Why didn't your wife stand by the casket with you?" He answered, "It's not her boy." I suggested to him that he go off somewhere by himself and have a good cry. "And," I added, "tell God how you feel. He will understand." A few days later he came to me and whispered that he had cried. Strange! Those people were often so emotional, and yet at funerals they seemed to hide their feelings.

The time had come to return home. The air was very turbulent on the way home, and we had quite a bumpy ride. Most of the way it was like riding on a rough road.

The same year I went to Lynden for a few weeks. Since I was alone in Lynden's parsonage, the daughters of Ralph and Etta Vander Meulen called every day to inquire about my welfare. Many of the congregation either brought in food or invited me over so that my main meals were usually supplied.

Hudsonville Protestant Reformed Church continued to grow. Every week it became increasingly difficult to find seats in the auditorium. We were soon compelled to place some of the people in the basement. Later closed-circuit television was installed for those who sat downstairs, but that could be only a temporary measure. Almost everybody talked about building a new church.

We looked at a piece of land off 32nd Avenue, which is the present site of Hudsonville church, but the farmer who owned that entire section and raised corn on it demanded an exorbitant price. So the congregation bought land by the water tower on 36th Avenue. No one was happy with that, especially because New Holland Street did not yet run through and the people coming from the south had to go way around to get there. Then someone bought the entire cornfield off 32nd Avenue for condominiums. He was interested in having people move into the condos, so he offered to sell the land at the top of the hill, exactly the piece of land the congregation had wanted to buy originally.

A ground-breaking ceremony was held and the work began. The congregation had an opportunity to sell its old building, so the public high school auditorium was rented, and we met there until the church was built. Thanksgiving Day in 1977, the cornerstone was laid, and a short ceremony was held.

At first there had been some objection to building a new church. Some of the older members were attached to the church edifice where they had worshiped for so many years. The architect suggested that we acquire as much help from the members of the congregation as possible. That had a very favorable result, for even those who had been opposed felt that the new building belonged to them because they had done some work on it.

In every congregation there are quiet, unassuming members of the church who are virtually unnoticed, yet are a real blessing to others. They are often wives who are submissive to their husbands, yet in a kindly way guide their mates with spiritual wisdom. As mothers in the home they teach by both word and example. They often have a word for the weary, encouragement for the distressed, and a pot of soup or some baked goods for the sick and aged.

One of those saints had seen her children grow up and leave the shelter of the home. She had experienced the loss of her husband and was now in a home for the aged. One morning I found her poring over her psalter. To my inquiry, she answered that she was reading the Lord's Day on which the minister was to preach the following Sunday. She said that her memory was so bad that if she did not read the Lord's Day every day she would not be prepared to listen properly on Sunday.

I often saw her in the audience listening so intently that, unbeknownst to herself, she was sitting on the very edge of her seat. That alone is an inspiration for any minister. Besides, what an untold blessing those women are for their children and grandchildren as well as for others. Those saints may far exceed us in glory.

Chapter 27

WORLD TOUR OF 1975

In her book A Watered Garden, *Gertrude Hoeksema refers to the 1970s as a time of outreach for the Protestant Reformed Churches.[1] Some of our contacts included those from New Zealand and Australia who were unhappy with the pastors coming from the Reformed Theological College in Geelong, Australia. Other contacts included those of the Gospel Literature and Tract Society in Singapore. Those who desire to read more about this trip can consult the late 1975 and early 1976 issues of the* Standard Bearer.[2]

In 1975 I took a world tour with Prof. Homer Hoeksema and his wife, Gertrude, and in the meantime did some work for the churches. We had a layover in Los Angeles. Homer and Trude left me, my granddaughter Beth Bos, and her friend Verna Klamer temporarily on another flight to visit some islands in the southern Pacific. Beth was paged to have some error in her tickets corrected. When that was taken care of, we left for Hawaii. We arrived in the hotel in Hawaii about six o'clock in the evening, which was midnight in Hudsonville. After dinner everyone was ready for bed.

The next morning we took in some of the scenery, but in the

---

1 Gertrude Hoeksema, *A Watered Garden: A Brief History of the Protestant Reformed Churches in America* (Grand Rapids, MI: Reformed Free Publishing Association, 1992).

2 The archived issues of the *Standard Bearer* can be found at www.rfpa.org.

early afternoon Beth and Verna had to take a plane to Hong Kong and then to Singapore, where we would meet them in about four weeks.

At one o'clock in the morning I boarded the plane for New Zealand. It was a large plane, and I was amazed to see people streaming in with hats, overcoats, and all kinds of winter clothing. Wednesday at eight o'clock in the morning I arrived in Auckland and came to the full realization that it was the first day of winter there. It was actually a nice day, but we should have been wearing more clothing than we were wearing. We had just left Hawaii, where the temperature was ninety-two degrees.

Mr. Van Dalen and his son Rich, members of the Orthodox Presbyterian Churches in New Zealand, met me at the airport. I stayed with them overnight after they had taken me around to see the city. There I had my first experience with the cold of winter. Their home, as the others, had no central heating. The only warm room in the house was the kitchen, where we sat until bedtime. As I prepared to retire, my feet became like blocks of ice. After a short time in bed I decide to go to the bathroom, where I might be able to warm up. Instead I met the wind blowing in from the vents in the wall. On the way back to bed I discovered a sheepskin rug, which I wrapped around my feet and soon fell off to sleep. My first lesson down under: don't take your shoes off until you are sitting on the bed, ready to crawl in!

The next day I met Homer and Trude in Wellington, where we went to a restaurant with Mr. Van Rij, Mr. Van Herk, Mr. Kuppa, Mr. Vooys, and some ministers in the area. Homer and Trude went with Mr. Van Rij to Christchurch, while I stayed in Wellington to preach for ten people twice on Sunday. On Monday I went to Christchurch. We spent the evening in discussion with a large number of people, and the next day we went on to Dunedin. After a few days there we went north to the city of Nelson to meet with a mixed group of people. I stayed with Mr. and Mrs. Button, who were definitely English even in their way of living. They had been Episcopalian and had left their church, yet were far from being Reformed. At the cottage meeting that evening Mr. Button burst forth, "Do you mean that God creates people to burn them up? What a conceit to think you are elect, while others are damned." After he quieted down, we referred him to Romans 9. Later, before we left, I had a calmer discussion with him. Thereupon we returned to Christchurch, had another meeting there, and then went off to Australia.

Tuesday morning at nine-thirty, we arrived in Melbourne, where we were met by Mr. Van Beelen, who was under censure because he opposed Rev. S. Woudstra, professor in the Reformed Theological College in Geelong, Australia, for his views on creation and predestination. Regarding the latter, Rev. Woudstra taught that God chose Abraham, later Israel, and then the church to win souls for Jesus.[3]

Prof. Homer Hoeksema with the Bosveld boys

---

3   Rev. Woudstra was a Christian Reformed minister on loan to the Reformed Church of Australia.

After a five-hour wait, we took the plane to Tasmania and went to Wynyard, where we had a discussion on the covenant in the afternoon and a lecture at night. There we met the Kleyn and Bosveld families.

I stayed with and had a pleasant visit with the Bosveld family. From there we went to Launceston, where we met a group of about thirty people, and where we discussed the subjects of supralapsarianism and infralapsarianism. On Sunday morning Professor Hoeksema preached for Rev. Rodman in Launceston.[4] I preached in St. Andrew's cathedral, where Rev. Miller was the minister. That was a wonderful experience, especially listening to the large pipe organ and preaching from a pulpit on the wall. After the service we all had dinner with the Connors family, after which Rev. Rodman took us to Winnaleah, where we met in the home of the Cairns.

On Monday we saw a farm of kangaroos, wallabies, and foresters (a large, gray kangaroo), after which Rev. Rodman took us through the rainforest between Winnaleah and St. Helens, and then on to the peninsula and Port Arthur, where in previous years English prisoners were kept.

In the evening we met the Terry Kingston family. I enjoyed my stay with them very much. The next morning the people showed us their little church in the woods, which meant so much to them. Rev. Rodman took us to the plane that brought us back to the mainland. There we spent the day in the hotel, since all three had the diarrhea, resulting from the water we drank on the island of Tasmania.

The next day Mr. Van Beelen met us and took us to a motel in Geelong. We found the seminary in Geelong to be nothing more than an old pickle factory, remodeled to suit the needs of the school. The rooms were large, cold, and bare, with a few

---

4   Rev. Rodman was a leader and a minister in the Evangelical Presbyterian Churches of Australia.

chairs and a small heater located somewhere in the room. There was a dungeon below where classes were held. The school had three professors and twelve students. We invited the professors to come to the motel for a dinner at Mr. Van Beelen's expense, but they refused. One student, Mr. De Graauw, arranged to have the students meet with us at the Commodore Motel, where we were staying. As a result twelve students came, along with three professors to keep an eye on the affair, and two ministers. We spent an interesting afternoon with them, since they pressed us with many questions about common grace and the free offer, most of which we had heard often in the past. One professor remarked that it was like Paul and Silas sitting there answering questions. Only one student, Mr. De Graauw, lingered afterward to show some real interest.

At five-thirty we took the train to Melbourne, where we met Mr. Morgan, whose son David had come along with us from Geelong. We talked long into the night, since Mr. Morgan was a theologian who had many books lining his living room and dining room walls. A good-sized group came together the next evening to discuss a variety of subjects: common grace, Christian education, and the Association for the Advancement of Christian Studies.[5] Once more it was late before we retired.

Saturday morning we were on our way by air to Sydney, where Rev. Stafford met us.[6] Mrs. Stafford was a concert pianist, who taught teachers how to teach music. They had three children, Naomi, Markus, and Matthew. In Sydney Professor and Mrs. Hoeksema stayed with Miss Marjorie Martin, while I stayed with the Stafford family. On Sunday afternoon I preached to about thirty people in Stafford's congregation. In the evening

5 The Advancement of Christian Studies later became the Institute for Christian Studies, still located in Toronto and dedicated to neo-Kuyperianism and the philosophy of Dooyeweerd and Vollenhoven.
6 Rev. Stafford was a minister in an independent church. Miss Martin and John Steele were members of his church.

Professor Hoeksema preached in a Baptist church, where Rev. Kastelign of the Free Reformed Church was present to spy on our activities.

Monday Miss Martin took us to the botanical gardens, which were of special interest to her, since she was a high school botany teacher. Tuesday John Steele and Miss Martin took us downtown, where we saw the famous Sydney opera house. The largest auditorium was five stories high, the upper floors could be reached by elevator, yet the acoustics were perfect even up there. We also took a sightseeing tour through the channels. The congregation there donated five hundred dollars toward our traveling expenses.

Wednesday morning we boarded the train with John Steele, Rev. Stafford, and two other persons to travel north to Wauchope. There we met Rev. and Mrs. Tripovitch of the Free Presbyterian Church. They did not understand the covenant. Mrs. Tripovitch was looking for a conscious or dramatic conversion in her son and was concerned because although his walk was proper, he had not shown signs of conversion. While she was making supper on a cook stove heated with wood, I explained to her our view of the covenant. She became extremely interested. In fact, while Professor Hoeksema spoke at night on John 3:16, she could hardly contain herself, moving restlessly on her chair. I wondered whether she strongly disagreed, until she whispered to me, "I can hardly resist crying out 'Hallelujah!'" After the lecture she said to her husband, tapping him on the chest, "I want you to keep a copy of that lecture, learn it, and preach like that." I doubt whether he ever did.

The next morning we went by a small, two-engine plane to Lismore. The pilot was very willing to describe the scenery as we flew over banana plantations, the ocean, and tropical areas. At Lismore we met Chris Coleborn, who took me to the home of Peter Torlach. After I disposed of my luggage we took a ride through the country and engaged in a serious discussion on God's covenant. That evening Professor Hoeksema lectured, which was followed by a long and interesting discussion.

The next morning I had devotions with the Torlach family in the living room, after which Chris took me to the plane. We were so involved in a discussion on the covenant even as we sat at the airport that if the pilot had not come to call me, I would have been left behind.

We returned to Sydney, where a package was made up of winter clothing and various souvenirs that were sent to our home in Michigan. The next day Rev. Stafford, John Steele, and Miss Martin met us at the airport, where we had coffee together before boarding the plane. The plane took us to Jakarta, Indonesia.

We had enjoyed our stay in Australia and especially appreciated the people's wonderful hospitality, but the time had come to move on. It was a long, wearisome trip of nine hours across the alkali flats of inner Australia, to the famous resort in Bali, and then on to Jakarta. The hostess in the plane asked, "Why don't you stay in Bali? That is a much nicer place." But our schedule directed us to Jakarta.

As we returned to the plane in Bali I remarked to the stewardess that she looked rather distraught. She answered, "You would too, if you had been searching under the seats for a small alligator that escaped out of a box carried in by a small boy." I could hardly disagree with that.

We were met in a crowded airport in Jakarta by Kornelis Kooswanto and Paulina Wangedorm, who ushered us through the teeming crowds of sweating humanity to an auto nearby. On the way I was warned not to lay my arm by the window lest someone take the wristwatch at any amount of damage to the hand or arm. Kornelis brought us to the Boroburur Hotel, a beautiful building only a year old, overlooking a filthy city.

The next morning Kornelis and Paulina were at the hotel to pick us up for the early service at seven o'clock. At the church we were given tea and cakes before the service. The service was conducted by Kornelis in the Indonesian language. The sermon on John 14:6 was delivered in English by Professor Hoeksema to an audience of about one hundred fifty people and translated as he went along.

After the service we had sandwiches and tea and then went to Paulina's home. Mrs. Surengo was also there. She took us to see her home and apothecary. Mr. Surengo was away to Europe to attend the American Association of Christian Schools (AACS) meetings.

At ten in the morning we had another service. I preached on Psalm 91:1–2 in the Dutch language, which again was translated into Indonesian.[7] That was the first time we experienced women elders, one of whom led in prayer before the service.

After the service we had an elaborate meal at the church, consisting of rice, barbecued chicken, chop suey, and numerous side dishes. Professor Hoeksema and I were each presented with a batik shirt, while Trude was given a table set of batik. In the evening we met and had a discussion with the young people of the congregation.

The next morning Cornelius Marinus, who worked for Mr. Van Rij, took us to the bookstore that had been receiving some of our literature. He also took us outside the city, which had about seven million inhabitants, to show us the canal that once was kept clean by the tide from the sea. Then the tide no longer swept into the canal. About a million people were living along its shores in cardboard huts. Occasionally some were driven away by the police, but they soon returned because of the work nearby in the banana plantations, the rice paddies, and the tea fields. Pickers were picking the small, tender leaves from the plants. We also saw the huge estate where the governor lived. It covered about a section of land, fenced in, containing streams, deer, and other animals, all in their natural settings. We had a real Indonesian

---

7   Some of the people could understand Dutch because Indonesia was part of the Dutch East Indies.

lunch at Pumpuk and then had to return to the airport to catch our plane.

What struck us about Jakarta were the remnants of the Dutch influence, since the East Indies had been under the Netherlands before World War II. There were Dutch names on the streets, the offices (*kantoor*), the garages that advertised *remmen* for brakes and *aku* for generators.

We were also deeply impressed by the total confusion in the traffic. Everyone drove like maniacs, cars missed each other by fractions of an inch, and everyone fought to be first. We would not have been able to drive there. It was bad enough to ride through the pandemonium with someone else driving.

When we arrived at the airport, we met Cornelis, Paulina, Mrs. Surgaro, and her daughter, who came to see us off. Since the plane was delayed forty-five minutes, we had a little while to visit together.

At eight-forty in the evening we arrived in Singapore, where Beth Bos and Verna Klamer had been waiting since seven that morning. They were glad to see us, and we were glad to see them. Ong, whose girlfriend we had met in Christchurch, took Professor and Mrs. Hoeksema, while Peter, who had harbored the girls, took me to Mrs. Paauwe, at whose place we would lodge.

Mrs. Paauwe was the wife of a minister, who at that time was away to attend the AACS meetings. That mother of a four-year old child usually left home at six o'clock every morning to work in a nursery where she cared for children from pagan homes and gave them Christian training. Intermittently, she would come home to supervise the Chinese woman who took care of her child. At eleven o'clock in the evening her day was complete. She arranged to come home to visit with us at ten o'clock the last evening we were there.

The next day Ong and Peter, along with Beth and Verna, took us sightseeing. First we went to Peter's father's shop, then to the observation tower of the hotel, where we had a nice view of the entire city of two hundred thousand inhabitants. We had lunch in a Chinese restaurant and then took a sky ride to Sentosa Island, where we spent part of the afternoon. After we ate supper in a restaurant, Professor Hoeksema spoke to a rather large audience of young people between the ages of eighteen and twenty-eight, who had been converted from heathendom to fundamentalism. He spoke on the marks of the true church. Afterward they asked, "Do we have those marks?" When Hoeksema told them to examine themselves, some answered, "We fear that we don't." There was a couple wearing Indian garb who showed great interest. When I bid them goodbye, they assured me that they would be back the next night.

Wednesday it was raining, but at nine-thirty Peter picked us up to take us to Singapore Botanic Gardens and the campus of the American university, which covers many acres of land. After that we went to the Calvary Baptist Presbyterian Church, where Peter was a full-time evangelist. We had lunch there and then went up one of the high rises to get an idea of how the people lived in those crowded areas.

At five in the evening, Ong picked us up to take us for supper to the Salad Bowl, where we had eaten the evening before. Early that morning someone had asked me to speak on assurance of faith. He said, "That is what we lack." So in the evening I took the viewpoint of Lord's Day 1 of the Heidelberg Catechism and spoke on "Our Only Comfort." It is quite obvious that the Arminian has no real assurance or comfort, since his salvation depends at least in part on himself. In the question hour, one of the most important questions was, "How do we attain that comfort?"

At five-thirty the next morning, Ong was at the door to take us to the airport. Soon after, Peter brought the girls over, and we headed for the airport. The plane left at seven-thirty, so we had time for a cup of coffee with Ong. He presented each of us with a beautiful tablecloth as a remembrance. We were again on our way, the girls with us.

When we left Singapore, we felt that we had enjoyed the visit very much, more than our stay at Jakarta. However, we had been so strongly impressed by the group's Arminian tendencies that we never expected to hear from them again. Yet shortly after we arrived home, a letter arrived from Chin Kwee,[8] seeking more permanent contact.

It was a three-hour trip to Bangkok, Thailand, our next stop, where we would spend a couple of days. A bus took us to Narcis Hotel, where we had lunch in a Bavarian restaurant. In the afternoon we took a tour through some of the elaborate temples.

Friday Trude stayed in her room, and Homer stayed with her. Verna also preferred to rest, so Beth and I went out to see the town. Later in the day Trude went with the girls, and I went with Homer to buy a few souvenirs.

At seven-thirty in the evening we were brought to the airport, where we had to wait until ten-thirty for our flight. We had a DC-8, a long narrow plane that took us on a fourteen-hour flight to Switzerland with only one layover.

The layover was in Iran, where we were forbidden to take cameras or any other luggage from the plane. We were herded like a flock of sheep into the airport, with guards in white robes and turbans all around staring at us. All in all, it made us very uncomfortable and created the idea that we would never care to come back to Iran.

The next morning around six o'clock in the morning we flew over the Alps. It was an unforgettable sight—the massive snow-covered peaks in the dazzling brightness of the morning sun, with small towns and lakes stowed away in the valleys below.

Upon our arrival at the airport, we soon discovered that there was no guide to direct us. We had planned to go to the mountains,

---

8   Chin Kwee was Pastor Lau of Covenant Evangelical Reformed Church. He has since died. At that time he was a leader of the Gospel Literature and Tract Society.

where we would spend Sunday in a missionary retreat, but we had no idea how to get there, and there was no one who could give us directions in the English language. As we stood with our luggage in the center of the terminal, a guide came, but we could not get through to her what we wanted in either English, Dutch, or German. In disgust we turned to the ticket office for the Netherlands, intending to buy tickets to go directly there.

A woman there could speak both Dutch and English and informed us how to get to the railroad station to board a train that would take us into the mountains. When the train reached its destination in the mountains, we were directed into the depot, where we could obtain our noonday meal, which was served to us in pans that were kept warm on a small heater.

Then we boarded a bus that took us to our destination, which was a hotel with small cottages. We were assigned rooms in the cottages and also assigned a seat at the table in the main building where we would eat our meals.

We spent a very enjoyable Sunday in that retreat, even though we soon discovered that the Roman Catholic Church was the only church in the area. We had our worship services at the bank of the river with Professor Hoeksema speaking on a passage from Isaiah. As we sang, people walked past slowly to listen to us.

In the afternoon we saw men harvesting grain with scythes and carrying bundles on their shoulders, so that we could only see two legs and a bundle of grain moving toward us and disappearing into the barn. We also took a walk to enjoy the scenery.

Monday morning the bus was at the hotel very early to pick us up and bring us back to Zurich, where we took the train through Germany past Cologne to Amsterdam, where we arrived at the depot about ten o'clock.

The girls and I thought we had reservations at a certain hotel, but there must have been some misunderstanding. Yet there was lodging for us. The next day Homer and Trude went to Stadt Groningen, while we took the train to Alkmar, where we met a bus that took us over the Afsluit Dijk to Harlingen. There we tried to call a Mr. Dykstra in Zeksberen, but we reached the wrong Dykstra. So we sat in the restaurant, discussing how best to spend our time by going into Groningen. While we were eating our lunch, the Dykstra whom we wanted to contact came to the door and asked, "Are there Americans here?" He had been informed by the other Dykstra of our call and decided he might find us in the restaurant. The two girls went with his daughter, who was supposed to be able to speak English, while I went to the home of this Dykstra (a relative of the Miedema family in Hudsonville Protestant Reformed Church), who took me sightseeing, a tour that ended on the dike as the sun was setting.

Dykstra had arranged for me to preach in his church, an old cathedral, the next Sunday, but that did not fit in with our plans. He complained of the modernism in his church and was eager to talk about the Reformed faith. The next day the girls went with me to Harlingen, where we did a bit of shopping.

Early the next morning Dykstra took us to the train in Harlingen, which would take us by way of Leeuwarden back to Amsterdam. When the train pulled out, Dykstra went by car and met us in Leeuwarden, where we had a cup of coffee together. He urged me to try to come again in the near future and slipped into my hand a twenty-dollar bill.

All day Beth, Verna, and I traveled by train, the same train Homer and Trude were on, except that we did not see each other until we reached our destination in Luxembourg. There we were once more confronted with the problem that we had no interpreter. We finally found out that our hotel was outside the city and what bus we had to take to get there. The bus driver set us with our luggage out on the road about a half mile from the hotel. Our next problem was how we could get to the hotel with our luggage, which was far more than we could carry. The girls went to the hotel to inform them of our arrival, and they sent a bus to pick us up and bring us to the lobby. There we obtained rooms for the night, and the next morning we went back to the city to board the plane that would take us by way of Newfoundland to Grand Rapids.

Luxembourg has an old walled city within a new city. We would have liked to see the old city, but the difficulty with the language prevented us from doing any more than was absolutely necessary.

The next day a bus took us to the airport, where we boarded a plane for our last flight to the United States. The plane was packed with people, and the girls and I had seats so close to the back that we could not put the backs of our seats down to take a rest. All day we sat upright in our seats, enjoying very little other than seeing the ice floes in the water below.

A large crowd came to welcome us as we arrived in Kent County Airport, but we were so tired that we could hardly appreciate that. We had one desire, and that was to go home and get some rest.

Chapter 28

RETIREMENT YEARS
—1977 TO 1992

Rev. Hanko was apprehensive that he would not stay busy enough in his retirement years. He soon found out that he had no cause for worry. He taught Dutch in the seminary for a number of years; he was a church visitor for classis from 1979 to 1989; he traveled extensively on behalf of the churches; he took two overseas trips; and he traveled to Bradenton, Florida, to preach there for parts of every year from 1980 to 1992.

In 1977 when I was seventy years old, I retired. That was not an easy decision. I had lived an active life and did not fancy the idea of sitting home and twiddling my thumbs. If retirement meant doing nothing, I would put that off as long as possible, but the opportunity was offered to me to teach Dutch to the students in the seminary. That would give me something to do. With that in mind, I informed Hudsonville's consistory, which reluctantly agreed to approve my action.[1]

The Hudsonville congregation had just moved into the new church building on Beechtree Avenue. The consistory also offered me the new parsonage in which to live, but since I had in mind to retire, I declined their offer. It was a good thing, for my

---

1   See appendix six for a congratulatory letter from Hope Protestant Reformed Church in Redlands on the occasion of Rev. Hanko's emeritation from the ministry.

last duty as minister of Hudsonville was to install Rev. Gise Van Baren as minister there.

In the summer of 1978 I had hip surgery. Dr. Avery had consulted a bone doctor about my Paget's disease,[2] which had been developing for some time. The doctors in Beaver Clinic in Redlands had mentioned to me that I had the ailment, but they said that it likely would never bother me. On the world tour of 1975 I had begun to limp a bit, and I stumbled readily. Later I fell without realizing what caused the fall. I began taking shots, but Dr. Avery wondered whether more could be done to prevent the disease from developing further. One doctor Dr. Avery consulted said that I should have hip surgery, replacement of the ball and socket. Another doctor strongly advised against it. After some time the doctor who advised the hip surgery won out.

For a few days I was in a private room in Blodgett Hospital, after which I went through a period of therapy to help get the left leg to move again. Only by concentrating on it could I finally get the leg to move. While the surgery did help for a time, that leg was shorter than the right one.

All the while I had not even given thought to where I would live after I retired. Somehow that problem never came up. It was Gordon Van Overloop who came over and asked me what I had in mind. He suggested the possibility of going to Sunset Manor, a retirement home, or buying an old house somewhere. He also mentioned that he had ordered a new condominium among the Beechridge developments on 32nd Avenue, which he would turn over to me if I so desired. We went to where some condominiums had already been built, looked over the lot he had intended to buy, discussed the price, and decided that that would be the best thing to do. Gord made all the arrangements with the owners, managed to get a cut in the price for us, and gave us the privilege

---

2 Paget's disease is a chronic bone disorder that results in enlarged or deformed bones in the spine, pelvis, thighs, or lower legs.

of deciding how we wanted the various rooms arranged, particularly allowing room for my library.

At the beginning of 1979 Allie and I moved with the assistance of some of the family and many members of the congregation. It was a stormy day with snow flying, but we managed to get all the furniture moved in without any damage, so we were settled in a condo, in contrast to the eight-room house on School Street. At first it felt as if we were living in cramped quarters, like a motel, but we soon became accustomed to it and were glad that the place was not any larger.

In 1980 I had an opportunity to take a trip to the Holy Land for a mere three hundred dollars. That sounded good to me, so I sent a down payment. Later I was glad that it fell through, because upon further investigation, I found out that it was a tour of charismatics who would spend prayer time in Jerusalem and on the Sea of Galilee.

The trip fell through because Allie developed cancer in the thyroid gland, for which she had surgery that same summer. The surgery was done in Zeeland Hospital, but she had to go to Ann Arbor for treatments with radioactive iodine. She was in isolation for four or five days; we could only come as far as the door to see her. After she returned home she had to go to the University of Michigan every year for a checkup.

On July 8, 1984, we left for our unforgettable trip to Palestine. It all happened because Elaine had a brainstorm, thinking that if she could get a group of our own people together, that would be a nice trip. That is what made the trip especially enjoyable; all but three of the twenty were our people, and a number of them were schoolteachers. Twelve of us left a week earlier to visit Egypt also.

We visited Cairo, Memphis, Luxor, and Karnak. We found that the Land of Goshen is no longer the fertile country of onions, garlic, and leeks known to ancient Israel. The Aswan Dam has taken care of that. From Karnak we crossed the Nile to the Valley of the Kings, where many of the pharaohs are buried. On our way to Athens from Cairo, many of us sickened, most likely from the water we had been drinking.

In Athens we met up with the rest of our party, including Rich and Elaine Bos. It was a pleasure to have the group complete. We had a meeting with the guide that night to make plans for the week, but most of us were eager to get some rest. John Kalsbeek Sr. was my roommate for the rest of the trip. Some of the cities we visited in Greece were the same ancient cities that the apostle Paul visited: Athens, Corinth, and Thessalonica. We were often amazed at the hilly terrain that he had had to traverse by foot on his journeys.

We arrived at the port near Ephesus and then visited Turkey, which was another outstanding experience on our trip. A bus took us to the ruins of the former city, about the best-preserved ruins of any old cities. There we saw the ruins of the former Roman temple, library, and amphitheater. The guide told us to imagine about a thousand people gathered there as he gave a big shout that resounded against the hill. We could well imagine what a riot that was when the mob turned against Paul, shouting, "Great is Diana of the Ephesians" (Acts 19:28).

From Ephesus we took a ship to the Island of Patmos. That was an especially interesting part of the tour. There is only one very small city on the island and only one cave where likely the apostle John lived in exile. From that spot one can look over the broad expanse of the sea, and it takes little imagination to see what John saw and described in the book of Revelation. We did not stay very long in the cave because there was a baptism ceremony going on there, and the people did not appreciate interference.

We returned to Athens, from whence we departed for Palestine. We spent a great deal of time in Jerusalem, in both the old city and the new. We saw such sights as Hezekiah's tunnel, the Mount of Olives, the Wailing Wall, the Pool of Bethesda, and Mount Moriah, where Solomon's temple supposedly stood.

We were especially keen to see what many think is Golgotha, the place of crucifixion, and the garden of the tomb, where Jesus was perhaps buried.

Other places of interest we visited were the cities of Nazareth, Bethlehem, Megiddo, and Capernaum. It was interesting to see the cities mentioned so frequently in the Bible and envision them as they were in the days of the Old and New Testaments.

I think it would be well for every minister and every schoolteacher to take a trip to that area to get a mental picture of Egypt, Palestine, and the many places referred to in scripture.

August 12, 1987, we left for a trip to Europe. We packed the Oldsmobile at the house of Rich and Elaine and then drove to Detroit. From there we flew to the Netherlands, the land of our forefathers.

One Friday morning we went to Franeker. A Reformed university was established in Franeker soon after the Reformation in the Netherlands. It had some outstanding professors, the name of one, Johannes Cocceius,[3] was still engraved above the entrance. At the time of our visit the building was used as an old people's home. A nearby café was once the meeting place for students, and it is said to be the oldest café in the whole of Europe. A row of houses in front of the old university was once called professors' row, for all the professors lived in them.

In the afternoon we went to Ulrum, where Don Rietema was raised. But our interest was especially focused on the Reformed church where Rev. Hendrik de Cock was minister and where the Secession of 1834 originated.[4] This church had a pulpit built up on the wall over against a section enclosed for the consistory. There

---

3 Cocceius was a Dutch theologian from the seventeenth century.
4 In 2004 the church became part of the Protestant Church in the Netherlands, which is a new denomination formed by a merger of the Netherlands Reformed Church (the state church), the Reformed Church in the Netherlands, and the Evangelical Lutheran Church. The denomination is totally apostate.

were hard wooden seats and a small opening in the wall where it is thought the lepers could come and listen to the sermon. We toured the town and went to 't Sandt, where my father was born and raised. We saw the *Hervormde Kerk* that he likely attended.

Then we went on to the capital of Groningen, Stadt Groningen, which is a rather large and old city. There Rev. Herman Hoeksema spent his early days.

Another city we visited was Kampen, where the Schilder Theological School is located. It took us a while to find it because of poor directions. In fact, we rode past it once without seeing it. But we finally found the red brick building set between others of similar design, and the name was clearly written above the doorway.

We were about to leave the Netherlands, a country that had a strong appeal especially because for years it had been the seat of Calvinism. There the great Synod of Dordt was held. There was the history of reformation in the nineteenth century that still affects our lives today. Besides all that, there we had our roots, since our forefathers came from that little country.

We joined a tour group and headed into Germany. Before long we were traveling along the autobahn, the freeway built by Hitler to speed up the transport of war supplies. Our driver brought us to Heidelberg, where we took a tour of Heidelberg Castle. There the Heidelberg Catechism, which we still cherish today, was written by Caspar Olevianus and Zacharias Ursinus.

We drove through the Austrian Alps but were unable to see much because of low-lying clouds. From Austria we traveled to Italy. The highlights of our travels there would certainly include the cities of Venice and Rome and the ruins of Pompeii, the ancient city destroyed by the eruption of Vesuvius.

We left Italy with all its attractions and arrived at Monaco, where we saw the palace of Prince Rainier, who was married to Grace Kelly. Monaco is an attractive city, built on the hillside overlooking the sea. From there the Protestant Reformed

Churches had sent a broadcast through Trans World Radio, which was focused on England but spread to Germany and was even heard on short wave in Tasmania. That broadcast had brought a splendid response, and through the broadcast the denomination came into contact with the churches of Jamaica.

We stopped at Calvin's city, Geneva, Switzerland, and made a short visit to a garden of flowers, but our chief interest was the university. We spent considerably more time viewing the wall with its carvings of the four reformers: William Farel, John Calvin, John Knox, and Theodore Beza. We would have liked to see Calvin's church also, but that was not included in the tour. What we did see brought back a strong appreciation for what God has wrought through those reformers and for preserving the truth for us even to this day. The guide remarked that the followers of Calvin are called Calvinists, who never have any fun. We disagreed.

Our next stop was Paris, where we rode through Paris and saw the city all lit up at night.

We left Paris with all its points of interest. So often we had heard of those things and saw pictures of them, but it was far more interesting to see them as they are. The trip through Belgium was very scenic and pleasant. We rode through "Flanders Fields, where the poppies bloom" and which was made famous in World War I.[5] That did not look like a war-torn battlefield any more, but then France and Germany did not either.

We took a boat across the North Sea to England and its capital, London, where we spent a few days sightseeing before we left for home.

Our trip home was pretty much without incident. We arrived in the wee hours of the morning, tired but thankful that we had made the trip under God's watchful care.

---

5   The author refers to a poem written by Major Mc Crae, who fought in World War I. Flanders Fields refers generally to the site of many World War I battlefields.

For a few years I enjoyed teaching Dutch in the seminary. Allie worked in Hudsonville Public Library and also for Vern Klamer on his celery farm. There were also opportunities to do a bit of traveling and church visiting for the classis.

In 1980 Allie and I started going to Florida. I preached at services for Protestant Reformed snowbirds in Bradenton. At first we went there for a very short time, only a month or two every year, but that was gradually increased so that by 1989 we stayed the whole

Rev. C. Hanko and Allie

year, except for visits to Michigan in the spring and in the fall.

We often traveled to and from Florida with Owen and Irene Peterson, Bertha Dusselje, and Nell Reitsma, my sister-in-law. If nothing else we were a small voice in the Reformed church world presenting Reformed preaching.

After one winter in Bradenton we returned to Michigan briefly, and shortly thereafter Owen Petersen, Allie, and I started out for Ripon, California, to work there toward possible organization of a congregation. I had received a request to work there for four or five months. Rev. Steven Houck joined me in the work there for a short time.

During our stay in Ripon Allie and I made a trip to Redlands. We spent a week there, and I preached twice on Sunday. On our way back to Ripon we visited Sequoia National Park.

During the early years of my retirement I was able to help out the Protestant Reformed congregation in Lynden a number of times. Once we stayed for six weeks.

During that visit to Lynden I went by plane to Calgary to meet Rev. Tom Miersma, then minister in First Edmonton

Protestant Reformed Church. We spent two days visiting with a family who was connected with the churches that had separated from the *Gereformeerde Gemeenten* (Reformed Congregations) in the Netherlands in 1953. That group left with Rev. Cornelis Steenblok, who had a view of God's covenant similar to the Protestant Reformed view.[6] We could agree on many things, but the strong mystical tendency in that family stood between us. We were well received, sat up late talking, and were treated like royalty. The threat of a blizzard cut our visit a bit short. Rev. Miersma brought me to the plane to return to Vancouver and Lynden. Shortly thereafter Allie and I returned to our home in Hudsonville.

On another preaching trip to Lynden, I stayed for three months. I had a bit of trouble with cataracts developing on my eyes, and I could not see very well. My biggest problems were the narrow roads, the stop signs, and stop lights, but Allie assisted me as copilot, just in case I should fail to see the signs. Once more we enjoyed our stay in Lynden, especially because it was during the summer months and the longer days of the year. Various members of the congregation took us to see the places of interest in the area.

I might remark in passing that about that time, my sister Corie Vander Woude felt that she could no longer be alone and decided to join her husband in the Christian Rest Home.

During the summer months of 1986 Southeast Church was vacant, so I taught a Bible class there for young adults. I had my second eye surgery late in the summer, and the Bible class sent me fruit at the time of my surgery.

I had another request to come to Modesto, California, because Rev. Houck, our missionary there, needed back surgery. His wife was also there. During those few hours I learned

---

6 Rev. Steenblok was also opposed to the well-meant offer of the gospel, and over that issue that he left the Reformed Congregations.

to know her and admire her spiritually. I also spent some time in the Houck home. They had a nice family, and the children felt free to come and talk to me. I was especially impressed by the training they received at the close of the meal, when the Bible passage that had been read was also discussed.

Soon afterward, we were back in the trailer in Florida. Whenever we were in Florida, I got up each weekday morning while it was still dark to bike at the crack of dawn until sunrise. I went to the mall where the whole parking area was open for biking.[7]

Since the mission in Venice, Florida, was then under the supervision of the Protestant Reformed mission committee, pulpit supply was sent on a regular basis. Usually a minister came for two Sundays and I took the third Sunday, but special arrangements were made when I went to Michigan, as I did when we received word that my granddaughter, Ellen Dick (second daughter of Fred and Ruth), had died. At times like that one wants nothing more than to be with family.

I always enjoyed the times in Bradenton, but my health was starting to deteriorate. On one visit to Michigan I tripped and fell as I went out of church. I did not hurt myself, but from that time on, I felt safer on crutches. Soon I was entirely dependent on them. It was also necessary that if I preached, I sat on a stool. I could no longer stand for that length of time.

I visited the doctor about my increasing difficulties with walking. He took a number of X-rays and spent about two hours with us. The conclusion of the matter was that if anything were to be done, hip, knee, and femur would need replacement. That would have been a big and dangerous surgery, especially with a view to possible bleeding, so we were advised to go on as long as possible with the crutches.

In July 1992 while in Florida, I came down with a blood clot

---

7   Rev. Hanko biked daily to improve the movement and strength of his leg that was affected by Paget's disease.

in my lung. George Yonker and Owen took me to Blake Hospital, where I spent a week. Allie also was experiencing various health problems at that time.

A short time later I developed a pain in my chest, which proved to be bronchitis. I lost considerable weight during my illness and tried to regain some of it. Because of our health problems, we decided to return to Michigan in the near future and to take all of our belongings back with us. Owen Peterson and Menno Smits took care of selling the trailer.

On March 15, 1993, Herm, Fred, Elaine, and Rich came with the van. On Sunday I preached my last sermon and bid the fold of Venice goodbye. They gave me a present of over a thousand dollars. Herm preached for me that night. Thus my work in Florida came to an end. I then considered myself officially retired and took up the work of writing this memoir.

Chapter 29

RETIREMENT YEARS— 1993 TO 1995

The Protestant Reformed Churches first had contact with Rev. George Hutton and the Bible Presbyterian Church in Larne, Northern Ireland, in 1983. The church suddenly broke off relations with the Protestant Reformed Churches in 1987 and joined the Free Presbyterian Church of Scotland. Some of the members of Rev. Hutton's group refused to join the Free Presbyterians, believing that those churches were not doctrinally pure. The Protestant Reformed Churches continued to work with that group of people and sent Rev. Ron Hanko to be their missionary. During Rev. Ron Hanko's tenure, Rev. C. Hanko went to visit Northern Ireland.

Those Northern Ireland saints suffered another setback in 2002, when dissatisfied members disbanded the church. Again, God preserved a remnant. Since then the group has reorganized as the Covenant Protestant Reformed Church of Northern Ireland and has established a sister-church relationship with the Protestant Reformed Churches. Rev. Angus Stewart currently serves as the pastor of Covenant.

I n March 1993 Ron (oldest son of Herman and Wilma), his wife Nancy, and their family moved to Northern Ireland to take up mission work among the Covenant Reformed Fellowship there. On May 19 Herm, Wilma, Allie, and I left on a trip to visit Ron and his family. We drove to the Detroit airport, where we left our car. British Airways took us by way of Montreal to London, where we changed planes. From London we went to Belfast, where Ron was waiting to meet us.

For the first time in our lives Allie and I were on the soil of Northern Ireland. The cities, the small towns, the houses, the verdant fields with their lichen-covered stone walls and their flocks of sheep on the hillsides appealed to us.

Soon we were at the gate that marks the entrance to the manse, or parsonage. The manse was large, with four bedrooms, a study, two bathrooms, a large kitchen and dining area, as well as a large living room. The house was set on a large lot bordered by beautiful rhododendrons, azaleas, and other flowers and surrounded by shrubbery and trees.

It was a pleasure to meet the family again. When Ron was minister in Wyckoff, New Jersey, I had the privilege of visiting there from time to time, but after the family moved to Houston, Texas, I had not been to their home.

We made up quite a family with four extra guests. There were fourteen of us at meal times. It was a pleasant time as we were all gathered around the table. Ron's daughter Jessica usually sat next to me. At the end of the meal we ended our devotions with singing from the Scottish psalter they used in the worship services.

The day after our arrival we went for supper to the home of Ivan and Lily Reid. While we were there, Mrs. Reid, Nancy, and Allie took a walk to a nearby church. Later we joined them and walked through the cemetery and along the stream and bridge on the side of the church.

May 22 we drove to Belfast Lough, where we walked around the tower built as a memorial to the soldiers who had died in the war for freedom from Catholic control. Those men had been led by William of Orange of the Netherlands. It was a raw, windy day, so we did not stay long.

At home we settled in the living room. It should be added

that the three older girls took great delight in teasing their grandpa and getting him to jostle with them. Without fail they got the worst of the deal, but they always came back for more. In our more quiet sessions, the girls joined me in working crossword puzzles.

Saturday, May 23, we rode along the Irish Sea. Particularly Allie and I had to get accustomed once more to riding on the left side of the road. We stopped at a rest area to allow the kids to expend some of their energy by climbing over huge boulders. At noon we went to a park near the beach just outside of the small town of Carnlough to eat lunch. A number of boats were docked in the harbor on the other side of the road.

Sunday we went to church in Ballymena. The meetings were held in a second-floor hall. To get there we went through a gateway and an alley to a back door. We ascended a flight of narrow stairs and thus entered the hall. Nancy, Allie, and I sat on chairs. The others sat on benches. Mr. Desmond Callendar was a very capable precentor, or lead singer, who led us in singing from the Scottish psalter. Herm preached in the morning and evening worship services.

Monday, May 24, we went to Carrickfergus Castle by the sea. On the way we stopped at the home where Herm and Wilma had stayed on their previous visit. Carrickfergus Castle is large, has numerous rooms, and is lined with fortifications. The castle was given to William of Orange as a gift for gaining the victory over the Catholics at the Battle of the Boyne. It has a large harbor open to the sea. While the rest of our party explored the castle, Wilma and I sat in the coffee shop and entertained ourselves there. The kids had a good time climbing around on the lookouts and viewing the many rooms.

The next day we went to Giant's Causeway. As we traveled the countryside we saw the fields of yellow flowers, more sheep and cattle, and everything that makes the countryside interesting. We stopped at a foot suspension bridge at Carrick-a-Rede and spent a little time there. The sway of such a bridge always gives a bit of a thrill to those who venture across. As you can imagine, I did not try it.

Arriving at the Causeway, a number of our party started down to the sea on foot. A few of us took the bus. The bus driver was extremely accommodating, putting my wheelchair in the back of the bus. As soon as we reached our destination, Neal was out on the rocks climbing as high as he could. Soon the others followed, that is, as many as were interested in clambering over the rocks like mountain goats. Giant's Causeway extends under the sea all the way to Scotland. The scenery is very interesting, and we spent some time walking around there.

Since two of Ron's children, Rose and Herman, had to go to school that day, they missed out on the ride, but we picked them up on the way home. They were cute in their neat uniforms, book packs in their hands, coming out of the school and ready to go. Occasionally Herm and I would ride along with Ron in the morning to bring them to school or in the afternoon to fetch them home.

May 27 we went to the home of John and Marlene Clarke for supper. They had six children, two boys and four girls. Upon our return to the manse, we gathered in Ron's dining room to celebrate the fortieth wedding anniversary of Herm and Wilma.

Taking full advantage of our short stay, on May 28 we went to the Antrim seacoast. On a long, winding, narrow road we came to Murdock Cove, a most scenic spot and a nice place just to enjoy the broad expanse of the sea.

That evening we were invited by the fellowship to come to a college in Ballymena where the cafeteria was reserved by John Clarke for our use for the evening. The purpose of the gathering was to celebrate the fortieth anniversary of Herm and Wilma. Tables were set up for groups of four to eight. Everyone enjoyed the delicious food that was so lavishly spread out before us. Then came the cake cutting. Margaret McAuley had made the cake. Of particular interest was that Neal, the handicapped son of Ron and Nancy, sat right next to his brother Herman, eyeing the cake with extreme interest. Suddenly Neal's finger shot out to take a lick of the frosting, but just as suddenly Ron, who was on the watch, said, "Neal." As quickly as that, the finger drew back. Afterward a beautiful vase with the inscription "40th anniversary" was presented, and Herm made a thank you speech that was quite fitting for the occasion. When the celebration came to an end, the women had the responsibility of cleaning up the place. The men helped move the tables, and for some time the women were engaged in washing dishes in the kitchen.

We also spent a day in Belfast. Let it be known that although Belfast has a reputation for riots, Chicago is said to be ten times more dangerous than Belfast. The women went shopping and Ron, Herm, and I visited some bookstores. One dealer had his business in his home. One room on the first floor was used for books, but the main display was on the second floor. The man formerly had a warehouse, but it was burned by the IRA.[1] He moved his business in his home and seemed to do very well.

Sunday, May 30, we went to church twice in Ballymena. I had the privilege of preaching in the morning on Isaiah 43:1–4, some of which reads, "When thou passest through the waters, I will be with thee; and through the rivers, they shall not overflow thee: when thou walkest through fire, thou shalt not be burned; neither shall the flame kindle upon thee." Herm preached in the evening to a very attentive audience. Allie took some pictures of the various families present.

May 31 we went to the sea by way of Belfast. At noon we stopped at a park to eat lunch. It was very cold, with a cold wind sweeping in from the sea. I wore two jackets. But we enjoyed the

---

1   The IRA refers to the Irish Republican Army, a paramilitary group that sought to unite the Republic of Ireland in the south and Northern Ireland, which is part of the United Kingdom.

lunch and the kids enjoyed running around. Ryan caught a crab that he carried around to show us. Later we took a ferry at Porta-ferry and enjoyed the ride.

The evening of June 1 we went for dinner to the home of Brian and Edna Crossett and their two children, David and Cher-ith.[2] Brian played the flute for us. Edna had a brother there who spent a bit of time with us discussing various doctrinal problems that seemed to bother him. We had an interesting and friendly discussion.

Since June 2 was the last day with Ron's family, we stayed home and enjoyed the warm sunshine. In the evening we went to the Bible class, as we had done the week before. Again we met and had fellowship with the group, but that was the last time. After the meeting we all went to the Salvation Army Hall and looked around it, because the fellowship was hoping to buy it. All too soon the time came that we had to bid them goodbye. We had enjoyed being with them, but now we parted ways. Back at Ron's house we sat together for a while. There was an atmosphere of sadness in the room, for the time had come to bid each other farewell. We gathered in the dining room, had a lunch, and sang from the book of psalms.

In the morning of June 3 Ron took us to the Belfast airport, where we made our final farewell. We took the plane to London, transferred to another part of the airport, and boarded the plane that took us by way of Montreal back to Detroit. We arrived in Detroit about three o'clock in the afternoon and arrived home about seven-thirty at night, thankful for a safe and pleasant trip.

In the fall of 1994 my eyes began to fail me. The right eye never was very good, but now the fluid was collecting in the cornea of the left eye. It became increasingly difficult to read, since everything was blurred. I had a number of preaching

---

2   Brian and Edna Crossett have been with the Covenant Protestant Reformed Church through all of its history.

appointments scheduled yet for the end of the year but decided to cancel them. When the time came to renew the insurance on my car, I decided also to give up driving, even though it was very handy for Allie and me to drive in the vicinity of our home.

In May 1995 I underwent surgery for a cornea transplant. Three weeks later I still could see very little with that eye, since it was still officially blind; but my sight gradually improved. Reading ordinary print was still difficult, but for a while I had sufficient sight in that eye to be able to read the church papers and other writings with the aid of a magnifying glass.

In June 1995 Allie and I accompanied Rich and Elaine to Loveland for grandson Bob's wedding. We went out for a day with Rev. Gise and Clara Van Baren to Rocky Mountain National Park, where I spent a few enjoyable hours at Bear Lake while the others hiked.

It was a real pleasure to attend church in Loveland, to hear our former minister once again, and to meet the many people we knew from earlier contacts. Way back in the 1950s, Rev. Lubbers and I had visited Loveland to talk to folks who had heard about the Protestant Reformed Churches and were unhappy with the situation in their church. At that time they belonged to the German Reformed Church, a small group that hired a Lutheran preacher. The minister preached for the Lutherans in the morning and for the German Reformed group in the afternoon. Occasionally he got his lines mixed and introduced the Lutheran doctrine of consubstantiation. Clara Sur, a founding member of Loveland Protestant Reformed Church, complained of that to the consistory. After the group heard of the Protestant Reformed Churches through Rev. Mensch,[3] the people sought contact with the denomination.

On that first stay in the 1950s, I was with the group for five

---

3 Rev. Mensch was a minister for a time in the Reformed Church of the United States (German Reformed). He later resigned from the ministry and joined Hope Protestant Reformed Church of Walker, Michigan.

days and stayed over Sunday to preach. The result was that the people who had requested help from the Protestant Reformed Churches were banished from the church. Then they requested the Protestant Reformed mission committee to send Rev. Lubbers to labor there. Later a church was organized. Today Loveland Protestant Reformed Church is a healthy, growing congregation.

Even trips such as the one to Loveland were becoming overwhelming for me; so our lives became quite routine. Occasionally I was still able to preach, although I had to do so from a stool because my bad leg did not allow me to stand for long. I preached a bit for the group that is now Grace Protestant Reformed Church but soon, due to failing eyesight, had to give that up.

Thus I am about to write *finis*. Years ago the Dutch Men's Society of First Church held an annual banquet. On that auspicious occasion there were three essays of great length read by members of the society. Coffee, lunch, and cigars were served between the essays. When an essayist finished his lengthy discussion, he would sometimes remark, "I could have said much more." I could say the same of these memoirs.

I have always considered Rev. Hoeksema to be my spiritual father, since he taught me from the time I was fourteen years of age. His favorite psalm and mine is Psalm 89:17–18, "For thou art the glory of their strength: and in thy favour our horn shall be exalted. For the LORD is our defence; and the Holy One of Israel is our king."

Here I raise my Ebenezer with the inscription: "Hitherto hath the Lord helped us" (1 Sam. 7:12).

Chapter 30

A FINISHED COURSE

Since Rev. Hanko did not write about the last ten years of his life, it was necessary that I write a final chapter to bring his memoirs to a fitting conclusion. I have relied heavily on my own memory and the memories of his three surviving children in assembling the material for this chapter. However, the reader can hear Rev. Hanko's own voice one last time at the very end of the chapter.

Rev. Hanko wrote these memoirs after his retirement, adding to them every few years or so. But as far as we know, he added nothing after 1995. However, he continued to look for ways to be of use to the family and the churches.

He asked his son Herm what he thought of the idea of translating the Dutch book *Van Zonde en Genade* by Herman Hoeksema and Henry Danhof. Herman's answer can be found in the editor's introduction to the book *Sin and Grace*.

Because he was fluent in Dutch and because he needed work to keep him occupied, I readily agreed that the book should be translated. I was a bit skeptical whether he was able to do it, though. He was, after all, in his eighties, very nearly blind, and weary with the burdens of many years in the ministry. But if it could be done, it would be well worth it.

I got out his copy of *Van Dale's Woordenboek*, the authoritative dictionary of the Dutch language; set up a word processor; installed a program that would enlarge the text on the screen of his monitor; and encouraged him to do what he could.[1]

Grandpa took every opportunity to tell others of the history of the churches that he had served. For example, Doug Dykstra's young people's class from Grandville Protestant Reformed Church came to visit Rev. Hanko once a year for many years, so that he could talk with them about 1924 and 1953.

His last great effort on behalf of the churches was to speak to Professor Hanko's Monday night Bible class and other interested people, a group of about one hundred fifty, on the schism of 1953. By that time, two years before his death, he could see and hear very little and was confined to a wheelchair. Yet his memory remained keen, as did his love for and interest in the Protestant Reformed Churches.

He and Allie moved to Walden Woods, an assisted living home, in the spring of 2000. When he first toured the place with his children, he remarked in Dutch, "I am weary of life." Yet the Lord spared him for another five years. While he lived there, his days were filled with the difficult work of growing old. Grandpa had to say with Paul, "I have learned, in whatsoever state I am, therewith to be content" (Phil. 4:11).

Almost to the very end of his life, he loved to go for long drives and out to eat with his children. His afflictions were many—congestive heart failure and increasing stomach problems. Yet he continued to attend church in the evenings and listened by telephone to the morning service.

At one point Grandpa contracted pneumonia and nearly died. He was disappointed and a bit resentful when he rallied. Grandpa said that he felt as if he had been in the narthex of

---

1   Henry Danhof and Herman Hoeksema, *Sin and Grace*, trans. Cornelius Hanko, ed. Herman Hanko (Grandville, MI: Reformed Free Publishing Association, 2003), vii.

heaven and God had pushed him back out the door. At times he grew impatient that the Lord tarried so long, especially when the Lord took members of Rev. Hanko's own family who were much younger than he was.

The family members closest to him felt the brunt of his impatience at times, but often for most visitors he had a ready story, usually one about the visitor himself or the visitor's relatives. The story was always told with dry wit, Rev. Hanko's shoulders shaking with silent laughter. As his son fondly recalled, he was ardently loved by his grandchildren, who never failed to stop in to see him when they were in town. They loved his stories taken from his own life and the rich and varied experiences through which the Lord had led him. Those stories, while captivating and told with zest, were nevertheless all geared to instruct those who listened in the ways of faithfulness.

Rev. Hanko ceased going out to eat with his children, a weekly occurrence for many years, in the early winter of 2004, for he was very afraid of falling on the ice. He fell in his room in early January 2005, and on January 29 he was admitted to the hospital for pneumonia and congestive heart failure. Although he returned from the hospital and recovered from the pneumonia and the fall, his strength was sapped, and he began the decline that led to his death.

Rev. Hanko's life spanned nearly a century. He had lived through two world wars, the Great Depression, and the Korean and Vietnam wars. He had seen the rise and fall of communism, the advent of the space age, and the rise of terrorism, and he lived during the terms of eighteen presidents of the United States, from Theodore Roosevelt to George W. Bush.[2]

It is just as well that God does not reveal to us the length or the sorrow of our days.

In all his life Rev. Hanko lived first for the church and that

2   See appendix eight for a timeline of Rev. Hanko's life.

had not always been easy. He pastored six Protestant Reformed churches from the Midwest to the far West. He lived through two heart-wrenching church splits and never wavered in his commitment to sovereign grace. His children can confirm that, especially when they think back on a Thanksgiving morning long ago.

The schism of 1953 nearly killed him. On a Thanksgiving morning when his wife was in the hospital because of a heart attack, he called his son into his bedroom early in the morning in a feeble voice. He was scheduled to preach, but his ulcer had begun to bleed. By the time his son had called an ambulance and it arrived, he was unconscious from loss of blood. He literally spent himself in the cause of the church.

Truly he had kept the faith.

Grandpa had one last enemy to face, and that was death. He was confined to bed for a number of days prior to his death. While he began to lose interest in life, he still received great comfort from singing and reading the Dutch psalms with his visitors.

He responded less and less to those around him as the days progressed. He slipped into a coma, from which he never awakened, during the second week of March 2005. On March 14 the Lord granted him victory over the last great enemy. He had finished the course.

We did not really have the sorrow that is usual when a loved one is taken to glory, for we saw him in those last few years as a weary and worn-out warrior in the battles of faith. We witnessed his almost pathetic eagerness to be with the Lord, and we watched the slow decline of his eyesight, hearing, and physical well-being. He had been for many years a faithful, covenantal father and grandfather who encouraged us in the ways of the Lord, instructed us in what they were, and chided us when we did not show proper zeal.

Because he outlived by so many years those of his generation and even many of the succeeding generation, Rev. Hanko would from time to time express apprehension that there would be no one at his funeral. He need not have worried. His four children, most of his nineteen grandchildren, most of his seventy-one great-grandchildren, as well as two great-great-grandchildren, were in attendance. Many of his fellow saints and former parishioners also appeared to hear Rev. Gise Van Baren, a friend of the family and Rev. Hanko's long-time pastor, speak on Revelation 3:11–12:

> Behold, I come quickly: hold that fast which thou hast, that no man take thy crown. Him that overcometh will I make a pillar in the temple of my God, and he shall go no more out: and I will write upon him the name of my God, and the name of the city of my God, which is the new Jerusalem, which cometh down out of heaven from my God: and I will write upon him my new name.

As we stood together at the side of his coffin, it seemed totally inappropriate to wring our hands and weep. It was a time for thanksgiving and rejoicing, and that we did with hundreds of God's people who came to offer their condolences through visitation, their presence at the funeral service, and cards and letters. Rev. Hanko had exchanged his spiritual sword for a palm branch, his helmet for a crown of life, and his armor for the white robes of the righteousness of Christ. He is a little ahead of us, for we too shall go to join the company of just men made perfect.

His lasting legacy was his total devotion to the church that has made its indelible mark on us all. But people in the churches remember him chiefly for his quietness, his meekness, his humility, his unwillingness to be in the limelight, his understanding of people, and his sympathy for them. The latter was because he knew himself to be a very great sinner, saved by grace. That enabled him to empathize with others in their struggles with temptations and their weary walks through the valley of the shadow of death.

All his life, but particularly toward the end, Allie's care

weighed heavily on Grandpa. He wondered how she would carry on when he died. He need not have worried. Six months after the Lord took Grandpa, Allie contracted pneumonia and died. Their lives had been closely intertwined, and once Grandpa died she felt she had little reason to live. They had cared for each other for many years, and because of her, Grandpa never needed to be confined to a rest home. She too had fought a good fight and has now obtained her crown.

Grandpa spent a great deal of time in his retirement writing these memoirs. The vast majority of the chapters in this book are verbatim from his writings. Thus it is only fitting that I end these chapters with Grandpa's own words:

> Looking back, there were a number of firsts in my life. My family was the first in the neighborhood to have electricity and an automobile. I was among the first students in Grand Rapids Christian High when the doors were opened for the first time. I experienced the opening of our seminary and was with the first class that graduated. Later I was delegate to our first synod meeting. And in Oak Lawn we held our first young people's convention. Striking, isn't it?
>
> My wife was delivered from her suffering and taken to glory many years ago. She suffered much, most of her life, yet she never complained. Since that time, my sons, my daughters, my son-in-law and daughters-in-law, my grandchildren and my great-grandchildren mean more to me than ever. I can never be thankful enough for the family God gave us and for the blessing my children and grandchildren are to me.
>
> As I look back upon the past I must say that I have had a rich and full life. Even in the years of my retirement I could keep active. I know that the real life is still to come and this life is but a preparation, but the Lord has

been good. I can well say, as the patriarchs of old, that I am full of days, for I have seen all God's promises realized in my children's children to the second and third generations. Let me quote one of my favorite psalter numbers. "When I in righteousness at last / Thy glorious face shall see, / When all the weary night is past, / And I awake with Thee / To view the glories that abide, / Then, then I shall be satisfied."[3]

I think also of the Dutch psalm that was a tremendous support to me through the years, a versification of Psalm 27:13–14:

My heart had failed in fear and woe
Unless in God I had believed,
Assured that He would mercy show
And that my life His grace should know,
Nor was my hope deceived.
Fear not, though succor be delayed,
Still wait for God, and He will hear;
Be strong, nor be thy heart dismayed,
Wait, and the Lord shall bring thee aid,
Yea, trust and never fear.[4]

Soli Deo gloria!

---

3 No. 32:4, in *The Psalter*. Psalter 32 was one of the numbers sung at Rev. Hanko's funeral.
4 Rev. Hanko quoted this psalm in Dutch, but I give the English translation in psalter 73:5–6, in ibid.

Appendix One

Letter from Rev. Hoeksema to Rev. C. Hanko (January 28, 1947)

First Protestant Reformed Church
FULLER AVENUE AND FRANKLIN STREET
GRAND RAPIDS 7, MICH.

REV. HERMAN HOEKSEMA, PASTOR
1139 FRANKLIN ST., S. E.
PHONE 31999

Bellflower, Jan. 28-47

Rev. C. Hanko
Manhattan, Mont.

Dear brother:-

I just learned that you received the call from Fuller Ave. Congratulations. I am glad of it! And I sincerely hope that the Lord's way may be for you to accept it. You know that I am not in the habit to advise anyone in matters of this nature. But I want to express my opinion in this particular case, which is that you are just the man for this call, both from the viewpoint of preaching and of cooperation with Rev. DeWolf, which is, of course, rather important. Of course, with me you will find it easy to cooperate. The work is manifold, but now there are two of you, and I can help a little, too, once in a while.

And so, brother, you have my opinion. Perhaps, it can help you to reach a decision.

Regards to your wife and family, also from the Mrs.!

With love in the Lord,

H. Hoeksema.

299

Appendix Two

"Walking with God"
(*Standard Bearer* 24, no. 12, March 15, 1948)

Rev. Hanko wrote his first Standard Bearer *article, entitled "Unprofitable Servants," for the April 15, 1935, issue. He continued to write for the magazine for many years, even into his retirement. Some of the rubrics for which he wrote were "From Holy Writ," "In His Fear," "The Lord Gave the Word," and "Meditation." If one looks through the archives of the Standard Bearer, one sees that he was also the stated clerk of Classis West for a time. He filed many reports in the* Standard Bearer *in this role. By his many writings on various topics, one can assume that Rev. Hanko considered writing for this magazine an important part of his work as a minster of the gospel.*

What follows is an article written at the height of his ministry. See appendix seven for an article he wrote during his retirement years. Both have the same pastoral tone that pervades his writing.

Scripture says of Enoch that he walked with God. "And Enoch walked with God after he begat Methuselah three hundred years, and begat sons and daughters. And Enoch walked with God: and he was not; for God took him" (Gen. 5:22, 24). That is by far the most unique biography that you can find anywhere in the annals of history or in the scriptures. Whatever else Enoch may have done during the three hundred and sixty-five years of his life on the earth, or whatever cherished memories he may have left behind, the outstanding feature of his life that governed them all was that he walked with God.

This is also said of Noah as a reason he alone found grace in the eyes of the Lord, to be spared with his family by the waters of the flood. "Noah was a just man and perfect in his generations and Noah walked with God" (Gen. 6:9).

Otherwise this expression is not very freely used in scripture. We do often read of walking before the face of God, or of walking after God, or following after him, or even of walking in God's statutes and judgments. But the expression "walking with God" is a unique description of the intimate fellowship and friendship between God and his covenantal people.

That is the meaning of the expression. It is evident it cannot possibly refer to a physical, outward walk with God. That would be impossible. Whatever physical association there may have been between God and Adam in paradise was destroyed by the fall. God did establish a new relation of friendship between himself and his people in Christ, but this is not a physical contact. How can an earthly mortal, who is bound to time and place, walk about with the omnipresent, infinite, and sovereign God, who is a Spirit. Moreover, no one can actually see God alive. So that physical association is at once impossible.

But it does refer to a spiritual relationship between God and his saints, an inner association and communion through the Spirit. Walking in this case means going about, associating, and living in fellowship and mutual friendship. It is the fruit of God's grace in the hearts of his people whereby they know that he is their God and they are his people. They count it their highest good that they are privileged to fulfill their "part" in his covenant by walking with him.

That was originally Adam's blessedness in the state of righteousness. Genesis 3:8 states, "And they heard the voice of the LORD God walking in the garden in the cool of day." This is significant, for God is walking alone. Adam and Eve are hiding from before his face. They dread his coming, because they have broken their relationship of friendship with God by entering into a friendly alliance with the serpent. That covenantal communion in which they walked together and spoke together in mutual friendship has been destroyed. And as far as man is concerned, he is neither able nor willing to restore that relationship. It is broken forever. But God himself promises to restore his covenantal fellowship with them in Christ, by a declaration of war, creating enmity between the prince of darkness and his whole host on the one side and God's elect covenantal people in Christ on the other.

As a result Enoch and Noah, the seed of the woman, walk with God. Later God assures his chosen Israel, "And I will set my tabernacle among you: and my soul shall not abhor you. And I will walk among you, and will be your God, and ye shall be my people" (Lev. 26:11–12). This promise is also given to the Israel of God in the new dispensation: "For ye are the temple of the living God; as God hath said, I will dwell in them and walk in them, and I will be their God and they shall be my people." This same promise is finally realized in heaven, according to Revelation 3:4: "Thou hast a few names even in Sardis which have not defiled their garments; and they shall walk with me in white; for they are worthy."

Walking with God implies a living faith, humble obedience, a devoted love, and an implicit trust and constant prayer.

Faith is the bond that unites us to Christ and to God. By that living bond of faith, a relationship of friendship is established between God and his restored image-bearer. "Can two walk together, except they be agreed" (Amos 3:3)?

You can be sure that anyone who walks with God does not regard him as an emergency measure, someone to be called in conveniently when we are no longer able to take care of ourselves. That man' religion is not a conventional side issue, but fills his whole life. God had first place in Enoch's life. God was his God and his sovereign Lord, before whom he humbly bowed to ask, "Lord, what wilt Thou have me do?"

How else can a mere earthly creature ever walk with God? He must be deeply conscious of his own emptiness and insignificance. Compared with God he is but an insignificant speck of clay, less than nothing and vanity, for God is God, the almighty, omnipresent, sovereign God, in whom we live and move and have our being. And we are his creation, his handiwork, existing each moment by his power that sustains us. The Most High God is worthy to be praised, for even as all things are of him and through him, so he has also prepared all things unto himself, to show forth his praises. He has even called his people unto himself, not that they should live unto themselves, but that they should live unto him in worship, fear, and obedience.

That service must be a willing service in love. Our relationship to God is not that of a wage-servant. Nor may we regard it as our duty for duty's sake, since God demands love from the heart. No man can walk with God without a deep conviction of sin and guilt. Because of our sins we are unworthy and unfit to enter into the presence of him who is spotlessly holy. We deserve only to be banished from his presence forever. But God himself has removed our guilty stain through the perfect sacrifice of his Son upon the cross. He takes us unto himself, makes us like unto him in the true knowledge, righteousness, and holiness of Christ, who is our complete salvation. In holy awe his saints worship him as their God and Father, who calls them out of darkness into his marvelous light.

Such love manifests itself in implicit trust. Have you never noticed how confidently a child will walk next to his father, no matter how strange the way may be, how dark the night, or how many dangers may threaten? Asaph expresses exactly that in the seventy-third Psalm. When he had ventured a step alone without his God, his feet had well-nigh slipped. He was ready to question the wisdom of the Most High, and allow the doubt to take root whether God was actually good to Israel. He almost mistook the prosperity of the wicked as a token of God's favor, and the adversity of the righteous as a sign that God had forsaken them. He went into the sanctuary, where he met his God, and soon his problem was dissolved. He learned to hold to God's hand and to walk confidently at his side. In child-like trust he confessed, "Nevertheless, I am continually with thee; thou hast holden me by my right hand. Thou shalt guide me with thy counsel, and afterward receive me to glory" (Ps. 73:23–24). Such confidence, Asaph teaches us, is possible only by abiding in the sanctuary in constant prayer. Walking together implies talking together, revealing the thoughts and secrets of the heart to one another. He who walks with God knows him as his friend. He draws near to God as to the overflowing Fountain of life and blessedness. He delights in God's presence, seeks his face, pours out his heart to God, and makes all his needs known in prayer and supplication with thanksgiving. He prays without ceasing, in devotion and fear, for from his heart arises the confession, "Whom have I, Lord, in heav'n but Thee, / To Whom my tho'ts aspire? / And, having Thee, on earth is nought, / That I can yet desire" (Psalter 203:3).

But that life of fellowship with God requires a spiritual separation from the world of sin and evil. Friendship with God precludes enmity with the world. God says to Israel, "And if ye will not for all this hearken unto me, but walk contrary to me, then I will walk contrary unto you also in fury; and I, even I, will chastise you seven times for your sins" (Lev. 26:27–28). If Israel walks away from the Lord to seek other gods or the pleasures of sin, God will walk in the opposite direction away from her. A breech will be established that only grows wider as Israel departs farther from the Lord. The Holy Spirit can have no fellowship with sin, so that he withdraws himself in sore displeasure, causing us to experience his disapproval until we are brought back in repentance. Therefore Micah admonishes Israel, "He hath shewed thee, O man, what is good; and what doth the Lord require of thee, but to do justly, and to love mercy, and to walk humbly with thy God?" (Micah 6:8).

Enoch walked with God in the midst of an evil generation, and so did Noah. It was the time before the flood when a rapid degeneration was hastening the world toward judgment. Cain's city exalted itself against God and his church as a kingdom of antichrist. Wickedness abounded everywhere, persecution ran rampant. As almost a lone witness of his God, Enoch testified, "Behold, the LORD cometh with ten thousands of his saints, to execute judgment upon all, and to convince all that are ungodly among them of all their ungodly deeds which they have ungodly committed, and of all their hard speeches which ungodly sinners have spoken against him" (Jude 14–15). Noah, likewise, was a preacher of righteousness, boldly defying and condemning the world. Every hammer blow was a witness that he believed in his God, who is holy and righteous and a consuming fire against all the workers of iniquity. The fact that they were friends of God made them enemies of the world. Should they not hate those who hate their God? And though they were hated by the world, they had the testimony of God that they were pleasing to him (Heb. 11:5—7). They walked with God as a friend with a friend. And God took Enoch unto himself in heaven, while Noah was delivered from an evil world by the waters of the flood; for God is a rewarder of those who diligently seek him. He takes them into his glory and clothes them with garments of righteousness in Christ, that they may enjoy his fellowship forever. God is faithful. His covenant never fails. Blessed is that people whose God is Jehovah.

Rev. Hanko's handwritten sermon on Ephesians 3:8–11 preached in First Protestant Reformed Church on November 25, 1956

Rev. Hanko made approximately 3,500 sermons in English alone. This does not include his sermons in Dutch, which probably numbered nearly as many, nor does it include the numerous sermons on the Heidelberg Catechism (which he figures he preached through at least thirty times). His sermon files included 177 sermons on the book of Ephesians, by far the most of any other book of the Bible. When asked why he favored the book of Ephesians he said, "I chose the book of Ephesians because of its doctrinal, as well as its practical character. The main theme is: "The glory of the church in Christ Jesus." I enjoyed that strong emphasis throughout."

What follows is a sample of one his sermons on Ephesians. While he did own a typewriter, many of his sermons are written out in their entirety in beautiful penmanship.

4. Our text for this evening is very closely related to the passage we discussed a week ago.

1. There the apostle spoke of the mystery of Christ, which in times past was hidden from the sons of men, but now is revealed to the holy apostles & prophets. a. This mystery consists in this, that the Gentiles are fellow heirs, fellow members of the body, & fellow partakers of the promise of the Gospel with the church of the old dispensation.

b. The apostle was deeply stirred in the depths of his soul that he might be the recipient of that glorious revelation and might preach that wonderful gospel.

2. Here he continues to express his amazement that he should be called to such a high calling.

a. He refers to the contents of his message as the riches of Christ.

b. He points to the fact that from the beginning of the world these riches were hidden - hidden, so he says in God.

c. And that now they are revealed

as the wisdom of God made known
to the church of the new dispensation
d. And that with the amazing purpose
that we, in turn, should make this
wisdom of God known to the angels
in heaven.
B. An amazing truth is revealed to us
here.
1. Amazing to the apostle himself, as is obvious from everything he says. He speaks
in superlatives with exclamation marks.
Note: less than the least of the apostles!
Many-multiple wisdom of God, as the original expresses it. Unsearchable riches.
Eternal purpose. The creation of all things in N.J.
2. Besides, in these few brief statements he
joins time & eternity. Creation & recreation,
heaven & earth, Christ & His church, preaching & faith, divine purpose & faith, the
beginning of the ages & the ultimate glory
of all things in one great exultant
eulogy of praise.
3. It makes the apostle deeply humble. It
fills him with awed reverence. It fills
him with a strong desire to tell the praises
& wonders of God.
4. May the Holy Spirit so work in us, that
we, too, are aroused to humble, reverent & praise.

Theme: The Revelation Of The Riches Of Christ.
    I. The Contents. II. The Time. III. The Purpose.
    What.   When.   Why.

I. The Contents of The Revelation.

  A. It is very obvious that the riches of
   Christ, of which our text speaks, and
   the mystery, which he repeatedly refers
   to are closely related.

    1. Some would insist that they refer
    to one and the same thing.

      a. There are interpreters who speak
      of the mystery somewhat as if
      it were nothing more than a
      general well-meant offer of sal-
      vation.

        (1) According to them, the riches of
        Christ were made known only to
        the Jews in the old dispensation.

        (2) But now these riches are pro-
        claimed and offered to all man-
        kind, so that every one has an
        opportunity to know them and
        accept them as their own.

      b. There are others, a little more sober,
      who say that the riches of Christ
      now consist in the fact that
      Gentiles as well as Jews are in-

cluded in the church), that is, that the church has now become universal.

(1) It may be granted, of course, that the church of the old dispensation was poor in comparison with the richer blessings of the church of the new dispensation.

(2) It is unquestionably true, that we have a richer Spirit, a richer revelation, and a richer life than the church of the past ever could have. The riches of Christ do include the revelation of the mystery.

2. Nevertheless, the riches of Christ, of which our texts speaks, include much more than that.

   a. The text speaks of unsearchable riches. Not only were they hidden in times past, but even now after being revealed, they are still unsearchable, unfathomable, past finding out.

   b. He speaks of them as hidden in God, and adds in the same breath, who created all things in Christ Jesus.

   c. He speaks of manifold wisdom of God revealed in these riches.

   d. And he adds that the church now makes this wisdom known to the principalities & powers in the heavens.

3. The riches of Christ are something exceedingly great & magnificent, that can only fill us with awesome wonder eternally. That raises the question: What are they?

B. In one word, we can say that the riches of Christ are all that Christ is, all that is contained in Him.

1. We can speak of these riches as they are in Christ Himself.

   a. And then we are immediately reminded that He is God. Let us pause a moment to allow that thought to live before our consciousness.

     (1) He is one with the Father & the Holy Spirit, co-equal with them.

     (2) He is eternally generated by the Father & eternally He breathes forth the Sp. as Sp. of the Son.

     (3) He possesses all the divine attributes of infinity, ~~independency~~ ~~contingency~~, knowledge, wisdom, power, grace, ~~truth~~, holiness & righteousness.

   b. But He is also the great Servant in the council of God. "God reveals Himself in the Son." The Son shows forth all the glory of God. He works all things with the Father and the Spirit.

     (2) Yet He is also the servant. He is the Head of all the elect, of all the church.

(3) As such He is God's prophet, God's priest & God's king.

c. In a few weeks we shall commemorate His incarnation. For the Word became flesh, Immanuel, God with us. And that fact, too, includes inexhaustible riches for the Christ of God.

(1) He was born in all the weakness of sinful flesh, as a mere Babe in the manger.

(2) God lay in the Manger. The Infinite born of the finite. The Holy One born of the unclean. Life from the dead.

(3) Yet He was born in abjest poverty & shame. In deepest humility, like us & yet the lowliest among men.

d. Go with me to the cross a moment, for there you see the great Servant of God in perfect obedience casting Himself into bitter disrepute & agony of soul for our sins. Consider that the Good Shepherd lays down His life for His sheep. God was in Christ making reconciliation for sin. God was forsaken of God to bring us into eternal fellowship with Him.

e. And see Him in His resurrection as Victor over death, hell & the grave. See Him exalted to the right hand of power in the heavens. The Head of the Church is now Lord over all unto the consummation of the world.

2. But even so we have not expressed all the riches of Christ, since Christ & His church are always one, and the revelation & participation in these riches by His church are forever inseparable.

a. Christ gathers His church by His Spirit and Word. He knows His own & He calls them all by name. He blesses them from heaven. He rules over them as Lord over all for the sake of His church. No wind blows, no hostile nation arises to warfare except by His power for the sake of His church.

b. But he blesses us also individually.
(1) In Him is all our salvation. He is the Bread of Life. The Resurrection & the Life. He is our Peace. Wisdom, Righteousness, Sanctification & complete Redemption.
(2) He regenerates, converts, gives faith & makes it active, justifies, sanctifies, preserves. He makes pilgrims, causes us to suffer & gives grace accordingly, prepares trials that also purifies us by them.

3. Yet the fulness of the riches of Christ is not realized until the day of Christ, when all things will be subjected under His feet in the kingdom of the Father.

a. Christ is the center of the new creation, even as He is the center of all things in the counsel of God.

b. And the church will be united with Him to share those riches forever to the glory of the Father.

4. All that belongs to the unsearchable riches of Christ. No wonder Paul refers to them as unsearchable.

a. The word means literally that they cannot be traced out.

b. They 'defy' all our comprehension & exceed our fondest hopes. Even as God is incomprehensible, so are His works & His blessings prepared in Christ.

c. But they also are inexhaustible. As you try to trace them you never come to an end. They are riches eternally in God.

(a) They are riches made known in time. How little we appreciate them, how readily we take them for granted. How lax some of us are in searching them out. How lacking in zeal we are — even increasingly more so. Where is zeal of C. High.

(b) But God is faithful. He carries out His work. Now we still see in a mirror, but then we shall see face to face.

II. The Time Of The Revelation.

A. These riches, our text tells us, were hidden from the beginning of the world in God.

1. Even at the dawn of creation these things were hidden.

a. When God created the world He made an earthly home for man & temporal creation. Heaven & earth were two separate creations. God's friend - servant Adam was of the earth / earthly.

b. ~~Therefore~~ Adam did not know Christ. He did not even know about heaven.

c. The things to come were entirely foreign to him, for God had kept them hidden from him.

2. Even after the fall these things still remained hidden to a great extent.

a. Not as if the church of the old dispensation knew nothing at all about the riches of Christ! God lifted, as it were, the corner of the veil, and gave them a glimpse of it. But the riches as such remained hidden.

b. There was the promise which came immediately after the fall. God promised a ~~seed~~, promised enmity, promised ~~salvation~~ atonement by blood. Already then God spoke of the Lamb for sinners slain.

c. That promise was renewed, repeated, even enriched. They did not have the Bible as we do today, but God spoke, sometimes directly, sometimes thru angels, through dreams, through types & shadows, through prophets. (Pointed to Christ.)

d. Believers longed for day of Christ's coming but most of them died without seeing it.

3. The riches of Christ remained hidden for the most part in God.

  a. That is, God had His own wise purpose in keeping them hidden.

  b. Moreover, God would make them known in His own time and in His own way.

B. Divine wisdom reveals itself in the revelation of these riches of Christ

  1. Paul speaks of the manifold, many-colored, variegated wisdom of God.

    a. God's wisdom is that divine virtue whereby He knows to appoints and employs the best means to the best end.

    b. That wisdom has many colors, many facets. No matter how you look at it you see some new beauty of amazing wisdom.

  2. In this case, you may be sure, that we could never know the riches of Christ, except that God had taken all these special efforts to reveal them to us throughout all of history.

    a. The first paradise was a small replica, a working model, so to speak, of the paradise to come.

      (1) That we know to be a fact because the earthly is always a picture of the heavenly.

(2) But that is also very pointedly expressed in the text. Paul speaks of God as Creator of all things. But he also adds that God created all things by Jesus Christ. That, by the way is quoted in art. 10 of our Belgic Confession to show that Jesus is the Son of God. That can only mean, that God's purpose never was centered in Adam, or in the first creation, but that when God created this world, He did so with a view to the renewal of all things in Christ Jesus.

b. That first paradise passed away, but the coming of Christ was not yet. The first world had to perish in a flood. Abraham had to be called out of Ur of the Chaldees into the promised land. The church had to go to Egypt & be delivered. Had to be placed under the strict discipline of the law & taught by pictures.

c. These things happened as much for our sakes as for their.

3. Finally the fulness of time came & Christ was born.
a. A new day dawned. The day of the Son of man, the day of His coming, the last hour.
1. We have Christ in heaven. Spirit in hearts Word as mirror & to be changed in His likeness from glory to glory.

4. Even so not all accomplished. God will once more shake heaven & earth. Make all new. Face to face. Revelation of riches of Christ complete.

III. The Purpose Of The Revelation.

4. Thus the apostle has a glorious calling.

   1. Unto me, he says, is this grace given that I should preach amongst the Gentiles the unsearchable riches of Christ.

     a. It was God's grace that he also personally should share in and experience those riches of Christ. He speaks from personal experience & conviction.

     b. But it was also free and sovereign grace that he should be called and qualified by the Holy Spirit to preach the gospel to the Gentiles.

   2. That makes him very humble, so that he adds: to me, who am less than the least of all the saints.

     a. In other places he referred to himself as one that was born out of due time, an abortion, and not worthy to be called an apostle.

     b. But here he makes it even stronger, for he calls himself less than the least of all the saints. No one is worthy to know the riches of Christ and to tell about them. But he least of all, for he once persecuted the church.

   3. God called him by the effectual working of His power. Saul was changed to Paul & blasphemer to a servant, a persecutor to an apostle.

a. That continues to fill the soul of
the apostle with holy amazement.
He can never fathom it.
b. But it also fills him with zeal to
preach that gospel according to his
calling.
B. But then the text also adds that, according to the purpose of God, the church
also makes known the riches of Christ-
that is, you & I do — & to no lesser
audience than the principalities and
powers in the heavens.
1. According to some, the idea is that
the church serves as a mirror, or
as a beautiful painting.
a. We are passive in this respect,
and only the angels are active.
b. God causes the glory of Christ to shine
forth in the church, so that the angels
see it, & worship the wisdom of God.
2. Now it is true enough in itself, that
the angels are always as a spell-
bound band of spectators, intently
watching the unfolding of the counsel
of God throughout the history of the
world. a. Peter speaks of that in his
first epistle.

b. Moreover, Scripture shows us that they are always present at every one of the outstanding events of history. At Jesus' birth, Gethsemane, resurrection, ascension, second coming.

c. They know much more about us than we do about them. And they are very active in the work of God in saving His church & sending His judgments.

3. But here Paul says more than that. The church is the angels' seminary, so to speak, & the believers are the professors, who are instructing the angels.

a. We speak the manifold wisdom of God In our worship, in our songs, in our prayers & in all our spiritual conversations with each other.

b. And the angels are listening. We are much richer than they. But we enrich them, so that they sing praises to God.

4. Finally that will be in perfection in heaven.

a. Then we shall see all principalities & powers in their places. And know them perfectly.

b. They shall hear us worship God – see our salvation, & worship before Him.

c. All things' yours – ye are Christ's, He is God's. Makes you small? It should. Amazes you? Prayer, feed study & praise? It should. Cause you to say: Blessed Lord! Amen.

Call letter from Hope Protestant Reformed Church in Redlands (April 27, 1964)

FORM FOR CALL-LETTER.

The Rev.. *G. Henke*.................

....

Grace, Mercy and Peace, from God our Father and Jesus Christ our Lord!

Dear and Esteemed Brother:-

The consistory of the Protestant Reformed Church at.. *Redlands*... *California*.....herewith has the honor and the pleasure to inform you, that from a previously made nomination of... *you*,...you, Rev........ .... *G. Henke*......., have been chosen by.. *popular*...........vote at a legal congregational meeting, held on the. *twenty-ninth* day of *April* ....,19*64*, to be their minister of the Word and of the Sacraments.

On behalf of said congregation we therefore extend to you the call, and come to you with the urgent request: "Come over and help us."

The labours that we expect of you-should it please God to send you to us-are: Preaching twice on the Lord's Day, attending to cate- chetical instruction, to family visiting and calling on the sick, and furthermore of all things that pertain to the work of a faithful and diligent servant of the Lord, all these agreeably to the Word of God, as interpreted by our Forms of Unity and the Church Order of Dord- recht, as amended by the rules of our churches.

Convinced that the labourer is worthy of his hire, and to en- courage you in the discharge of your duties, and to free you from all worldly cares and avocations while you are dispensing spiritual blessings to us, we, the elders and deacons of the.. *Redlands. Hope*. Protestant Reformed Church do promise and oblige ourselves to pay you the sum of .... *4,400*.....dollars,.. An.. *semi- monthly*. payments, yearly, and every year as long as you continue the minister of this church, together with free use of parsonage, the free use of a tele- phone.. *and hot water heater*...............................

Moreover, we promise free transportation of yourself, your family, and your belongings (under provisions as stipulated in arts. 5, 10 and 11 of our Church Order).

Now, dear Reverend Brother, may the King of His Church so im- press this call upon your heart and give you light, that you may arrive at a decision that is pleasing to Him and if possible for us mutually gratifying.

Done in Consistory, this *twenty-ninth*.....day of . *April*........., 19*64*.., and subscribed with our names.

The Consistory of the Protestant Reformed Church of............. ....

DEACONS	ELDERS
Harry L. Sawyer	*M. Gaastra*
Everett Van Voorthuysen Jr.	*Jr. Kerseneyd*
Dick Van Helder	*William F. ____, clerk*
	Rev. David J. Engelsma....Counselor.

Call letter from Hudsonville Protestant Reformed Church (August 16, 1971)

CALL LETTER

The Reverend ...... *Rev. C. Hanko* ....

.... *817 Habbleton St.* ....

.... *Redlands, Calif.* ....

Grace, Mercy and Peace from God our Father and Jesus Christ, our Lord:

Dear and Esteemed Brother:

The Consistory of the Protestant Reformed Church at ...... *Hudsonville* .... herewith has the honor and the pleasure to inform you, that from a previously made nomination of .... *called* ...you, Rev.... *Hanko* ....have been chosen by.. *Majority* .. vote at a legal congregational meeting, held on the .....*16*...day of .. *August* ..... 19.*71* . to be their minister of the Word and of the Sacraments.

On behalf of said congregation we, therefore, extend to you the call, and come to you with the urgent request: *"Come over and help us!"*

The labors that we expect of you, should it please God to send you to us, are: Preaching twice on the Lord's Day, attending to catechetical instruction, to family visiting and calling on the sick, and furthermore of all things that pertain to the work of a faithful and diligent servant of the Lord, all these agreeably to the Word of God, as interpreted by our Forms of Unity and the Church Order of Dordrecht, as amended by the rules of our churches.

Convinced that the laborer is worthy of his hire, and to encourage you in the discharge of your duties, and to free you from all worldly cares and avocations while you are dispensing spiritual blessings to us, we, the elders and deacons of the ... *Hudsonville* .....Protestant Reformed Church do promise and oblige ourselves to pay you the sum of.. *8,000.00* .... dollars, in ....payments, yearly, and every year as long as you continue the minister of this church, together with free use of parsonage, the free use of a telephone and:

Utilities & Soc. Security. ....

....

Moreover, we promise free transportation of yourself, your family and your belongings (under provisions as stipulated in Articles 5, 10 and 11 of our Church Order).

Now, dear Reverend Brother, may the King of His Church so impress this call upon your heart and give you light, that you may arrive at a decision that is pleasing to Him, and, if possible, for us mutually gratifying.

Done in Consistory this .....*16*.......day of .. *August* .. 19.*71* . and subscribed with our names.

THE CONSISTORY OF THE PROTESTANT REFORMED CHURCH OF

Kenneth Lanning. Vice Pres. H.A. Kuiper. ..... Clerk

Elders	Deacons
John B. Lubbers	*Jay Lubbers*
John C. Lubbers	*Leonard Nienhuis*
Kenneth Lanning	*Robert Banninga*
Arnold Havenga	*Leonard Holstege*
George Boverhof	*Leon Lanning*
H.A. Kuiper	*Richard Dykstra*
	John R. Heys
	Counselor

325

Congratulatory letter from Hope Protestant Reformed Church in Redlands on the occasion of Rev. Hanko's emeritation (July 18, 1978)

Hope Protestant Reformed Church

1309 EAST BROCKTON AVENUE
REDLANDS, CALIFORNIA 92373

REV. JASON KORTERING
PASTOR

July 18, 1978

Rev. C. Hanko
5046 32nd Ave.
Hudsonville, Michigan 49426

Dear Rev. Hanko,

The Consistory of the Hope Protestant Reformed Church of Redlands, California, wishes to extend our best wishes to you on the occasion of your emeritation from the ministry.

We want especially to express our appreciation for the years of labor you devoted to the congregation of Redlands. The Lord certainly blessed your work in our midst. Your life and work has given testimony to the fact that you BELIEVED - - therefore, you SPOKE!

It is our prayer that the Lord may continue to bless you with health and strength so you may in a new way be active in the work of His Kingdom and in the fellowship of the saints.

Best wishes for a Blessed Retirement!

Yours in Christ,

The Consistory - -
Hope Prot. Ref. Church

Edwin B. Gritters, Clerk

"Foretaste of Eternal Joy"

(*Standard Bearer* 69, no. 17, June 1993)

Rejoice in the Lord alway: and again I say, Rejoice.
—Philippians 4:4

Rejoice!

God's people are a happy, a blessed people.

Have you noticed how often scripture speaks of the joy, the happiness, and the blessedness of the people of God? Have you taken note of the many times we are encouraged, urged, and even admonished to rejoice? Or have you considered how often the church of Jesus Christ has spontaneously broken forth into singing?

Think of Psalm 95:1: "O come, let us sing unto the LORD: let us make a joyful noise unto the rock of our salvation." Or think of Psalm 100:1–2: "Make a joyful noise unto the LORD, all ye lands. Serve the LORD with gladness, come into his presence with singing."

We have good reason to rejoice, for "Great is the LORD, and greatly to be praised in the city of our God, in the mountain of his holiness" (Ps. 48:1). He is the living God, who lives his own blessed life in intimate covenantal fellowship as three persons in one divine essence. He delights eternally in all his virtues and all his mighty works. He is the light, and in him is no darkness whatever. In his light we see the light (Ps. 36:9). "For this God is our God for ever and ever: he will be our guide even unto death" (Ps. 48:14).

We have reason to rejoice in all the works of God's hands, for "the heavens declare the glory of God; and the firmament sheweth his handiwork. Day unto day uttereth speech, and night unto night sheweth knowledge" (Ps. 19:1–2).

We rejoice in our Lord Jesus Christ, of whom the prophet of old declared, "Rejoice greatly, O daughter of Zion; shout, O daughter of Jerusalem: behold, thy King cometh unto thee: he is just, and having salvation; lowly, and riding upon an ass, and upon a colt the foal of an ass" (Zech. 9:9).

His birth was announced by the angel who said to the shepherds, "Fear not: for, behold, I bring you good tidings of great joy, which shall be to all people" (Luke 2:10). He now has a name above all names. Every knee must bow and every tongue must confess that he is lord, to the glory of the Father (Phil. 2:9–11).

We rejoice as church of Jesus Christ in the midst of this present world. "Glorious things are spoken of thee, O city of God" (Ps. 87:3). "How amiable are thy tabernacles, O Lord of hosts! Blessed are they that dwell in thy house: they will be still praising thee" (Ps. 84:1).

God's people are very special in the eyes of God. "Ye are a chosen generation, a royal priesthood, an holy nation, a peculiar people; that ye should shew forth the praises of him who hath called you out of darkness into his marvelous light" (1 Pet. 2:9).

Our God supplies all our daily needs, far more than we can ask or think. He watches over us, cares for us, and even uses us for the ingathering of his church and the coming of his kingdom. He entrusts to us his holy, infallibly inspired word, his own self-revelation, wherein he reveals to us the secrets of his heart, his eternal thoughts, plans, and promises, for the purpose of uniting us with himself in heavenly perfection and fellowship. By faith we embrace him as the God of our salvation in Jesus Christ, in whom is all the fullness of blessedness.

And, as if this were a small thing, He has planned, has merited, and now is preparing for us a home with him in glory, where we shall eternally sing the song of Moses and the Lamb.

Rejoice always!

This joy is unique, for it is not a momentary experience, soon to be lost in the routine or turmoil of our daily existence. Earthly joys at best are only for the moment. We often plan for them some time in advance, only to discover that the anticipation was better than the reality. For these joys belong to the passing things of this world. Still worse, hidden sorrows, griefs, and disappointments interfere with a full enjoyment of the happy occasion. Natural man never experiences true, pure joy.

The joy of which scripture speaks is unhampered, complete, all comprehensive, and eternal. Even the sorrows of this present time cannot frustrate it. It is true that many are the afflictions of the righteous; yet the apostle Peter speaks of smiling through our tears. Referring to the inheritance that awaits us in the heavens he says, "Wherein ye greatly rejoice, though now for a season, if need be, ye are in heaviness through manifold temptations" (1 Pet. 1:6).

James tells us, "My brethren, count it all joy, when ye fall into divers temptations; knowing that the trying of your faith worketh patience" (James 1:2–3). Jesus adds to that, "Blessed are ye, when men revile you, and persecute you, and shall say all manner of evil against you falsely, for my sake. Rejoice, and be exceeding glad: for great is your reward in heaven: for so persecuted they the prophets which were before you" (Matt. 5:11–12).

That makes it possible for believers to sing psalms in the night. We are reminded of Paul and Silas, sitting with feet and arms cramped in stocks, the bloody, raw wounds of their backs pressed against the cold stone wall, singing psalms of praise to God in the long hours of the night. We as children of God are able, and therefore are encouraged, to rejoice always!

Rejoice in the Lord! There is no true joy apart from him.

Joy! Who does not seek it? We are told to have a good day, or a good weekend. We are surrounded with superficial mirth that cannot satisfy. Many seek happiness in entertainments, sports, or hard-rock music. Many others only add to their misery by trying to drown their cares in wild orgies, immoral living, drunken debauchery, or drugs. A world that is at enmity with God knows no peace, no contentment, and certainly no true happiness.

True happiness is only from and only in the Lord.

Our God lives a life of perfect joy. He rejoices in his glorious divine, perfection, and he delights in the intimate blessedness of covenantal fellowship as Father, Son, and Holy, Spirit.

Christ, the great servant of Jehovah, experienced throughout his earthly ministry the joy of doing his Father's will. As Man of Sorrows he was burdened with the guilt of our sin that brought him to the cross, yet he always had the assurance that he was well pleasing to God. Is it not remarkable that even in the hour of utter darkness on Golgotha, when all the billows of divine wrath continued to sweep over him, causing him to suffer indescribable anguish of hellish torments, that Psalm 22 still rang in his soul and caused him to reach out to God with the bitter cry, "My God, My God, why hast thou forsaken me?"

This Christ is now the Lord of glory who blesses us with every spiritual blessing for time and eternity. He has united us with himself by the bond of faith, so that we can confess, " belong to my faithful Savior Jesus Christ." We can say triumphantly with the apostle Paul, "I am crucified with Christ, nevertheless I live; yet not I, but Christ liveth in me" (Gal. 2:20).

"The Lord my Shepherd holds me within His tender care, / And with His flock He folds me, / No want shall find me there. / In pastures green He feeds me, / With plenty I am blest; / By quiet streams He leads me / And makes me safely rest" (Psalter 55:1).

Timeline of events before and during the lifetime of Rev. Hanko

March 4, 1893 — Grover Cleveland inaugurated as the 24th president of the United States

September 11, 1895 — Herman Hanko and Jantje Burmania marry

1893–97 — Cleveland Panic

1898 — Spanish American War begins

1900 — Population of the United States exceeds seventy-five million

November 8, 1904 — Teddy Roosevelt elected to a second term as the 26th president of the United States

May 19, 1907 — Cornelius Hanko is born

April 14–15, 1912 — The *Titanic* sinks

1914 — World War I begins

May 7, 1915 — *Lusitania* is sunk, killing 1,198 passengers

April 6, 1917 — United States declares war on Germany

June, 1919 — Treaty of Versailles

1920 — Rev. Herman Hoeksema installed as the pastor of Eastern Avenue Christian Reformed Church

1922 — Prof. Ralph Janssen controversy

October 1, 1924 — First issue of the *Standard Bearer*

January 1925 — Rev. Henry Danhof, Rev. George Ophoff, and Rev. Herman Hoeksema are deposed

March 6, 1925 — Deposed consistories and ministers form a temporary organization called Protesting Christian Reformed Churches

November, 1926 — The Protesting Christian Reformed Churches organize as a classis and adopt the name Protestant Reformed Churches

1927 — Charles Lindbergh's first trans-Atlantic flight

December, 1928 — Cornelius Hanko and Jennie Griffioen are engaged

June 1929 — Classical (synodical) examination of the first seminary class; Cornelius Hanko is declared a candidate for the gospel ministry

September 18, 1929 — (Classical) examination of Candidate Hanko

September 19, 1929 — Cornelius Hanko marries Jennie Griffioen

September 23, 1929 — Cornelius and Jennie leave Grand Rapids for Hull, Iowa, his first charge

October 29, 1929 — Stock market crash

March 4, 1933 — Franklin D. Roosevelt takes office as the 32nd president of the United States

1934 — Dust Bowl

1935 — Rev. Hanko moves to Oak Lawn, Illinois

1940 — First synodical meeting of the Protestant Reformed Churches

January, 1941 — Publication of the first issue of the *Beacon Lights*; Rev. Hanko is the editor

December 7, 1941 — Japanese attack Pearl Harbor and the United States enters World War II

1942 — Jantje Hanko dies

June 6, 1944 — Invasion of Normandy

January 4, 1945 — Rev. Hanko leaves Oak Lawn for Manhattan, Montana

August 15, 1945 — World War II ends

May, 1948 — Rev. Hanko moves to Grand Rapids, Michigan

1950–53 — Korean War

1953 — Schism in the Protestant Reformed Churches

July 8, 1959 — First United States' casualties of the Vietnam War

June 12, 1962 — Rev. George Ophoff dies

November 24, 1963 — President John F. Kennedy is killed

June, 1964 — Rev. Hanko moves to Redlands, California

September 2, 1965 — Rev. Herman Hoeksema dies

July 20, 1969 — Spaceship *Apollo 11* lands on the moon; Americans Neil Armstrong and Buzz Aldrin walk on the moon

October, 1971 — Rev. Hanko moves to Hudsonville, Michigan

March 8, 1973 — Jennie Hanko dies

February 15, 1974 — Dedication of the new seminary building of the Protestant Reformed Churches

1975 — World tour to Australia, New Zealand, and Singapore on behalf of the denomination

1977 — Rev. Hanko retires

1979 — Iran hostage crisis

January 28, 1986 — Space shuttle *Challenger* explodes

January 16, 1991 — President George H. W. Bush announces the beginning of Operation Desert Storm

December 26, 1991 — Dissolution of the Soviet Union

1993 — Rev. Hanko visits Northern Ireland

January 20, 2001 — Inauguration of George W. Bush as the 43rd president of the United States

September 11, 2001 — Attacks on the World Trade Center

2003 — *Sin and Grace*, translated by Rev. Hanko, is published by the Reformed Free Publishing Association

March 14, 2005 — Rev. Hanko dies

www.ingramcontent.com/pod-product-compliance
Lightning Source LLC
Chambersburg PA
CBHW060754100426
42813CB00004B/807